HAVE YOU EVER WONDERED:

Why the Klingons are such a warlike, aggressive race?

How the *Enterprise* was created?

What makes Mr. Spock such a popular character?

How the crew of the *Enterprise* traveled through time?

What the various actors and actresses who worked on *Star Trek* are doing now?

The answers to all these questions may be found in this collection; the most comprehensive anthology ever written on the show, the stars, the fans, the aliens, the monsters, the special effects, and every other aspect of the beloved television series that became a way of life.

The Best of TREK

From the Magazine for *Star Trek* Fans

The Best of
TREK®

*from the magazine for
Star Trek fans*

EDITED BY

Walter Irwin

AND

G. B. Love

A SIGNET BOOK
NEW AMERICAN LIBRARY
TIMES MIRROR

ACKNOWLEDGMENTS

We would like to voice our appreciation to the many people who have made the success of *Trek* (and consequently this collection) possible. Uppermost among them are: Earl Blair and Jim Houston, who helped us to launch *Trek:* Janet Smith-Bozarth, for articles and encouragement; Helen Young, working with the Star Trek Welcommittee, for material, advice, and support; Margaret DeStefano for the painstaking chore of typing the manuscript; and the many Star Trek organizations around the country who have given their unfailing support; our editor at NAL, Sheila Gilbert, for getting this project off the ground. An extra nod goes to Jim Van Hise, publisher of the *RBCC* and *Enterprise Incidents,* both for his articles and for allowing us to use many pieces of artwork in this volume. Our many contributors (both those represented in this collection and those, equally deserving, who are not) get a special vote of thanks, as they provide the words for the blank pages we start out with each month. But our biggest thanks go to our thousands of loyal readers; for without them, there would be no *Trek.*

Thank you all. We constantly strive to be worthy of your confidence and support.

CONTENTS

INTRODUCTION

When we were preparing this collection of the best of *Trek*, it was suggested that we use the introduction to give our views on why Star Trek has been such an enduring success. We only wish we could.

Many reasons are given for Star Trek's popularity. The vision of hope and peace for mankind's future. The feeling that the characters are warm and close friends. The promise that we can finally reach understanding and love of others, even aliens. The excitement and sheer escape of flying through space and visiting strange new worlds. And there are many others.

While all of these reasons help explain the appeal of Star Trek, they seem to be a little too glib. They roll too easily off the tongue. Once one has heard them thousands of times, they begin to sound like excuses, not reasons, for loving Star Trek.

And it's a shame. Star Trek is a very personal thing to each and every individual fan. His hopes and dreams are embodied in what he perceives Star Trek to be. He acts on that perception, builds on it, and, ultimately, it changes his life. A *very* personal thing; too deep and special to be explained away by pat answers to those who do not share it.

Perhaps the *why* of Star Trek is a question better left to psychologists and sociologists. And, we feel, eventually to historians.

Why historians? While our overview as editors hasn't given us the answer to why Star Trek is so enduring and popular, it has allowed us to see something which really can be called a phenomenon (a word which, unfortunately, is often used as interchangeable with "craze" by many writers when referring to Star Trek).

That phenomenon is the gradual absorption of Star Trek into our cultural heritage. Characters, things, concepts, words from Star Trek have slowly become part of our everyday lives. It is an ongoing process, and one which seems to be picking up speed.

Captain Kirk and Mr. Spock are almost as well known as Tarzan, the Shadow, and Sherlock Holmes—a sure indication that they are about to join that exclusive club of characters who are instantly recognizable to the general public.

Even things associated with the series are commonly known. President Ford named our space shuttle *Enterprise*. "Spock" has replaced "egghead" as a disparaging name for a brainy person. And a highly secret energy-damping device developed by the Israelis has been dubbed a "phaser" by many scientists.

Perhaps the best indication of this acceptance is that instead of calling SF "that crazy Buck Rogers stuff," critics have started calling it "that Star Trek stuff." The landing on the moon seems to have made most of them drop the "crazy"; but SF is still met by the average critic with as much love and understanding as integral calculus.

So, for bad or good, Star Trek is making a place for itself in our culture. It may not be as honored and exalted a place as many fans would like, but they can comfort themselves with this fact: *There will always be a Star Trek.*

That's right. Once something is absorbed into our culture, it becomes a special sort of thing which is never allowed to die. Star Trek will live on, in one form or another, as long as our civilization does. In continual reruns, new productions, books, articles, fan clubs, plays, movies, records, scholarly researches—plus whatever forms of entertainment the future holds—Star Trek will always be around, along with Sherlock, Tarzan, the Lone Ranger, and the rest.

It is exciting and enthralling to think about. And it is something we all should be proud of, as we all had a part in it.

But there remains another facet of this absorption of Star Trek into our culture. And it is far more exciting and important than the mere fact that a fictional presentation will continue.

Thanks to Star Trek, our society and technology is about to take a quantum leap in the next fifty years or so. Why? Consider this: Millions of young, impressionable people are out there, right now, watching Star Trek. And they see a wonderfully advanced technology; men and aliens working together. They see what *could* be. And then they go out into the world and see what *is*. Can anyone wonder that these people are going to prefer the idealized Star Trek vision, and carry it with them all their lives?

And here's the exciting part. Some of these people (not all of them, or even most of them, but *some*) will go on and gain the necessary skills to change our technology and society. And with the enthusiasm and determination that the idealized view of Star Trek has given them, they will indeed start to transform our world into that vision.

It's wonderful, and it will happen. We have no doubt. It's one of the primary reasons we started *Trek*. Sure, *Trek* is a labor of love, but it is also our statement of belief in this wave of change which will happen because of Star Trek.

We started *Trek* almost three years ago with a specific purpose in mind: to give Star Trek fans a professionally produced magazine in which their interests would be uppermost. We wanted to augment the personal views; to push the dreams along a little bit.

So, no facet of Star Trek has been too small (or too big!) for us to cover, as long as we felt that it would be interesting, entertaining, and educational to our readers. In this vein, we have run articles on everything from the mechanics of the *Enterprise* warp drive to a guide for making a Star Trek needlepoint wall display. And we are constantly on the lookout for new writers with fresh ideas. So if you have an article or feature which you feel would be suitable for *Trek*, please send it to us.

As we know our readers are very much graphics-oriented (thanks to the wonder of television), we supplement these articles with photos and artwork, and constantly strive for a fresh and exciting presentation of our articles and features.

Thanks to the enthusiasm of our readers and contributors, *Trek* has become the leading Star Trek magazine. This is especially gratifying as *Trek* is sold only by mail and is not readily available to most of our readers. (If you would like more information about ordering *Trek,* please see our ad at the back of this book.) And now, our efforts, and the support of our readers, have culminated in this collection of *The Best of Trek*.

In choosing the articles included in this book, we were faced with the problem of giving readers who had never seen a copy of *Trek* a good idea of what our magazine is. Because books are produced differently than magazines, we could not use as many photos as we do in a typical *Trek* issue, so we had to choose articles which can stand on their own without the aid of graphics. Nevertheless, we feel we have achieved a good "mix" of articles, so that new readers will be able to realize the scope of *Trek*.

Herein you will find almost every facet of the intricate world of Star Trek—enough, we hope, to stimulate your dreams and determination to make this world come about. We, and countless thousands of others, are working on it. Come and join us.

WALTER IRWIN
G. B. LOVE

October 1977

1. STAR TREK THEN AND NOW
by G. B. Love

G. B. Love is considered the elder statesman around the Trek offices, as he is about ten years older than the rest of us (and we never let him forget it!). His exposure to the world of radio, television, and film science fiction is firmly rooted in the fast-changing world we lived in during the 1950s. And thus it was as an adult that he sat down to watch the first episode of Star Trek way back in '66, with an adult's tastes and an adult's viewpoint. What he saw that night, and the way he reacted to it, was only a hint of what the future was to bring, not only for him, but for millions more of us.

1966 and something called Star Trek was going to go on the air. "Another half-baked attempt to put a good science fiction series on the TV," I thought. You people and children of the 70s must remember that television's few feeble attempts at producing anything closely resembling a science fiction series were few and far between to the SF/TV fans of the fifties.

We post-Alamogordo kids (aka Postwar Baby Boom) had been science fiction fans almost by ordination. After all, we and the atomic bomb were about the same age, weren't we? So we had waddled to the movie theaters to see *Destination: Moon, The Thing, The Day the Earth Stood Still, War of the Worlds, When Worlds Collide,* and other SF films of the fifties. We also jumped out of the coolness of our Saturday-morning beds to marvel at *Space Patrol, Tom Corbett, Captain Video, Commando Cody,* and the other superscientific heroes of the distant future.

Between that night in 1966 and all of the television years past, there had been only sporadic science fictiondom. There was *Tale of Tomorrow*, filmed in England and hosted by Boris Karloff; and the imaginative (at times) *Invisible Man* series. Occasionally *The Twilight Zone* would go SF, as in the version of Asimov's *I Robot*.

But there had yet to exist a weekly series that employed a regular cast dealing in an adult and imaginative manner with SF adventures.

Then came Star Trek.

I remember that Friday, having just been disappointed by the last half of *Tarzan* (I had to see *The Green Hornet* with Van Williams and Bruce Lee!), when I yawned awaiting this new show . . . Star something or another. I had been really turned off by the promos on the show, especially since they were playing up some pointed-eared fellow in the advertising. But the special effects looked good, which made it better than most of the SF shows on television to that date. So, pessimistically, I waited for Star Trek.

Sixty minutes later, I was beside myself. Nothing that great could be a television series! Oddly enough, I also thought, "It'll never last. It's just too good."

As it turned out, I was right—even though it took NBC two and a half years to cancel the show, at the height of its popularity. But fans of Star Trek are a hearty bunch; and we have written, cajoled, and otherwise badgered studio heads, television executives, and just about anyone who could bring Star Trek back.

We were given a reprieve when the animated series began in 1973. As good as it was—and it was about a light-year ahead of the other banal "kiddie" shows on Saturday morning—it just didn't hold a phaser to the original. And now production has ceased on that, leaving us with nothing but reruns.

Will, we wonder, that feature film of Star Trek that has been talked about and murmured about throughout Star Trek fandom ever become a reality? With the most devoted legion of fans ever assembled for a single cause awaiting the answer, Paramount (which owns the film rights to the show) sits on its thumbs.

No one has yet convinced them that there are thousands of Star Trek fans who would pay many dollars to see a well-made film about the *Enterprise* and its crew.

And you can multiply that figure by three or four (and in some cases ten or twelve!), as many of Trekkers would see it many times just to watch in awe new adventures of our favorite space explorers.

In this age of an erratic economy and box-office flops at our local Bijou, what could be a safer bet than a Star Trek film?

Even if a Star Trek movie is never filmed, we Star Trek fans have our fandom. And what a wonderful fandom it is. By and large, it has been this author's experience that although there ain't no such animal as "bad" fandom, Star Trek fandom has to be the best fandom for communication among its members.

Science fiction is far too pseudointellectual, comics fandom is too money-conscious—but Star Trek fandom is like a universal session where we can share our mutual feelings about a very personal thing to each of us: Star Trek.

Sure, we've seen the Star Trek programs time and time again. It's gotten to the point where some people can quote whole segments or even complete programs! I personally turn the show on out of habit, occasionally catching a show that I haven't seen six or eight times. I do it as a favor to a friend—a friend I like to be close to whenever possible. For one hour a day I have the whole crew over. That is the wonder of television.

It's been a long—pardon the pun—trek for all of us from the days of *Captain Video* and *Destination Moon* to that September day in 1966 when thousands of us first saw Star Trek. I am sure that it will be years hence when the last of us who saw the program on that day die, leaving the memories of an energy that binded all of us together in our devotion—no, love—for Star Trek.

But that is the beauty of Star Trek. It will endure in new generations of people until those star dates become a reality. It will have served its purpose. It will have given us dreams and imagination to carry us on into the future.

2. THE KLINGONS:
THEIR HISTORY AND EMPIRE
by Leslie Thompson

To have a program with a hero, you must of necessity have a villain. Star Trek had several, but as a whole, none were more popular with viewers than the Klingons. This article by Leslie Thompson appeared in the very first issue of Trek, *and helped set the standard for the in-depth type of look at Star Trek that* Trek *features. This article also introduced Star Trek fans to the type of writing which Leslie calls "speculative faction," in which a fictional hypothesis is woven around a set of known or proven facts in a way which complements and expands those facts. It has led to a whole new facet of Star Trek fan involvement, and has provided hours of both reading and creative pleasure for fans.*

Klingon: The very word suggests a sheer villainy. Evil. Corruption. Treachery. Torture. And, incidentally, one heck of a Star Trek episode.

When one stops to think, it is surprising just how few Star Trek shows featured the Klingons. They were always around, sure, plotting some new scheme against Kirk and crew, but rarely were they the focal point of an episode.

In fact, of the five shows that are generally considered Star Trek's best ("The Menagerie," "Shore Leave," "The Squire of Gothos," "The City on the Edge of Forever," and "The Trouble with Tribbles"), the Klingons are featured only in "Tribbles."

Why then are the Klingons so closely identified with Star Trek? What makes them so much more "special" than, say, the Romulans?

To begin with, let's look at some comments on the Klingons, as excerpted from Stephen Whitfield's excellent book *The Making of Star Trek:*

"Their only rule of life is that rules are only made to be broken by shrewdness, deceit, or power. Cruelty is something to admire; honor is a despicable trait ... Their society is totally devoted to personal gain by the cleverest, strongest, or most treacherous."

But the main reason for the Klingons' great popularity lies in the fact that they are completely and totally rotten just for the sheer fun of it.

Every Star Trek fan knows this. The Klingons enjoy being villains; it shows in every move they make, every scheme they hatch. And we enjoy watching them do so.

To understand why the Klingons are what they are, and why their entire empire is dedicated to conquest, we have to first examine their lifestyles and history.

The home planet of the Klingons is called Kazh (which, strangely enough, translates to "Earth").

Kazh is the second planet from its sun, and is about one and one-half times the size of Earth. It is an entirely inhospitable place, hot, dry, and sparsely vegetated.

It is not, as most Class M planets are, divided into continents by oceans; but instead is an almost solid land mass spotted with salty and shallow seas.

Because of its proximity to its sun and the absence of large oceans and great mountain chains, climate is the same over much of Kazh. Except for the poles, which are slightly cooler, and the equator, which is slightly warmer, one part of Kazh is pretty much like any other part of Kazh. This blandness of climate is not helped by the fact that Kazh has very little tilt to its axis, so the seasons change very little.

All in all, a dreary place, and one which would be expected to produce a technology which enabled the Klingons to seek out planets with a little more to offer. In other words, the Klingons became a people of conquest.

Life on the planet Kazh in the time of Star Trek is pretty good. That is, if you can consider a total dictatorship "pretty good."

Klingon government is much like the communistic system of Earth. Rule is by the council of thirteen men, whose order and influence is in direct proportion to their power in the empire.

The chief of state is called the Senator in Chief, others in the Council are Senators and territorial governors. Although the Senator in Chief is the absolute ruler of the Klingon Empire, his orders and edicts can be overruled or superseded by the rest of the Senate. It is simply power politics in the purest form; those with the most control make the rules.

The average Klingon is considered to be owned by the empire. No matter what his rank (achieved by assassination and treachery), he is basically a "front-line soldier," and thinks of himself in that way.

From the time a Klingon male is born, he is raised to be a warrior. The lessons of life as a Klingon are brought home to him in the most graphic way: through example. He is taught to cheat, to betray, to steal, to lie. He is likely to find his teachers changing from day to day, as they are either replaced or moved up in the order of power.

The main thing he is taught is that on Kazh, no one ever moves down from power, only up. Those who lose power also lose their lives.

Women on Kazh are also educated. They are taught to be scientists, computer technicians, factory laborers, and the like. In other words, the women are given jobs that no self-respecting Klingon male would consider doing. Males want to fight.

Women of Kazh are considered really little more than chattel, owned by whoever is strong enough to keep them. Natural childbirth is a rarity on Kazh, and is actually illegal among the lower orders.

Children are bred in the laboratory at a specific rate. They are raised by the state, and educated to a specific design. The concept of family is unknown among the Klingons, along with the inherent weaknesses of family life: love, loyalty, and tenderness.

Although the Klingon technology is as advanced as that of the Federation, the average Klingon receives little benefit from that technology.

His life is an unending struggle for survival against his fellow Klingons. He must continually make the effort to gain and keep power. And the farther he rises and the more power and influence he gains, the more he must try to protect his power and gain even more.

The weak fail. The strong survive and conquer. So it has always been on Kazh.

Because of the absence of climatic change on Kazh, life has remained virtually the same there for millions of years.

The mere fact that humanoid life could develop on Kazh, much less raise a civilization there, is a mystery to many astroanthropologists. The Klingons have no interest in this dilemma; indeed, they have little interest in any facet of their beginnings. A Klingon will merely state: "We are here and have always been here." Knowledge of the past, unless it can be used as a "weapon" of some sort, has little value to a Klingon.

The Klingons are all of one race. This is due in large part to the similarity of climate all over Kazh, but also to the fact that since their beginnings, they have been a nomadic people.

Early Kazh man found no area on his planet which offered enough food and water for permanent survival. So like the Arabs of Earth, he had to keep moving constantly, searching for new hunting grounds, new watering spots.

But unlike the Arabs, the Kazh man did not restrict himself to one area of his planet. One place was much like another place, and therefore familiar, so why not go there?

The distance covered by these roving bands was immense; some tribal elders could not remember ever having camped in the same place twice. Some bands moved almost halfway across the planet!

Life was hard, of course. The men of Kazh had no time for the luxury of repose and reflection. Survival was a full-time job, and the weak and fanciful were left to die.

There were no legends, no songs, no sympathy or compassion of any kind. No god favored them, for to have a god, a people must have curiosity about themselves, their world, and their origins; and the Kazhians had neither. And to live for a god, one must have faith and hope. On Kazh there was no faith or hope; there was only life and the day-to-day living of it.

Existence meant traveling, and constant traveling meant war. Kazhians formed tribes for strength, not companionship. There was never enough of anything for anyone, so whenever two bands met, they fought.

Victory was complete. No adult male captives were taken, only women and children. They became the property of their captors, and eventually, members of the tribe. Thus, over thousands of years, the people of Kazh eliminated the already slight differences of race, customs, and language through interbreeding.

Eventually, great "nations" of semi-nomadic Kazhians developed. Specific areas of the planet became the property of these nations, and the constant sporadic battling of the past became full-fledged warfare.

War, as it always does, brought advancement. Animals were trained to be beasts of burden, weapons were developed and improved, and most important, a system of command, of government came into being.

These governments were total dictatorships, ruled by the strongest and the most vicious warriors. Despots rose to power through assassination and subversion and remained in power through terror, torture, and sheer tenacity.

Now records of a sort were being kept; lists of conquered peoples, lands taken, enemies yet to fight. And fight they did. For ten thousand years, the people of Kazh battled among themselves with ever-increasing weaponry, and a viciousness unequaled throughout the galaxy. There seemed to be no end . . . that is, until the time of the Kazhian named Kling.

Kling was a veritable giant. Standing over seven feet high, he could move his 300-odd pounds with the speed of a man only half his size. Kling's arms could crush an enemy's skull. No one dared to stand up to him, and no group ever succeeded in doing so.

Many Kazhians were strong, some even more so than Kling. But Kling had a distinct advantage: He was also intelligent. Many of his opponents fell because they underestimated the superb cunning that lay behind his sleepy and stupid-seeming eyes. They paid for this error with their lives. By the time Kling was barely twenty, he ruled his nation.

Life became good for Kling's people under his leadership. They found battles aplenty, and lost none of them.' Their armies swelled, the lands they controlled increased, and nothing could halt their relentless advance.

With this success, a new emotion began to appear on Kazh. For the first time in their history, men felt pride in themselves, their accomplishments, their people, and most especially in their leader. And so, to show that pride and to prove themselves members of a mighty race, they took a new name: They became Klingons.

Seven years after he took control of this nation, Kling made a decision that was later to change forever the face of the galaxy.

A captured weaponeer of a conquered nation offered to make Kling a bargain: a certain secret in exchange for wealth and power. He slyly explained how his plans to use this power to conquer his own nation were thwarted by Kling's untimely invasion, but he was now prepared to share the secret with Kling. Kling readily agreed; and in short order possessed the secrets of atomic energy. And the atomic bomb.

Soon Kling also possessed a world. The treacherous weaponeer was then summarily executed.

Kling had achieved his objective. He ruled his planet. There was nothing left to conquer, no enemies left to fight. Now Kling could think about his true dream, building a dynasty of completely united peoples. A dynasty which would last a thousand years.

He found himself unable to. Or more specifically, his people were unable to. The instincts of hundreds of thousands of years could not be suppressed or controlled. A Kazhian had to fight to live.

Kling ruefully realized his people could never be at peace. It was impossible. Everyone on the planet was now a Klingon, but even a Klingon would fight another Klingon if there was no one else to fight.

Out-and-out warfare was prevented by Kling's firm control. But as the years passed, his people began to find other outlets for their inherent viciousness.

The local governments that Kling had so carefully set up were becoming bloody fiefdoms as the more wily of his subjects took control of them.

Dueling, thievery, personal treachery, petty lying, brawling, and cheating; all major characteristics throughout Kazhian history were readily integrated into the new society.

The hardness which had previously been a necessity had now become sport.

Kling was getting old. He found it more and more difficult to control his world. Small-scale revolutions were breaking out regularly, and assassination attempts against him came nearer to succeeding with each try.

Kling knew that after his death planetary unity would collapse, and his people would fall back into barbarism.

What was needed was someone to fight, to conquer; to give his people something to live for again. But where? When you control a planet, where do you look for enemies?

Kling's answer came roaring out of the skies one night.

The resulting explosion leveled several square miles, but curious Klingon investigators found much more than they expected to.

The wreckage was that of a space ship. Alien bodies were pulled from the rubble. Alien machines were pieced together. A report was made to Kling.

Kling was quick to grasp the significance of this visitor from another planet. If other planets were indeed populated, then there was hope for his people. There was someone left to fight after all.

The idea of space travel was an entirely new one to Kazh. Beyond the airships they had developed for war, they had little interest in flight or exploration. The twinkling lights in the sky had meant little more to them than an aid to navigation.

Now Kling speculated. Could the missiles which rained bombs on his enemies carry a man to these other worlds, to fight these other men?

Perhaps.

For the first time in the history of Kazh, a man lifted his eyes to the heavens. As he gazed upward, Kling smiled. Perhaps his empire would not only last a thousand years, but extend over a thousand worlds as well.

The Klingons, able to pour their total energies into space, achieved star flight in a little over a hundred years.

Their conquests were relatively easy, and they proceeded about their warring at a leisurely pace.

Then one day a battle cruiser failed to report back to Kazh. Instead a message arrived over subspace radio. Translated, it read: "Unprovoked attack by your ship has resulted in its destruction by Starship *Exeter*. Our intentions are peaceful. May we meet to discuss jurisdiction. United Federation of Planets."

The Klingons were overjoyed. At last, someone to fight!

Klingons are usually thought of as humorless stoic warriors. True, warriors they are, but one must not forget that they enjoy what they do.

In several Star Trek episodes, actors who played Klingons

were able to capture this spirit of fun, and therefore make their particular Klingon come more alive.

In "Errand of Mercy," John Colicos became the prototype Klingon.

Cold, unfeeling, and decidedly militaristic, his Kor was still a Klingon who enjoyed his power. Toying with the Federation (through its representatives Kirk and Spock), relishing the destruction of Organians, and commenting wryly on the fact that even he was under constant surveillance made Kor believable.

Michael Ansara gave us another side of the Klingons in "Day of the Dove."

His Kang was a Klingon who refused to battle simply for the sake of an outside influence.

Proud and haughty, Kang felt that the glory and fun of fighting were corrupted when it was forced upon him and his men. "Klingons fight," he said, "for their own objectives."

Also in "Dove," we got our first look at a Klingon woman. Kang must have been powerful indeed to have his wife aboard his ship, since Klingon women generally never leave a planet. Here we saw that even in the unfeeling Klingons, a kind of love can grow between two people. There's hope for them yet.

But the absolute best Klingon of them all was undoubtedly William Campbell's Captain Koloth from "The Trouble with Tribbles."

Campbell was everything a Klingon should be—cocky, arrogant, and superbly self-assured.

And he had humor. His verbal jibes at Kirk were exactly those of a man who has been bested before but is unafraid to battle again the very man who has bested him.

Campbell did so well as Koloth that, had the show continued another season, he would have become a semi-regular.

This, of course, would have meant an increase in the number of shows which featured the Klingons. And it probably would also have upped the quality of the shows from the third season.

Should Star Trek ever return on a weekly live basis, Campbell would now almost be a necessity as a continuing character. His interpretation of the Klingon is the one that is the most remembered and admired, and the show would not seem complete without him as Kirk's major adversary.

In actuality, Star Trek never told us too much about the Klingons. Mention was made of their empire, their tortures, their sonic disruptor pistols, etc.

This was mainly because of the necessity of getting on with the plot, but also because Star Trek wrote itself into a corner early in the series concerning the Klingons.

The episode was "Errand of Mercy," and it concerned a little something known as the Organian Peace Treaty.

The establishment of this treaty and how it was done made for an exciting story but was basically a mistake.

For how could you use Klingons as your major villains if you had some superpowerful beings who could automatically stop trouble before it had a chance to get started? Where is the drama? The suspense? When things got a little hot for the Federation, they could just call in the Organian cavalry, and it was all over.

So the Klingons couldn't be used to best advantage. Their actions were stifled by the existence of the treaty. They became simple plot devices, "bad guys" just as obvious and simplistic as the bad guys in black hats in second-grade western movies.

Thanks to the Organians, the Klingons couldn't really be Klingons and Star Trek lost some exciting shows.

When Star Trek returns as a regular weekly series, several major changes must be made.

First, all of the events in the James Blish novel *Spock Must Die* have to be completely ignored. It's bad enough to have to live with the Organian Peace Treaty, but to have the Klingons deprived of space flight is unthinkable.

Second, Koloth must be featured as a continuing character. The personal animosity between him and Kirk would serve as the focal point for stories, rather than the standard "Klingon interference" theme of earlier shows.

Third, there must be more shows featuring Klingons. This would be taken care of automatically by featuring Koloth regularly. But it should be done simply because of what the Klingons are: the Federation's major rivals in the galaxy. A major rival is always around and not just thrown in whenever the plot happens to call for it.

Klingons helped to make Star Trek, its people, and its world more believable and enjoyable. Sadly, we never got to see enough of them.

When Star Trek returns, the Klingons will return as well.

Let us hope that they will be just as corrupt, rotten, villainous, and lovable as ever.

HOME PLANET: Kazh

GOVERNMENT: Dictatorship

RELIGION: None

POPULATION: 7 billion

WEAPONS: Sonic disruptors (cannon), ship cannon, rifles and handguns

DRESS: Battle Standard (armor, handgun, communicator); Battle Presentation (gold armor, handgun, broadsword, shortsword, mace, helmet, and blaze of rank)

EMPIRE: 112 captive planets (East Quadrant of the galaxy); "influence" on 43 satellite planets

AIMS: Complete and absolute subjugation of the entire universe

3. STAR TREK MINIATURES:
THE STARSHIP ENTERPRISE
by Richard G. Van Treuren

The miniature spaceships used on Star Trek are among the primary interests of fans, and in Richard Van Treuren's article they can find just about the most complete nontechnical discussion of them anywhere. Richard is a flying-machine buff who resides in California, and he followed the progress of Star Trek's various vessels from their beginnings. In this article, he traces the development of what was to become the most famous star vessel of all time—the USS Enterprise—in a manner which is both entertaining and informative. Which is a difficult thing to do, especially when you are writing for an audience unfamiliar with the intricacies of modelmaking. However, Richard succeeds magnificently, and his article has proved to be one of our most popular ever, making the issue it first appeared in (Trek 5) one of the most sought-after and rarest Star Trek items in the country!

The story began in 1964 when Star Trek was just a series idea veteran producer Gene Roddenberry was trying to sell. A newly hired executive of the then faltering Desilu Studios, Oscar Katz, latched onto Roddenberry, and by June of that year, Star Trek was beginning to take shape.

Roddenberry called for a vessel to move his characters about, and designing it was one of the most difficult pieces of creative work ever faced by the studio.

Not only did it have to be a probable-looking spaceship with starflight capability, it had to be flexible enough to encompass what was to be an anthology of stories.

Further, once represented in miniature, it would have to

be practical to properly illuminate and photograph. Many projected spaceship designs created by technological experts would look ridiculous in miniature in spite of their logical architecture.

(This is a problem in films dealing with dirigibles, such as *Zeppelin* and the current *Hindenberg*. Perfect miniature airships look poor because the *real* dirigibles look fake on film.)

The aeronautical history of the producer, designers, and consultants was delightfully obvious when the spacecraft design neared completion. United States aircraft license numbers had NC and NX prefixes, depending on type. Lengthening this old prefix afforded an excellent method of spaceship classification for the coming series, so NCC was added. (If plans for other prefix classifications were ever made, they never reached the miniature stage.)

One of the designers, Walter "Matt" Jefferies, an antique-airplane enthusiast, whipped up the first rough model of the four-part design. The ship, said to be about 200 feet in length, was finally named after the fastest carrier in the United States Navy.

The approved prototype was turned over to the Howard Anderson Company, an optical-effects house down the street from the Desilu Studios. Working with Jefferies, a four-inch cardboard and balsa miniature was constructed. Upon approval, a three-foot wood and plastic miniature was fabricated without lighting effects. Shooting of the pilot had already begun, so the yard-long ship was taken out to the "Rigel Seven" exterior set, where Roddenberry and Jeffery Hunter, the first series lead, were photographed looking it over.

The largest spaceship miniature ever made for a speculative project like a pilot film was then begun. The finished product, a balsa and plastic miniature, much more detailed than its predecessors, was 134 inches long.

It was equipped with many lights, including some in the sixty-inch-diameter saucer that flashed. At this point the hangar bay was only loosely planned, if at all, so little detail was added to the rear of the lower cylindrical projection.

Evidently test footage was exposed with white coloring, but eventually the two major models were finished with a silvery-gray top coat. Variable film stock, lighting, processing, and optical quality would make the ship appear blue, white, and green in the coming years.

It is not clear just how much footage of each model was used, but the final cut of the first Star Trek pilot remains a science fiction classic and a television milestone. However, its believability was hampered by those static-looking miniatures. The tiny four-inch model, used briefly, was very unconvincing.

As is well known, the National Broadcasting Company thought the film was acceptable, but after a poorly conducted test, they decided not to buy the series. It looked as though the studio would take a near-half-million-dollar bath until, after some hounding, the film was retested and the network agreed to another pilot.

The making of the second pilot saw many changes, not the least of which was the enlargement of the theoretical size of the ship.

The four-inch miniature was not used, and has since been lost. However, probably to keep costs down, no major changes were made in the models in 1965.

Publicity drawings made for the film show flame and smoke jutting from the hangar bay; while this does not mean a hangar bay was not being considered, no reflective changes were seen in miniature.

The completed film, stalled from network viewing until 1966, was inferior but looked more professional and contained lots of action-adventure. NBC bought it and Star Trek was placed in production status.

A memo dated May 2 that year called for "revision" of the USS *Enterprise* miniatures, probably because the models constructed quickly for the pilot films would not stand up to weekly viewer scrutiny.

The actors were busied taking publicity pictures in borrowed sets with handy equipment since the regular sets were being torn down and moved to the main Desilu studio. The three-foot model was used to dress up some of these pictures, either being held up by an actor or suspended on quite obvious wires.

In April, the Anderson Company began modifications to the eleven-foot model, including removing the spiked nacelle caps and replacing them with an impressive light effect created with small winking lights on motor-driven plates.

In addition, the bridge section was lowered, crosshatched

panels were added to the nacelles and their struts, the "main sensor" screen was shrunk, and lighted pods were added to the nacelle exhaust cones. At last the hangar bay was established by adding detail to the "engineering section" rear.

It appears the heavy wiring required to run the new lighting effects could not be strung through the pipe the big model had been mounted on, so holes were cut in the port side and the cables run there. When the model was refinished with a beautiful 'weathered' effect, the port side was left unpainted.

Since the model could not now be filmed from the left side, one would think a set of numbers would be painted on the starboard side in reverse, then making it appear to be the port side by slipping the film over. (This happens from time to time by accident.) Instead, stock footage of the big model's original version was spliced into every one of the following 78 hour-long segments.

The smaller model, released from picture-taking, was refinished to incorporate as many of these changes as possible without adding lighting. This model wound up with an ugly, permanent mounting bracket dangling from the cigar-section underside so it could be easily mounted on a post for picture-taking. This knob stuck out whenever the model was suspended (particularly in views like the F-104 pilot's view in "Tomorrow Is Yesterday"), giving birth to hordes of "inaccurate" drawings of the ship.

It was necessary to use the three-footer in several episodes in the coming series, but stock footage of its original version was rare. An Anderson memo dated April 6 placed the two-model improvement cost at over $34,000.

Numerous publicity pictures were taken of both refinished models. The eleven-footer was illuminated on a darkened stage, allowing printers to add a star field without costly optical effect. The yard-long model found its way into more actor poses.

Unfortunately, the most widely publicized photo of the USS *Enterprise* was the static model hung by highly visible wires in front of the *sky*-textured backdrop. This shot was printed on the cover of the first edition of *The Making of Star Trek*, the book that slipped up slightly by reporting the large miniature to be fourteen feet long.

People unfamiliar with the show often printed pictures upside down. (Even *TV Guide* was guilty of printing a

"Tholian Web" clip wrong side up; but the magazine's editors argued that there is no up or down in space.)

Shortly after some regular filming, the saucer underside numbers were "rotated" 180 degrees to be more easily readable from the now necessarily popular camera angles.

Eventually the regular sets were finished, and regular shooting began late in May 1966. The first-season production, stretched well into 1967, saw the large miniature being moved to various optical-effect houses in Hollywood. It was photographed by many technicians, including the award-winning Linwood Dunn of Film Effects.

The first thirteen episodes ordered were well into production when AMT corporation, of Troy, Michigan, acquired the rights to reproduce the starship in model kit form.

AMT manufactures many of its models by first constructing a wooden prototype two and one-half times the desired kit size. Matt Jefferies made several trips to Michigan to be of service on the project, but no miniature was made available.

Despite evidence to the contrary, AMT did not use the popular plans printed in *The Making of Star Trek;* the plans had not yet been drawn. How their kit gained top-of-the-saucer deck lines is a mystery; perhaps the earliest models had such lines. A wooden *Enterprise* was fabricated.

Once the wooden model is completed, a machine called a Planograph "traces" it, running over its surfaces and sending out information. Through the control of a computer, a milling machine accepts the information and mimics every move the Planograph makes, cutting a steel mold exactly two and one-half times smaller than the original. AMT craftsmen then carefully engrave the high-grade, heat-treated steel mold. Having fulfilled their function, the wooden tool models are not stored.

An average run of *Enterprise* kits sees about 90,000 units manufactured. A box with artwork by AMT's Don Greer (duplicating the early "reversed" underside numbers) was prepared in 1966 with intermediate publicity pictures of Kirk and Spock. Advertising flyers were distributed to dealers, and the kits hit the stands in the fall. The initial response was excellent, and the kits have been selling very well ever since.

Gulf and Western acquired Desilu Studios in the summer of 1967, and combined it with its neighbor studio, Paramount. Slightly improved production facilities were used, reflected in the construction of a completely new "engineering room" set. Unfortunately, overall quality slumped for a variety of reasons.

The first episode filmed in the new bunch was "Catspaw," and it featured a brand-new *Enterprise* miniature, a tiny four-inch model made of metal. The script called for the ship to be held in a force field, so the representative miniature was encased in a block of lucite measuring 10.4 cm × 5.4 cm × 3.5 cm.

Few or no changes were made in the two regular miniatures during the second year, although there were many other changes. The dubbed-in ship operating noises were for the most part eliminated; phasers became constant streams of energy instead of one-shot bursts, and so on.

AMT Corporation provided a mold of their *Enterprise* kit, and complete AMT kits were assembled in the making of several episodes (including the wrecked *Constellation* in "The Doomsday Machine," the Federation starships in "The Ultimate Computer," and the ship seen orbiting outside Lurry's office in "The Trouble with Tribbles").

The three-foot model and an AMT kit were lent out to Don Jim, a Los Angeles photographer who took the space shot seen in GAF Corporation's View Master summation of the "Omega Glory" segment. An old trick used in war films was used in this shot—showing an angle of the ship without numbers so it cannot be identified. (This gimmick was used in a third-season episode to create the Starship *Defiant.*)

What could have been Star Trek's best season was ruined when NBC changed its plans and moved the show to late Friday nights. Inept or not, the people who remained with the show in the last year had no incentive for quality, and little emerged. A typical third-season episode, "Requiem for Methuselah," had Kirk looking at the three-foot model, supposedly seeing inside through what had long been established as a one-way television viewing screen.

When production halted, Paramount saw little chance of any more Star Trek productions, and few properties were kept. The eleven-foot *Enterprise* was shoved into storage; Roddenberry acquired the three-foot model. The big miniature was not kept in good repair, even though it was occasionally displayed; the nacelle caps and the "main sensor screen" eventually were lost. Jefferies got the "Catspaw" trinket.

Desilu had printed a flyer explaining Star Trek in many languages back when production first started. The show had actually premiered in Canada slightly before September 8, 1966. Japanese television was the next foreign country to buy the series, and the show became popular there in spite of the large number of Japanese imaginative programs.

Commercialism based on Japanese SF series like *Ultra Man* include high-quality action-feature model kits. When the Japanese model company Midori elected to manufacture an *Enterprise* kit, they added a propellor to the hangar bay.

The required motor and power supply caused the model to be out of proportion; the saucer and nacelles are smaller than those of the AMT kit, while the "engineering section" is larger. The model could be suspended with supplied nylon line, or mounted on a small wind-up cart.

Midori also manufactured a tiny five-inch *Enterprise*, which, after the ridiculous suspension wheels were removed, resulted in a reasonable miniature.

Although companies like Associated Hobby Manufacturers and Balboa Models import and repackage many Japanese kits from distributors like Miyano and Co., Ltd., neither of these kits were ever repackaged in the United States before Midori ceased manufacture.

In spite of the BBC's censorship policies (which resulted in three Star Trek episodes not being shown in England) the show became popular in England. Instead of making a kit of the starship or another vehicle, Aurora Plastics (U.K.) Ltd. made a kit of the most popular character, and then traded toolings with AMT to manufacture *Enterprise* kits for Europe.

Carried on Aurora stationery as simply "Startrek," the AMT kit was boxed in a slightly larger package bearing the words "as seen on BBC-TV." The kit continues to sell well across Europe, even though translated instruction sheets were not included.

Back in the United States the show was breaking records in syndication; more people became aware of the show, and AMT *Enterprise* kits sold like hotcakes. The company released several repressings (with the words "as seen on NBC-TV" removed from the box), but rising costs eliminated first the nacelle lights, then the saucer lights. More Star Trek model spaceships were tooled up as the years passed.

The show had not gone unrecognized in government circles, even in the sixties. Roddenberry went to Washington, D.C., in August 1967 to present Mr. S. Paul Johnson with the show's second pilot film; it has been placed in storage in the National Air and Space Museum.

The Secretary of the Navy eventually saw to it that Roddenberry went aboard the USS *Enterprise* (CVA(N)-65) for a mini-cruise.

The Smithsonian elected to create a display of science fiction's influence on actual technology (1973), and began accepting related material from many people. Miniatures were donated by, among others, Matt Jefferies, G. Harry Stein, and this writer.

Early in 1974, Paramount Studios graciously donated the eleven-foot miniature, and the museum staff performed cosmetic restoration, allowing it to be included in a late-1974 temporary exhibit. The completely restored model is now on display in the Life in the Universe Gallery of the National Air and Space Museum.

Another run of the AMT *Enterprise* kit introduced a new mold revision that allows easier assembly and a completely inaccurate decal sheet that reflects the company's less than rabid desire for quality. Though the various names and numbers assigned to imaginary starships is, of course, controversial, since little was established in the show, the decal style is all wrong.

In October 1974, a new dimension was added to Star Trek modeling when Estes Industries, the largest model rocket firm in the world, acquired the rights to manufacture flying rockets in the shape of the Star Trek spaceships.

Estes was intent on accuracy, and research for its V-2 rocket model included an interview with a veteran of the Peenemunde works! The Smithsonian graciously provided pictures, and this writer was interrogated for two days by Wayne Kellner and the model development staff out in Penrose, Colorado.

After almost a year of development, flying kits of the *Enterprise* and a Klingon warship were introduced in the spring of 1975. Though their first packaging was less than perfect, the kits show the quality obtainable by people who care.

The next AMT pressing saw the *Enterprise* and other kits repackaged in smaller versions of the original boxes. The kit has remained basically the same for many years, so if one desires to build an "accurate" *Enterprise* miniature, it makes no difference which AMT pressing is obtained. An Estes kit can be used to improve the individual's own starship miniature.

It is obvious that no one model can be an "accurate" version of the *Enterprise*, and the situation only worsens when the modeler looks over the plans available to him. The show miniatures were built from plans, which even if available, would be somewhat different than what was established, since the ship was to have been smaller.

The most popular plans, printed in *The Making of Star Trek* and sold by Lincoln Enterprises, were drawn by Matt Jefferies for that book in 1968. These drawings, while excellent and unquestionably "accurate," disagree with the miniatures on certain points.

The latest hat in the ring is the "General Plans" by Franz Joseph Designs (F. J. Schnaubelt). Although Mr. Jefferies was understandably not consulted, he echoed the sentiments of most fans when he said they were "a beautiful piece of work."

Unfortunately, not nearly as much thought and detail were possible when the show miniatures were whittled out of wood and plastic. All these things show that the individual modeler is at liberty to assemble the models as he or she sees fit.

The next version of Star Trek will feature new modifications to the starship; new models may be made, old models modified, great design changes may be incorporated.

We can be thankful that the original was excellent, since no amount of polish can make a poor design shine. If the new starship provides a believable platform for drama, then the effort will not be in vain.

ADAPTING YOUR OWN ENTERPRISE MODEL

To duplicate the professional *Enterprise* miniature as it appeared in the pilot films, start by scraping and sanding the cross-hatched panels off the nacelle struts and from inside the nacelle slots.

Also remove the top saucer deck lines, and half the underside concentric circles. The observation post atop the hangar bay doors must be cut off; fill in the underside saucer depressions as you cover the base mounting slot or hole and any cracks left after assembly.

The "main sensor" screen must be enlarged. One method is to glue a gasket-shaped object about one-quarter of an inch thick to the screen, then putty and sand smooth. Trim the stem so it will fit in close to the hull.

The bridge section of the saucer must be heightened; a fuse cap fits nicely and with some putty and sanding assumes the right shape.

After carefully finding the center of the nacelle caps, small spikes must be added; use turret terminals commonly used in electronic modules.

After studying film clips of this version, use the Estes decal sheet to add the proper details. Remember the underside saucer numbers must be reversed, and the lower side stripe must be recessed slightly.

If a production version is desired, the underside saucer numbers may be put on either way, as both versions were seen on film; one need not duplicate the ripped-up port side.

Spin the "main sensor" screen and reduce its diameter by about one-eighth of an inch, and again cut its stem to mount it closer to the hull.

Add filler generously to the nacelle caps, then sand to a diameter almost matching the nacelles. One method of adding spheres to the nacelle "exhausts" is to glue on hex nuts, cover with putty, then sand to shape.

The lip of the bridge cap must be filled in carefully to increase the bridge diameter without increasing its height. Again, after consulting photos, select the decals and details from the Estes kit to finish the model.

With either version of the model, maintain the alignment of the nacelles with the saucer, as they tend to sag. Navigation "lights" must be added to the top of the saucer, then painted green and red like those of modern aircraft. Real lighting can be added without storing batteries in the model by running wires out the "impulse power unit," then counterweighting the model to hang evenly.

Since many of the starships seen in the second season were

AMT kits, there is no reason why the modeler cannot assemble and damage kits in the same way the pros did. Studying film clips, you can use torches and heated tools to create the right amount of damage.

4. TREK INTERVIEW: WALTER KOENIG

The following is a three-part series of various articles by and about Walter Koenig that we have run in the past. We combined them in this way so that readers of this collection could see the various sides of Walter: introspective, irreverent, serious, joking, outgoing, close-mouthed. And more. The first is by Walter himself, the next a panel at a convention, the last an interview conducted by mail. In each of them, we see a different Walter Koenig, which is an indication of the many-faceted talents he possesses. Of all the Star Trek personalities, Walter is one of the most sought-after and popular as a convention guest, and we think that these looks into his personality will tell you why.

KOENIG ON STAR TREK
by Walter Koenig

I have decided to approach this piece in a kind of stream-of-consciousness style. I figure that way my feelings will register on more of a gut level and consequently provide for a more incisive personal record (I *think* I just said something). What we're talking about, of course, is *"Star Trek and what it has meant to me"* or *"the most unforgettable ego trip I have ever known."* No question about it, the most significant thing about ST for me was the public reaction to the character I played. All of a sudden there were 650 letters a week, my picture in dozens of magazines (with accompanying articles like "The Terrible Tragedy of Groovy Walter Koenig and his Malformed Small Intestine") and instant recognition on the street. To fully appreciate how novel and inappropriate it all seemed, put yourself in my shoes. It shouldn't be hard. I'm the guy, remember, who collects Big Little Books, Pep pins, and old bubble-gum cards—not a hell of a lot different from you.

In the beginning I found the public response downright embarrassing (in the first months I used to slink away from autograph seekers), but after a while I grew to enjoy the recognition. In my own defense I must say I don't think I ever got "hooked" on it. By that I mean I always maintained a healthy perspective about instant stardom and instant anonymity; today's rising young star is tomorrow's "Walter who?" Also, of course, it was the popularity of the show itself that was largely responsible for my personal success—even the androids received fan mail. All the same, I dug the idea that several million people knew who I was. Pretty heady stuff!

"Wait!" you say. "What about art, the exploration of the creative essence, what about, for goodness sakes, *money!?*" Well, as for my search for art and creative expression, there weren't a hell of a lot of opportunities in that area. I mean, you can do just so much with "Varp (warp) four, captain." There were meatier roles, of course, particularly in my first year (the show's second), but regrettably I don't think I ever really did them justice. I was on a show-to-show basis that first season, which means I could have been dropped at any time, and the weight of that knowledge spilled over onto the sound stage. I was tense a lot. I can't think of one show, in fact, in which I gave a really satisfactory performance. As for money, to be sure I made more bread than I ever had before, but it was still less than an industrious plumber. Anyway, money has never been a major preoccupation with me and would not have been of consuming interest in any circumstance.

About now is a good time to talk about my fellow workers. To be perfectly honest, I probably won't be. That is to say, the following is true as I know it but have the magazine space to fight back.

George Takei was always of good cheer. You never had the feeling that a particular role or even the whole business of acting was a life-and-death situation for him. Don't you hate people like that? One of the reasons for his good balance is the diversification of his interests. George is a political activist (he was a California delegate to the Democratic

National Convention), a successful businessman, and a community leader.

Nichelle Nichols is a very classy lady indeed; very hip, very together, and very strong-willed. She has the style to be as tough as nails and still come off very sexy and very feminine. Aside from a few black-white discussions, I never got to know Nichelle well and it would be presumptuous to elaborate on a personality I always suspected was mostly beneath the surface.

I've always felt that *Jimmy Doohan* was underrated as an actor. It's just a hunch, but I get the feeling that in the right part he could be positively brilliant. He's also a very clever craftsman. He makes really sensational hand-carved chairs, tables, etc. as a hobby. Along with Bill Shatner he was the most "actor-oriented" member of our group. It was Jimmy, I'm sure, who believed right up until the last—even after everyone else had given up—that the show would miraculously be picked up for a fourth year. Now doesn't that sound like an actor?

DeForest Kelley is one of a vanishing breed, a man of genuine warmth and sincerity. He was the only person I ever heard compliment another actor on his performance. Our relationship never extended beyond the set except for one time during the filming of the last episode when we were given an uncommon three-hour break. We decided to use the time to do some shopping. We began talking about ourselves, about the things we've done, about the way we feel, and after a while there was a rapport and a seldom-experienced sense of communion.

Leonard Nimoy is a very bright, very articulate, very involved human being. In many ways I concede Lenny a full measure of respect. Like George, his interests extend beyond acting into the sociopolitical arena. Furthermore, he produced a documentary film in Chicago, and his new contract at Universal calls for him to direct shows as well as act. On our set he was occasionally distant and a trifle aloof. I can't say I always appreciated this posture—it made me feel defensive and therefore a little angry. I seldom had the feeling he was really enjoying himself and was quite surprised recently to learn that he considered Star Trek the most enjoyable thing he had done as an actor. I guess all it means is that I'm not a very reliable analyst or that Leonard Nimoy is a complex personality. I've spoken to him a couple of times since the show closed down and on each occasion found him to be inordinately helpful.

Bill Shatner is a pro in many senses of the word. Whatever the backstage intrigue that was purported to have taken place, he was the one guy who did most to make the set fun and pressureless. Bill is also a hell of an actor. It is a credit to his technique that he could perform pages of dialogue that he memorized minutes before the cameras rolled and do it with authority and a measure of depth—no mean feat, believe me. He also had an extraordinary sense for comic timing. There are an awful lot of "leading man" actors who could have played the love scenes and the derring-do, but the quality of projecting humor is a very special talent. One curiosity: Bill's closest friends on the set were not the other actors but the stuntmen. Of all the regulars on the series, it is a four-to-one bet that Bill Shatner will be the one most likely to pop up again and again on the TV screen.

So much for my capsulized character assassination.

One of the things you sometimes forget as an actor is not to begin a scene too "down" if things are going to get worse as the action progresses. If you do this you have no place to go. With that in mind, it is safe to say that morale during the last season was pretty steady. We came back with foreboding and general pessimism and right up until the end we played the same note. The switch to Friday nights after it seemed that we had Monday nights on the schedule locked up was the most specific cause for depression. In my case it was everything. I had had a long talk with Gene Roddenberry prior to the third season and came away feeling very good about his attitude, the longevity of the series, and particularly the character of Chekov. Then they dropped the bomb and we were switched to no man's wasteland. So much for Chekov. On Monday at seven-thirty he could be cocky, impetuous, girl-chasing, and irreverent for the bubblegum set. At ten o'clock on Fridays he faded into the woodwork. The bubblegum set is either beddy-bye by ten o'clock or on a Friday night is out screwing around somewhere. I remember getting the news of the time switch and knowing instinctively by the feeling of nausea in the pit of my tummy that the ball game was not only over, it wasn't ever even going to be played. Gene, of course, had his own problems. The network had promised him one thing and then turned around and pulled a quickie. He felt deceived and it showed in his withdrawal from the active participation he had planned. Thus began the third and last year and thus it ended.

The new producer was a man who had seen front-line action in three wars, suffered numerous severely debilitating injuries, lost all his money supporting humanitarian causes, and endured unspeakable personal tragedy. Now, I don't know if any of this is true for a fact, but it is one possible explanation for a behavior pattern that at my most generous could only be described as "lack in sensitivity." I think I'll leave it at that.

My personal low point came with one of the episodes in which I played my biggest part. "The Way to Eden" had a subplot about a hippy Russian girl and an uptight anal-fixated establishment-type young officer. In case you don't recognize the guy in the figurative crewcut, it was supposed to be Ensign Chekov. The same character, you remember, that had originally been drawn to reflect an image young people could identify with. Not only did I have problems with the director who wanted me to block my big scene myself and then shoot it without a rehearsal, but the character being written this way was an unmistakable scream in the night that somebody somewhere had stopped caring about the quality of the show. (The fans picked up on this long before I did.) When Dorothy Fontana was story editor and Gene Roddenberry and Gene Coon were running the show, things like this could never have happened. It was about then I realized that the seeping water was past my kneecaps. There was one last gesture of grace from Gene before I was sent permanently back on unemployment insurance. He called each of us at home to thank us for our participation on Star Trek and to inform us personally that Star Trek had been canceled. I figure that was class.

Since ST (the article gets a lot shorter here on out) I spent the whole year of 1969 sitting at home. Not one interview, not one job. To keep myself from strangling my wife, the Avon lady, and my neighbor's emu, I decided to write a novel. Believe it or not I did it. Even sent it to two publishers—got back two very polite rejections. Immediately thereafter I buried the manuscript in a box along with my teething ring, modeling clay, and a course on Transcendental Meditation. I guess the novel served its purpose, though. It got me through the year and the emu still lives!

I started doing television again in 1970. At the same time

I was directing plays and appearing in others. One such play was a very successful production of Jules Feiffer's *White House Murder Case*. I played a CIA man who starts disintegrating on the battlefield—literally begins falling apart—and ends up—how do you say in this country?—with his own disembodied pecker in his hand. I guess you've got to see the play to think it's funny.

All the while I've been writing screenplays, and at last I have apparently come up with one that is, by the general consensus, worthy of production. At this moment my new literary agent is out trying to sell it—I hope. Oh yes, I am also teaching a course in Expressive Techniques to graduate psychology students.

So there you are. The only instant recognition I get these days is from my son (every time he sees me he says "Hi, Fred Flintstone"), but I'm still in there pitching. And who knows, maybe after many years of study, my nose to the grindstone, truly learning my craft, maybe then with decades of dedication and personal sacrifice behind me, perhaps, if I have at last really proven myself, I will finally and ultimately . . . complete my Big Little Book collection.

FOCUS ON WALTER KOENIG

In June 1973, Walter Koenig was the special guest of Houston's Star Trek 74 convention. In conjunction with the convention he appeared on a local talk show. This is an edited transcript of the segments of that hour show which were devoted to Walter.

Walter is introduced and a large round of applause is given him by the studio audience.

HOST: Ensign, I think they like you.

WALTER: That's very nice. It's nice to be liked.

H: We're going to talk to Ensign Chekov quite a bit. Mr. Koenig is his real name. Mr. Koenig, can we get on a first-name basis?

W: By all means.

H: Walter, are you Russian?

W: I'm of Russian extraction. I'm a first-generation American. My parents came from Russia.

H: Your being put into the cast of Star Trek, that in itself is an interesting story. How did that come about?

W: Do you want the truth or what the publicity blurb was?

H: Well, I'll tell you what. The truth.

W: All right. The publicity blurb, first of all, was that *Pravda* was complaining that they had gotten their astronauts out into space first and that there should be a Russian aboard the *Enterprise*. That was purely a fabrication of the people in charge of the publicity at Paramount. It's a nice story, though. I always enjoyed it. The fact of the matter was that they wanted somebody who they thought would appeal to the very young people, the bubblegum set, and everybody involved in making the decision to cast me, I had worked for. It was a very fortuitous thing that happens to an actor perhaps once in a lifetime. So when my name came up it seemed a relatively simple matter to make a decision. And that's what happened.

H: What in your estimation is the real magnetism of Star Trek in its reruns, and how many Star Trek episodes were made?

W: I think it was about seventy-eight. I think the magnetism of Star Trek has to be analyzed and interpreted on several different levels. I think that it stimulates the imagination; that the young people who are the most militant believers in Star Trek, have not yet had their thinking capsulized.

H: Sort of what Buck Rogers and Flash Gordon did for my generation.

W: I think that to a great extent that's true. It has that type of romantic appeal of the fantasy world, and yet there's still that possibility of reality. After all, our shows were very carefully and scrupulously researched so that everything that appeared on Star Trek was at least a possibility. I think that has a great deal to do with it. As for the older audience that was also addicted to the show, I think that it was generally a brighter audience. People who managed to keep an open mind, who had not yet become departmentalized.

H: But also what you're saying is that it's just doggone good entertainment.

W: There's no question about that.

H: Now, I want to be corrected if I say anything wrong here, but we're going to show you something that I think, and I hope you think, is absolutely hilarious. In Hollywood when you do a series, everything that you do in front of the cameras doesn't work out exactly right, and they clip it out and it just falls on the editing-room floor. It's called outtake, as I recall. Now sometimes a very enterprising person will come along and take those outtakes and put them together into a film. What we're about to show is the stars of Star Trek when they goofed. We want you to look at what happens on a set when things like this take place.

(Segment of Star Trek bloopers shown.)

We've just seen a part of this great cast of Star Trek in very unusual, and very humorous and very human situations. Those things do happen on the set.

w: Sure do. Of course you know they never happened to me because I never made a mistake. (*Laughter.*)

H: We're getting phone calls from people wanting to talk to you, so I'll just open up the lines."

CALLER: What I'd like to ask him is how they made the transporter work on Star Trek when they beamed down, and also how the hand phasers operated.

w: Well, in those cases the special effects were done in the laboratory. What we did with the beaming down is simply that they would shoot us standing very still in the transporter, and then we'd step out and they'd shoot some additional footage of just the transporter itself. They would fade us out on the film frame by frame and they would superimpose the shimmering effect in the laboratory. There was nothing like that happening on the set. And then phasers. When I said something about (*Russian accent*) "I'm going to take this phaser and make this rock warm," all I'd do is take this silly wooden thing and point it at a rock and pretend that it was doing something. Nothing actually happened on the set. It was all done in the laboratory. I don't know specifically how it worked, but that's what happens.

H: Walter, did the show ever get an Emmy for the special effects? Because they were tremendous.

w: Star Trek was nominated for an Emmy in—I believe it was 1968. I don't know if it won or not but it was recognized, the work that was being done was recognized by the Academy and by the industry.

CALLER: I have a question for Mr. Chekov. Are they going to bring the Star Trek series back?

W: There is a possibility that is a little bit more imminent than it was six months ago that Star Trek may come back in one form or another. Paramount has for the first time entered serious negotiations with Mr. Roddenberry, who is the producer of the show. As it stands now, if the show did come back it would come back first as a feature film with the idea of then going into a mini-series of six ninety-minute episodes. However, don't take that as gospel, because it's really in the initial stages now of discussion. A lot of things can happen between now and when the decision is ultimately made.

CALLER: Mr. Koenig (*Walter smiles at being addressed by his real name for a change*), I would like to know why you did not choose to participate in the cartoon version of Star Trek?

W: (*Russian accent*): Well, would you believe that it wasn't up to me? I wasn't asked to participate. What happened was that before the decision was made as to who would be in the Star Trek animated show, they had already offered me a script to do, which I did. Subsequently they decided they could not handle all of the actors on twenty-two minutes of film, so they said bye-bye Mr. Chekov.

CALLER: Well, what is your opinion of the actors who are doing it? Are they enjoying it?

W: I think they're probably enjoying it. I don't see why not. It's relatively easy money.

CALLER: At the beginning of the show when they have the numbers, what does that mean?

W: (*Laughing*): What does it mean? You mean the star date? That's what it it, it's the star date. I don't know if anybody really knows what's referred to. The whole concept was to make it as vague as possible so they couldn't possibly pinpoint it in time; so they couldn't say it was 200 years or 400 years from now. The general tacit understanding was that it was perhaps 400 years in the future. I think that it was consciously and purposely made to be vague.

CALLER: I'd like to ask Mr. Chekov a question. What was the Tribble that they had? Those little furry things.

W: The Tribbles. What were they made out of? They were just a synthetic fur kind of thing. The ones that were locomotive, that moved, had this furry synthetic skin over a wind-up toy, and they let it go across the room and shot it without sound or else you'd hear the whir. It was just a little toy that they used.

H: Well, that brings us to the end of the show, and I want to thank you, Walter Koenig, Ensign Chekov, for being with us.

AN INTERVIEW WITH WALTER KOENIG

Q: In retrospect, what is your opinion of the creative or aesthetic aspects of the Star Trek show?

A: In retrospect, I don't understand the question.

Q: Do you feel that the character of Chekov was used to its full potential on the show?

A: Is there dew in the desert? Igloos in Ireland? Magyars in Malaysia?

Q: What has been the effect of Star Trek on your career? Has it helped or hindered your career?

A: What's a career?

Q: What is your reaction to the tremendous following the show has received?

A: I consider it the most extraordinary phenomenon in the history of television.

Q: Since the show has an international following, have you ever been contacted by any Russian science fiction fans commenting on your Chekov portrayals?

A: No, but I've been threatened by the NKVD.

Q: Have you been offered a role in the new Star Trek movie?

A: Which version?

Q: Why were you omitted from the animated series?

A: I don't look good in ink and acetate.

Q: What was your reaction to the series after—say—the first few days on the set? Did you feel it was silly?

A: No, I felt I was silly. Swallows kept trying to nest in the wig they gave me.

Q: Do you feel that Star Trek will have a profound effect on its audience—especially the children who are so taken with the series?

A: Only after they come out with a Chekov doll.

Q: What changes would Walter Koenig like to see in his career? Would you do another series? A more demanding role?

A: What's a career?

Q: What role—either television, film, or stage—is your favorite? Most challenging?

A: The next one.

Q: Would you give a one-word description of your former cast members on Star Trek and then elaborate on your word choice?

A: Shatner: rich; when was the last time you didn't see him on television? Nimoy: humanistic; a man with a very strong social conscience. Doohan: brilliant; what else can I say—he's here with me at the convention! Kelley: human; a genuinely warm and likeable man. Takei: crafty; George would be offended if I didn't kid him at least once! Nichols: fiery; don't cross her! Roddenberry: character; a man of flawless integrity and fierce loyalty.

Q: What was Chekov's background? Did you base him on personal experiences or was he dictated by script motivations?

A: Chekov was invented by a little old lady from Leningrad . . . and a little old man from Minsk.

Q: How do you feel about Star Trek fans? Do you find them overbearing?

A: Only the ones that don't like Chekov.

Q: Do you have any thoughts on the Star Trek conventions? Do you find them a challenge in either a physical or performing sense?

A: The Star Trek fans always make them a tremendously enjoyable experience.

Q: How did you land the role of Chekov in the series?

A: I was working behind the counter of this drug store, see, and wearing this really terrific sweater . . .

Q: Does Walter Koenig have any thoughts about his purpose —or more generally, man's purpose—in life? Is it, as implied in many Star Trek episodes, to explore, to learn?

A: Man's purpose is to reaffirm the efficiency of his existence—to make his presence meaningful by the love, compassion, and respect he bestows on all living beings.

Q: What is Walter Koenig like? Can you describe him and his flaws?

A: The crystalized product of the distilled essence of the above answers compounded is what Walter Koenig is all about.

5. MR. SPOCK: A PERSONAL MEMOIR
by Leslie Thompson

One of the most amazing and most wonderful things about the characters in Star Trek is the way in which they seem to go beyond simple fiction and entertainment—many Star Trek fans can speak both eloquently and at length on how one or more of the Enterprise crew affected their lives. For our fourth issue, we asked Leslie to try to express the effect the character of Mr. Spock has had on her life, development, and personality, It was a thankless assignment, to be sure, as baring some of one's innermost thoughts in the pages of a magazine is no easy task; but the following article proved to be one of the most popular in our history. And we think that it is so because readers responded to the honesty, simplicity, and courage with which Leslie approached the subject.

You never get to know his first name, because you can't pronounce it. He comes from another planet, and his blood is green. His emotions are hidden behind a steely expression; he stands aloof. He is unbelievably smart, and insufferably smug about it. Women adore him, but he has nothing to do with them.

That's not all, but it's quite enough to convince any average producer that if this character was presented in any of his programs, he would find himself the proud possessor of one of the most hated, boring, and unpopular characters in television history.

Yet one producer had the courage to try to present this alien (in more than one sense of the word) in a sympathetic and realistic manner.

The producer was Gene Roddenberry, the show was

Star Trek, and the character was Mr. Spock. And it worked. Boy, did it ever work!

The development of Mr. Spock's character is an entirely different matter from what I want to discuss in this article. This is a personal account of Star Trek, and mostly a looking back on how I reacted to Mr. Spock way back in those dim and dusty years.

I saw the first show. I had read the press releases; about the "Martian," the green blood, the whole schmeer. And, I admit, I ate it up. Have a little charity for me, though. I was a child of, you know, *Attack of the Puppet People* and that sort of garbage. Aside from an occasional "Hey!" when something like *The Day the Earth Stood Still* or *Forbidden Planet* came along, mostly it was bug-eyed monsters who lusted after Julie Adams, and got theirs in the end through the use of electricity. Zap!

So I wasn't really ready for Star Trek, nor for Mr. Spock.

They did lead us in gradually. There was the good ol' salt monster, trashing people right and left, the heroic captain, and the ever-ready loyal crew. Not a particularly exceptional show, but in retrospect, a very wise choice for the premiere episode.

But there was this one character who was different. Sure he had pointed ears, and bled green (a lot of good that did on black-and-white TV), but he *acted* different from the rest of the space jockeys. This was Mr. Spock.

True, he didn't have much to do; and maybe not too coincidentally, he was kept pretty much in the background; but there was *something* there. Just how much was there I was to discover in the following weeks.

After only a few shows, I was hooked. A full-fledged, fire-breathing Spock Freak. And I thought I was the only one. Later I was to find out that my estimate was short by only a million or so.

Spock grabs you! The character so superbly portrayed by Leonard Nimoy just reaches out from the screen and pulls you in there with him.

Reams have been written about why this happens. Everything from "the secret, deep, dark, hidden, forbidden urge to be raped" to "the pure beauty of logic and reason." Ours is not to reason why.

Suffice it to say that Spock gets to people, for a variety of reasons. But back to a personal view.

Neither my life nor my thinking radically changed because of Mr. Spock. However, in many very subtle ways, I began to apply the philosophy taught by Mr. Spock.

The first was Keep Your Cool. If, like Spock, you could control your emotions, step back and look at a problem realistically and—yes—logically, then you could possibly control the situation as well. It worked for me. Instead of flying off the handle, I counted to ten, took a deep breath, and then took the necessary action. Spock would have been proud!

More important, however, was the influence of Spock (and other aliens presented on Star Trek) which helped me to overcome some deep-rooted prejudices.

Remember, I said I was a child of the fifties? Well, the sixties followed right after that. (More logic.)

Civil rights came of age in the sixties, and so did I—right here in the South. You can pretty well imagine my environment, so let's say that Spock and Star Trek did as much to change my views as my watching civil-rights workers being hosed down and badgered with police dogs.

You see, not only had all of the people of Earth settled their problems and differences, but they had *aliens*—completely different, in every way actual aliens—working hand in hand with Earthmen. It was a special and wonderful feeling to see such a vision at that time.

And Spock. Not only was I accepting an alien character, but actually liking and respecting him!

If that could be, then why couldn't it work with a person of a different color right here, right now? Another light dawned, and another debt owed to the characterization of Mr. Spock.

Spock. The memories come back, far too many to relate. The burgeoning interest in science and computers. The loosening of imagination as I wondered what Vulcan was like, and how a society had become a race of emotionless beings. Physics—*is* it possible for that damn ship to really go that fast?

Mr. Spock has undoubtedly now become one of the most famous creations of the TV years. Before long, he may join that small elite of characters whose names are instantly recognizable to anyone—Tarzan, Superman, the Lone Ranger, Sherlock Holmes, James Bond.

Mr. Spock may just turn out to be the folk hero of the

sixties and seventies. A pivot point for the intellectual development of thousands of adolescents—and a not too much
smaller number of adults.

The creation of Gene Roddenberry and Leonard Nimoy
has much yet ahead of him. He has much to do to help make
our world the world of Star Trek. And if we live in peace
and love and logic, then Spock will always be there as a
guide and beacon.

Mr. Spock didn't change my life. He helped *me* to change
my life. You can do the same.

Who is Spock?

A good many people will reply that he's that fellow on
the space show, the guy with the funny ears. But Mr. Spock
of Star Trek goes far beyond the pointed ears. He is the most
unique character in the history of television; for he was
the first continuing character in a series who was not only
alien to our society, but to our world.

In order to fully understand the character of Spock, we
must go all the way back to the beginning, before Spock
(and Star Trek) even existed.

When Gene Roddenberry was first playing with the idea
of a science fiction TV series, he wanted at least one regular
cast member to be an alien.

This alien had to be somewhat different in appearance—
but not so different that he would not mix with a group of
Earthlings. In addition, the alien would have to be played by
a human, so anything too far removed from *Homo sapiens*
would require a costume or makeup which would seem un-
realistic or even ludicrous to viewers. So, while he must be
different, he couldn't be *too* different. A pretty problem.

During this time (1963), Roddenberry was producing
The Lieutenant, and an actor by the name of Leonard Nimoy had a guest role in one episode.

As the story goes, Roddenberry told Nimoy that he
was working on a science fiction show pilot, and he had a
role planned that would be a challenge for any actor, but
that Nimoy was the actor he wanted.

Thus, in the minds of Roddenberry and Nimoy, the character of Spock began to emerge. But there would be more
problems to be overcome before Spock made his television
debut.

The main problem was the ears. It took some time before
the shape was just right, but after the first pilot, NBC

thought that Spock looked too Satanic, and would repel viewers. They wanted him dropped.

Roddenberry fought to keep Spock as a key component of the show, stressing how he added to the show's believability. There had to be at least one character to remind viewers that they were really out in space.

Thanks to Roddenberry's insistence, Spock was kept in the second pilot and managed to remain in the series despite the odds against him.

Now to regress a little. In the original Star Trek format, Spock was to be a minor character; the ship's science officer, half-Martian, and very emotional. Well, the red makeup looked pretty bad, so they changed it to a green base, and changed home planets for Spock at the same time.

Scenes cut from "The Cage" in making "The Menagerie" show a very emotional, almost human Spock. Two good emotional scenes remain in "The Menagerie": one on the planet's surface when Spock smiles at Captain Pike; and another in the transporter room, in which Spock screams, "The women!"

As viewer reaction proved cool to the character of Number One in the first pilot, her characteristics are merged into those of Spock. Spock remains the Vulcan science officer, but also becomes the cool, logical first officer. This is the beginning of the character we all know and love.

However, traces of emotion remain. In "Where No Man Has Gone Before," the second pilot, as the situation grows critical, Spock raises his voice. He smiles broadly when he says, "Ah yes, one of your Earth emotions."

It is also during this show that it is revealed that Mr. Spock is not supposed to have feelings, and that "one of his ancestors married a human female."

Most of this emotionalism continues through the first part of this first season, with Spock doing little more than feeding the Captain information, screaming "It's murdering the captain! Shoot it!" or placing his hands on his hips in frustration. (Something Nimoy must have felt like doing many times during this period.)

The outstanding Spock episode in the first part of the first season was "The Naked Time." Specifically, in the scene in the briefing room when we discover Spock's mother was human on a planet where emotion was considered to be in bad taste. We see for the first time the inner conflict between Spock's human and Vulcan halves.

It is not until the later part of the first season that Spock becomes a more rounded character through the addition of the Spock-McCoy conflict. Spock and McCoy are at the same time opposites and complementary to each other.

Both are men of science, but Spock is the logical, empirical scientist, while McCoy is the emotional, cynical doctor. This surface conflict continues, but deep inside each feels a great respect for the other's skills and abilities.

"Tomorrow is Yesterday," "The *Galileo* Seven," and almost every show in the second season contain excellent examples of the Spock-McCoy conflict. But one of the most touching scenes of mutual respect comes in "The Empath." After McCoy has been tortured (by his own choice to protect Kirk and Spock), Spock's only concern is the comfort of his friend.

Through Spock, during the later part of the second season, we discover that Vulcans are a superior race in many ways. They are phyically stronger and mentally superior to humans, but at the cost of their emotions.

Spock first exhibited the use of the Vulcan Mind Meld in "Dagger of the Mind" as a handy technique of getting information. Spock is reluctant to use it, since there is a merging of minds, and the recipient will gain knowledge of Spock's hidden human half. In later episodes, however, Spock uses the Meld more frequently, especially with the captain and others with whom he is close. Perhaps he had gained more control over what he "gave" in the process, or maybe he became less reluctant to express his inner self to his compatriots.

The great physical stamina of the Vulcan is demonstrated by Spock on several occasions, most notably in "The Enemy Within," which served to introduce the Vulcan nerve pinch. (Apparently humans cannot master this technique, since even the strong-willed and athletic Kirk is unable to learn how to do it.) In "The Naked Time," Spock hits Kirk and sends him flying across a table, and in "Mirror, Mirror," Spock manages to hold his own against Kirk, McCoy, Scott, and Uhura.

Another interesting aspect of the unemotional Mr. Spock is the number of his "love affairs." Five episodes contained a love relationship for the Vulcan: "This Side of Paradise,"

"Amok Time," "The *Enterprise* Incident," "The Cloud Minders," and "All Our Yesterdays."

In three of these Spock was driven to love by chemical or physical circumstances; one was a purely intellectual love affair; and only one was "true love."

In "This Side of Paradise," it was an alien spore which caused Spock to overcome his Vulcan half and fall in love with Leila Kalomi.

A trip through a time portal in "All Our Yesterdays" caused the Vulcan to regress to a primitive, barbaric state (as Vulcans were then) where he could both mentally and physically love Zarabeth.

In "Amok Time," it was the *pon farr* which caused Spock to return to Vulcan and seek out T'Pring. It is interesting to note T'Pring's reaction to Spock's *pon farr:* She rejects him in favor of Staun. She tells Spock that she wants Staun and that Staun wants her. Are no emotions involved here?

Spock's relationship with Droxine in "The Cloud Minders" is an intellectual affair rather than an emotional affair. But Droxine obviously wishes it was more, as she asks of Spock, "And is there nothing that can disturb that cycle?" (the every-seven-years *pon farr*).

The only episode in which Spock loosens his control of his own free will is "The *Enterprise* Incident." Of the five females with whom Spock becomes involved, only the Romulan commander is Spock's equal in personality and bearing. However, as involved as Spock becomes, he still places his duty above all.

Added to these five examples, of course, is the continuing involvement of Spock with Nurse Christine Chapel. Spock is aware of Christine's love for him, and while he cannot return it (especially in the enclosed environment of the ship) he always tries to treat her with compassion and understanding—traits one would hardly expect to find in an "emotionless" being.

But what about Spock's background? Little is discussed until "Journey to Babel," when we are introduced to Sarek and Amanda, Spock's parents.

Spock, it seems, had a difficult childhood. He was rejected by both Vulcans and humans. And his one friend was a pet *sehlat* (kind of a fat teddy bear—with six-inch fangs). When Amanda reveals this fact to Dr. McCoy, we can see the subtle and gentle chiding which she gives Spock for taking himself so seriously. His father, however, is a different matter.

When it came time for Spock to decide what he wanted to do for the rest of his life, he chose Starfleet. Sarek, not understanding the tensions which drove Spock from Vulcan, highly disapproved of his decision. So much so, in fact, that he and Spock did not speak as father and son for eighteen years. (Another Vulcan trait; they are stubborn.) How this impasse was resolved made for a fascinating story.

During the third and final season of Star Trek, everything in the show began to stagnate. No one seemed to care about the characters except the actors. Nimoy fought especially hard to keep Spock alive, but the regular writers and producers (who knew what to *do* with the character) were gone. So Spock slowly turned into a "yes man" for Kirk.

One of the best examples of this deterioration of Spock was in "Whom Gods Destroy," where Spock is unable to tell which is the real Kirk. He did not use logic and observation, or even the Mind Meld, but rather let himself be hit over the head.

But Spock has made his impression on the minds and hearts of millions. He brought many gifts to the Earth: the Vulcan hand salute, "Live Long and Prosper," and, of course, the concept of the IDIC—to be different is not necessarily to be wrong. We are all different, and should rejoice in our differences.

Spock was the first. He will not be the last.

6. THE MONSTERS OF STAR TREK
by Winslow Leach

Star Trek, like any other star-spanning series or films, often featured aliens in its episodes. And very often, the aliens were portrayed as the classical interpretation of a "monster" —a slimy, crawly, scaly, hairy, and just plain horrifying whatever. But in this area, as in many others, Star Trek always managed to rise above the accepted norm. The following article by Winslow Leach examines some of the monsters that appeared in various Star Trek episodes, and explains how on Star Trek, a "monster" was somehow different from anywhere else.

When it came to monsters, movies and television have always treated them pretty much the same. A monster is misshapen on the outside, therefore its personality and motives shall reflect that misshapenness, they *shall* be monstrous, of unrelenting evil intent.

But on Star Trek it was different. We were usually led along at first because we were accustomed to the cliché, and therefore took the bait, later to be surprised when a motive or a facet of the creature's personality emerged that we weren't prepared for.

It was Star Trek that showed us that just because something isn't human doesn't mean it can't have human traits and even feelings, or a personality that we can identify with under that harsh exterior.

The first monster that we encountered on Star Trek was in its premiere episode, "Mantrap." This was actually a monster in the most classic sense. The Salt Vampire (as the creature has been christened by the fans) was the last of its race. It was a highly intelligent creature, yet it would kill to eat, like any animal, no matter what.

Its hypnotic screen enabled it to disguise its true form so well that three different people looking at it would see three different versions of its false image. It plucked ideas for forms from the minds of others, or else from the image of those it had killed. When salt was not in ready supply, the Salt Vampire used stealth to gain it; stealth to get close to a victim before it killed.

Instead of using its intelligence to make a bargain with humankind and gain the salt it needed, the Salt Vampire's apparently bestial mind could only think of killing to get what it needed. In the end it was this primal, animalistic drive that brought about the creature's doom, and no amount of falsehood or disguise could save it.

In the "Corbomite Maneuver," we encounter the creature Balok and his gigantic starship the *Fesarious*. The Balok we see on the screen of the *Enterprise*, the fearful alien visage, turns out to be a ruse used to test the crew of the *Enterprise* to see how they would react to something totally alien from themselves, and perhaps reveal their true selves in doing so.

The real Balok turns out to be a puny being (played by Clint Howard) who is pleased at how they reacted when the frightful creature who had threatened them was apparently helpless and in need.

The voice of the false Balok, the loud booming one heard on the *Enterprise*, was uncredited on the show, but belonged to Ted Cassidy.

Ted Cassidy himself appeared in "What Are Little Girls Made Of?" as Ruk the Android.

Ruk was constructed thousands of years ago by the old ones, who died off and left him. Ruk is used to kill and shows no compassion. In fact it is the emotional weakness of his scientist master which makes Ruk turn on him, causing Ruk to meet his doom at the wrong end of a phaser.

In "The *Galileo* Seven" we face eight-foot-tall, monstrously strong barbarians who hurl spears six inches thick and roar defiantly at the stranded starcraft crew, whom they start killing off one by one. These beings are humanoid, but very low on the scale. They react by instinct, and their only thought concerning the strangers is to kill them.

In "The Menagerie" we meet the Keepers. These are apparently heartless beings who capture Captain Pike, and plan to mate him with an Earthwoman to create a colony of slaves.

This is later enlarged as being a last-ditch attempt of these people to save their race from extinction by beginning a new civilization on the surface of the planet.

When it becomes evident to them that Earth people are poor choices for captives, they release them. Later they display true compassion when they allow the hopelessly crippled Pike to return to Talos IV so that he can live out his life in his mind, "unfettered by his physical body."

The power of these creatures' minds is displayed when Pike captures one and it immediately changes into a weird apelike creature to try to frighten him.

Thus these creatures display many sides of their personalities. They are coldly logical in pursuit of their goal, and yet, when that goal is revealed as impossible, they show compassion for the being who has defeated them. These are not your run-of-the-mill aliens.

In "Shore Leave" the monsters are all mechanical contrivances cleverly built by the properties of the planet. They are real, yet unreal, and McCoy's increasing irritation over them (which began with his run-in with a large white rabbit) almost undoes him as he defies a charging knight to prove that it's real, which it promptly does by impaling him on its lance.

In "Arena" we confront the Gorn, the lizard being which is equal in intelligence to Kirk, but is more savage.

The Gorns wipe out an Earth outpost, as they feel that it is encroaching on their space. At first Kirk wants vengeance, but later he realizes that this creature does have its own point of view, and stops just short of killing it even though it would have been easy for him to do so.

So although the Gorn shows no compassion, Kirk sees within himself the same blind savagery for which he had planned to kill this creature; and having seen that it was wrong in the Gorn, he knows that it is also wrong for him.

But the important point is that Kirk accords the Gorn its own outlook, even though it is totally alien.

"The Devil in the Dark" introduces the creature which has endeared itself in the hearts and minds of the fans almost as much as the Tribbles, the Horta.

This creature too is accorded the right to have a point of view, despite its total alienness to humankind.

What appears at first to be blind, unreasoned attacks and brutal senseless murders turn out to be the Horta striking back in defense of its eggs. The miners have broken into the egg chamber, accidentally destroying some eggs, and threatening others. The Horta strikes back.

When Kirk and Spock establish communication with the creature, a settlement is reached. Both man and Horta viewed each other as invading monsters, and only when they stopped to communicate were the problems solved. It beats shooting the Horta off the Empire State Building.

In "Operation Annihilate," the monsters are parasites which take over the entire nervous system of the human body. These are more classical monsters, as they are just the "find some way to destroy them" type, and when their weakness is discovered, everything is cool.

"Catspaw" has aliens in human form. Their human forms are totally illusion and yet their minds are not alien at all. These beings are evil—although one is not as bad as the other when they argue over the fate of the *Enterprise* crew.

All manner of monsters materialize because of these beings, such as witches and even a gigantic black cat.

Upon their defeat and their loss of the source of their illusionary power, their true forms are revealed—forms only a few inches tall, and too fragile to exist without their power.

These beings are as alien as can be, and yet their personalities are as human and contradictory as that of any one of us.

"Metamorphosis" has an even more alien being in the form of a cloud creature. This creature at first seems of only instinctual intelligence, but it is revealed to be of humanlike high intelligence, so high as to be able to experience love.

What starts out as a being whose destruction is sought turns out to be a creature of compassion, whom we come to understand on the level of a fellow being. A monster? Well, everyone makes mistakes.

"The Doomsday Machine" is a monster on a cosmic level. It is a device constructed eons ago by a race now probably long dead. And yet its planet-killing abilities remain intact. Gazing into its maw is like looking down the throat of a monstrous whale, only instead of being able to swallow men and even ships, this whale "swallows" whole planets!

Although of the "how do we kill it?" school again, it becomes far more complex than that, as human factors become involved. In this case, the mindless monster causes the men involved to see what type of people they really are when they are forced to make great personal sacrifices, risking *everything* to bring about its destruction. Through this monster we see the men.

"Wolf in the Fold" introduces an entity which is revealed to be one of the most classic monsters in history, Jack the Ripper! Robert Bloch used a favorite concept of his in the form of the deathless Jack, this time transporting him to the stars.

This entity is mindless in that it thrives only on death, and is seemingly indestructible as it proves capable of taking over the *Enterprise*. This monster is interesting in the way it is able to manipulate men, murdering and seeing innocents suffer because of it, in this case the falsely accused Scotty.

A classic monster handled in a decidedly unclassic fashion.

"The Changeling" is a robot, the product of a collision of two deep space probes, one from Earth, the other from an alien world. The result is mayhem. The device demonstrates capabilities of vast magnitudes, redesigning the ship and even returning life to the dead.

But its misguided and damaged programming dooms it. It did not ask to be what it is. It gained intelligence through a fluke, but even that intelligence is not great enough to save it from self-destruction.

By the time "Journey to Babel" was aired, the viewers of Star Trek had matured enough not to look upon any of the various alien races represented here as "monsters" just because of a bizarre outward appearance.

"A Private Little War" presents us with the Maguto. Despite its strange appearance, what with the horn on its head and all, it is only a creature with poisonous fangs, seemingly just thrown into an otherwise undistinguished episode. It has no purpose, and is so two-dimensional as to not be worth a discussion. It was an animal; just leave it at that.

"Obsession" presents another cloud creature, this one a vampire. The creature itself has no demonstrable intelligence, other than cunning, and it is just used to show the foibles of men.

"The Immunity Syndrome" presents one of the strangest monsters used, an amoebalike creature which exists through a black hole in space. It makes for an interesting story of the "how do we kill it" school again, but one wonders where the devil something like that came from to begin with.

At least some speculation in the episode might have been interesting. As far as we know it is just a strange monster of sorts, of strange sorts to be sure, but that's it.

"The Ultimate Computer" presents one of the most interesting and multifaceted monsters of the series.

M-5 is a computer. But it also is a Frankenstein. Not out of revenge or any such human motives, but because it was made *too* well. But it is not because of this that its downfall is senility, reminiscent of the coldly logical Colossus of D. F. Jones' novel as well as the film that was based on it. M-5 does what is expected of it without the need for such complications as the pretend fight with the other four starships involved. M-5 is attacked, therefore M-5 defends itself, even if it means destroying a starship.

"Spectre of the Gun" confronts us with the Melkotian, the strange multi-colored, bulbous creature which pits Kirk and party to fight the strange duel. The creature is intelligent, but of an alien intelligence, ergo the problems. It's an interesting creature but more of a device as it's not nearly as fully explored as it could have been.

"The Lights of Zetar" are a colony of energy beings capable of killing all human beings they come in contact with. Their motives, etc. are explored to an extent and are interesting, but unfortunately this strange life entity has to be killed to save the crewperson.

"The Savage Curtain" uses a strange rock creature on a volcanic world. It is a perfectly intelligent entity, but needs Kirk to test whether good is stronger than evil. Since Kirk and the others in the test being performed aren't rock creatures, one wonders how anything could be settled anyway. It's a rather senseless episode with just a strange creature thrown in that looks like it would have been more at home on *Lost in Space*

"Day of the Dove" uses this creature-observing-conflict idea also, only in this case the energy being used is the hatred generated by conflict in order to survive. It is an interesting idea, although the creature's real thoughts are never investigated and it is pictured pretty much as just an ordinary alien monster.

But even when Star Trek resorted to the classic approach to monsters, it was interesting and still could not have been called average.

In "The Tholian Web" the bizarre alien, only the "face"

of which is ever seen, is a monster only due to its alienness; and it's because of the total difference of its mind and thoughts that communication fails. Despite what it does, the alien even in this case is not bad, just different.

This is what Star Trek so often strived to say when confronted with intelligent aliens which acted in ways we would find inexplicable.

They were different, but still, ultimately, understandable. This was the basic underlying optimism of the show. Don't kill what's different without trying to understand it first.

There was infinite diversity in infinite combinations; one of the underlying concepts which helped to tell what Star Trek was really all about.

7. STAR TREK AND ME
by Fern Lynch and Isobel Real

Some time ago we instituted a column called "Star Trek and Me," in which some of our readers told of the major effects that Star Trek had had on their lives. In a way, it was the predecessor of "Fan of the Month," but lacked that feature's photos, briefness, and general lightness. "Star Trek and Me" was an immensely popular feature, but ended in failure. Readers enjoyed the stories of others, but were obviously unwilling to reveal as much of themselves for the feature, so it died from lack of submissions. However, we feel that the stories of Mrs. Lynch and Ms. Real are important. Through them we can see the true beauty and wonder of the ideals of Star Trek and a fandom such as ours. Theirs is the story of every Star Trek fan. The difference is only one of degree.

FERN LYNCH

Finally, and at the ripe old age of sixty-five, I have become the expert! I have been watching Star Trek since my first heart attack in 1968, but never talked about it to anyone. I just thought I must be a little "peculiar" to have such a deep regard for a television program and its absolutely wonderful cast. So I didn't mention that I was a Star Trek gazer for years.

However, this March '76, I saw an ad for the con in Los Angeles (Equicon) and thought it would be wonderful fun to go. I thought about it for three days, and decided there was no time to waste! I wrote for my tickets, hotel room, theater tickets, banquet, made reservations to fly and was off!

I never saw a generation gap close so quickly! If you stood around more than three people you got into discussions. The most fascinating one I participated in was with a group of people of various ages. One college girl said she wears her IDIC everywhere and tells anyone who will listen the philosophy behind it. We ended up more or less on education and politics; and each one listened to the others, even though they might not agree.

I have twelve grandchildren, the oldest almost twenty-six and the youngest seven, and just this year I found out they watch Star Trek. For the first time since my own children were little, I was the expert! I have seen each episode ten to fifteen times, and never tire of them.

In discussing Star Trek with Adam, the youngest, he asked why I liked it. Now telling a seven-year-old how the courage, the optimism, and the hope for the future is the core of Star Trek's appeal is a little difficult. Children absorb this unknowingly, but the basic appeal to them is visual. They do not yet relate to the message Star Trek projects.

I think of it as a kind of "sleep teaching." By constant exposure to the show, I hope they will actually take in the message subconsciously, and emulate the characteristics of their heroes. And do we need heroes!

But back to the con: I registered on Thursday the 15th, and then sat in the lobby watching others checking in, trying to guess who was there for the convention. Of course, some already had their uniforms on.

The Hotel Marriott has 1,000 rooms, and it was jammed. The overflow was forced to go to an adjacent hotel.

I went to dinner in the hotel restaurant and was sitting adjacent to two young gentlemen (thirtyish), when a girl walked by wearing pointed ears and a costume. They remarked to each other that they couldn't figure out what was going on. Seeing I had my badge on, they turned to me for an explanation.

I told them that the girl typified the premise of Star Trek on diversity. That no one would laugh at her. That to herself she was beautiful, and therefore she would be regarded as beautiful by all who love Star Trek. They agreed that it was a wonderful thought, and said they would try to watch Star Trek in the future.

Now there may have been some complaints about this con, but I myself thought it was run very well. The Trimbles had a herculean task and achieved wonders. There were episodes of Star Trek three times a day. The programs were excellent and it was up to you to find what you wanted. It was all there, even though there were times when I wished I were twins so I could be in two places at once.

I think for myself I found the most satisfaction in listening to, and sometimes joining in, conversations that sounded interesting. The range was terrific; not limited to Star Trek, but spiraling off into education, politics, and the things that my generation had contributed to the young.

Several younger persons said they had never thought of us older people as having the same dreams they had and trying to do something about it, but without violence. As I pointed out, I had been seventeen, but they had never been sixty-five, so there was no way that they could validly believe that everything we had done was wrong.

There were writers' panels—one with Majel Barrett, William Campbell, Robert Clarke, Arlene Martel, and Kirk Alyn, the original Superman (a very good-looking man). At this panel, William Campbell was presented with the blue velvet coat he wore in "The Squire of Gothos." He was very touched and gave a nice speech, thanking the fans for their attendance in behalf of the Motion Picture and TV Actor's Home.

There was an excellent panel with George and Gene. Pal and Roddenberry, that is! Mr. Roddenberry said that the film had a stage assigned, but nothing else was firmed up. He thanked the fans for their continuing devotion and patience.

Now remember, this was a hotel and we had the ground floor, including all of the rooms on it. By Friday night, it was becoming very difficult to maneuver, but everyone was polite. Many times, because I had a cane, I was offered a seat or a better place in line.

I find that I can label fans only "good-mannered" or "bad-mannered"; the terms Trekker, Trekkie, etc. turn me off. By and large, 98 percent of the people I encountered were good-mannered and gentle. That is to me the typical fan: intelligent, willing to talk, but even readier to listen. The con "gofers" were lovely, very helpful indeed.

Bjo and her husband John gave great speeches and had an auction, which was fun. While I talked to Mr. Campbell and his wife and shook hands with Fritz Weaver, I made no attempt for autographs! I do not envy public personalities! When one appears, it is hazardous, even with the best of security. I cannot imagine going to a con with one of the Big Three. I want to more than anything but dare not.

Saturday there must have been at least 5,000 people in the confined space of the halls, meeting rooms, and hucksters' room. This was especially fascinating. I even bought myself a $10 record of Leonard Nimoy's "Mr. Spock's Music from Outer Space," and I don't even have a phonograph! (I took it home and left it at my daughter's and three weeks later finally persuaded myself to buy a tape recorder.)

I also bought some souvenirs for my grandchildren, including an Apollo patch for a grandson. I didn't even know if he would like that. He is twelve and we've always had trouble communicating. More on this later.

I saw Leonard Nimoy in "Sherlock Holmes" Saturday with a busload of people from the con. The show was fascinating and he achieved a remarkable feat with his voice; it was pitched higher—the delivery quick and sometimes slightly hysterical—which fitted the part perfectly, but took me a few minutes to adjust to after being used to the dignified, measured speech of Mr. Spock.

Because of my visit to the theater, I missed a panel of writers, including Robert Bloch and Theodore Sturgeon. I was very disappointed, but I had had to make a choice and I had made the logical one for me.

By Saturday night there was barely a square inch to move around in. I went to the costume judging, but because of the people in the row in front of me who kept getting up and the heat, I had to leave. However, I sat on a couch at the end of the hall and very soon a lady joined me.

She told me she was seventy-three and had been to every con within a decent distance. She had a big tape recorder which had just run out. She said she belonged to a club which met every week and showed me a beautiful photo album with candid shots of everyone from Star Trek and autographs!

While I was sitting with her, many people stopped by to say hello, including George Clayton Johnson, who wrote "The Man Trap." He is surprisingly young. We also had a corner where those who couldn't get into the big room were having their own photographic show, with some very beautiful girls and a Gorn. I think that boy will remember the con for a long while to come!

While sitting, we saw a Japanese outfit filming. We thought it was just a personal thing, but they turned the cameras on us too. We talked to them and asked if all of this type of thing happened in Japan and they answered yes! It is pretty hard to believe that the Star Trek craze (or whatever) is a worldwide thing, but I do believe it.

Sunday I attended what were my last two viewings of Star Trek episodes on the big 35-mm screen—and with no commercials, they were something to see. The reaction of each person at the screenings was so interesting. There was a sense of possessiveness about the show. I know; I felt it myself.

Sunday morning there were the usual episodes and science fiction films, but time was left from 11:00 a.m. onward in order to clear the room for the banquet. I went upstairs for a bath and when I came down, I heard Leonard Nimoy's voice! I was so disappointed, I wanted to cry, but couldn't. After all, I'm a big girl now. So I swallowed my disappointment and was doubly glad I had seen him in the play.

What made my disappointment doubly hard to take was the fact that in October 1973, he had come to a town thirty-five miles from where I live for a lecture and I had planned to go. But to my chagrin, I was in the coronary unit at the same time he was giving his lecture. And in the same town!

Now Mr. Nimoy had two performances Saturday night and one Sunday, and I think it shows a measure of the regard he has for his fans when he makes such a visit on a Sunday morning. From speaking with those who heard his talk, he is a witty, articulate, and gentle man who appreciates what the fans have done for him, just as we appreciate what he has done for us.

The banquet was attended by about 500 people, including the Roddenberrys (who sat at different tables) and the writers, designers, and the creative people who did sets, makeup, etc. Grace Lee Whitney, who had entertained with her band Saturday night, was there also. We were to have Robert Clarke at our table, but he didn't make it. There was no criticism from us. After all, he had been there all day Saturday and it was Easter.

All in all, it was the most memorable weekend of my life and one which brought some interesting sidelights with it.

First of all, I am able to be friends with my twelve-year-old grandson now. We really talk, and that we could never do before. Second, I stopped biting my nails! Silly, but I had started after the second heart attack and somehow, when I made up my mind to go to the con, I decided at the same time to stop. So now, for the first time in years, I have beautiful nails again.

I joined the Leonard Association of Fans, the Startrekennial News, bought records, sent a Leonard Nimoy tape to a girl in Australia, wrote to two ladies in Texas, and all in all, I am having a ball. For the first time, everything I do is for me, for fun, and because I love Star Trek and everyone who is connected with it.

ISOBEL REAL

Back in the latter part of 1966, I chanced to tune a TV set to the newly launched series Star Trek, thereby being introduced to its strong influence during my formative years. Although my age then was twenty-five, I was as uninformed about American customs and mores as a newborn babe. My country of birth (Cuba) had not prepared me for the American world of that period. I could not understand what was going on in my adopted country, and I did not accept the events taking place through lack of cultural empathy and background.

Language can be learned easily; culture cannot be learned at all, it must be absorbed, accepted, and later automatically adopted by the individual undergoing habitat transference. I am certain that erudite intellectuals have covered the subject thoroughly; my views are personal and unsupported and could, at times, contradict established norms.

At any rate, in 1966, I was not an American; I did not understand the cultural patterns of the society and, to be quite honest, what I saw on the surface I did not like. It may have been a normal rejection of the unknown when it conflicted with my natural patterns of behavior. But the country was also undergoing some unpleasant adjustments during the period and my judgment may have been clouded by a combination of circumstances, none of which made the process any easier.

That was the stage upon which Star Trek and I first met.

The first episode seen by me of what would become my favorite program and idealized environment was "Naked Time," a magnificent introduction to the series. Yes, I had missed the prior episodes and I have always regretted it; reruns filled in the empty spaces, but it was not the same.

My command of the English language was fair and I was fortunately able to understand the contents of that piece of Utopia. For years I had been an avid reader of science fiction (since childhood in fact) and I was prepared by the likes of Asimov to enjoy the new program. As the weeks went by, I continued to follow the characters as they developed, the story lines instilling a sense of belonging to a world that was, at the same time, mythical, well known, familiar, and truly fascinating.

One character made a particularly strong impact upon me, the alien with the pointed ears, the "biological computer," the unique and beloved stranger from Vulcan: Mr. Spock. It is imperative to note that, although I am female, there were no sexual overtones to my admiration. Nor were there any patterns for father replacement search in what developed. The alien, Mr. Spock, became my alter ego. It mattered not that the sexes were different; our positions in our worlds were so similar that nothing else was of consequence.

Slowly, ever so slowly and painfully, I began to realize that the society where I found myself (U.S.A.) could and would, one day in the future, give rise to the other world I was admiring, incomplete picture though it was. The best Americans could be, in fact, persons with the qualities of Captain James T. Kirk of the USS *Enterprise*.

It took longer still to reach another earthshaking conclusion: it had been Americans who saw the future world (and galaxy) united, accepting and welcoming all of us who contributed to the good of the society regardless of physiognomy or behavioral traits.

Mr. Spock, my alter ego, accepted and even understood a strange culture, without really approving of it. He, the ultimate giver of justice, was the Solomon of our *Enterprise*, with his controlled emotions and absolute impartiality, never suffering from our personal biases, ethical and devoted to duty. He would be the one I would attempt to emulate. What an ideal to copy!

The years passed, Star Trek and Spock kept alive in my mind. Wondering all the time how Spock would react to a given situation and following the answer as best I could, I was able to survive the difficult period of adjustment. An alien, me, copying an alien, Spock, became accepted as an American. To this day, no one knows the game I played with myself—that is, no one but me.

As I adopted American customs, as I strove to understand the ways of my society, I gained better depth of character. When I first saw Star Trek, I was a clerk in a government office with little or no chance of promotion. My desire to understand became curiosity about the work performed by the group. A similar curiosity is found in the Spock personality, although I did not realize it at the time. It was this consuming curiosity that made me devote many hours of leisure time to learning about everything we did.

Now, just ten years later, I find myself in a responsible position in government service. It is part of my duties to interpret laws and regulations (I am not an attorney) that relate to my area of expertise. It is also part of my duties to translate those regulations into semi-technical format, as "user's specification" for electronic data processing systems, a function for which I must display the powers of logical reasoning learned thanks to Mr. Spock. I now supervise sixty-two employees in various levels of service—I am now GS-12, and I plan to continue growing, loyally and justly.

For my life and my success, I have to thank Star Trek publicly. For making me a better person, I have to thank Mr. Spock. Now I am a fairly well-balanced person, fulfilled and content; then I was lost and disturbed.

Thank you, Mr. Spock . . . thank you, Star Trek.

8. A LOOK AT LEONARD McCOY
by Walter Irwin

When preparing material for Trek *No. 9, editor Walter Irwin began to get a nagging thought in the back of his head. Suddenly, it came to him: In the more than two years that* Trek *had been published, not one major article had been devoted to lovable and irascible Dr. McCoy. This was an oversight of serious proportions, as many of our readers are devoted McCoy fanatics. After deciding to run a McCoy article in that very issue, Walter began pooling our major contributors for one to do an article on Bones. For various reasons, no one was able to do the piece, but Walter was determined to have it in* Trek *9, so he did it himself. And from the result, we tend to think that Walter is one of those "McCoy fanatics" himself!*

It seems a bit of a shame that when Star Trek is discussed in newspaper articles and books, or by those who are not true fans, the character of Dr. Leonard McCoy is so often overlooked. The Kirk/Spock relationship is well known to everyone, and has indeed been the basis for much speculation, discussion, examination, and even fiction. But it is often forgotten that an integral part of this relationship is the third part of the triangle, McCoy.

He holds a special place in the relationship of the two primary officers, and to be able to understand what his very necessary place and function is, we must first examine who and what Leonard McCoy is.

McCoy is not the type of person that one would normally expect to find aboard a starship. His deep-rooted fear and distrust of machines and advanced (in his phrase "de-humanized") technology coupled with his innate tendency to greet everything with a touch of the cynical would seem to be completely unsuited to a life which is continually dependent on that technology, and in which the facing of the new and unexpected and the need for complete trust in one's companions is an almost daily occurrence.

However, there is much more to Leonard McCoy than just his surface peccadilloes. He feels, this man, very deeply and strongly. And in his chosen profession, those who care can soon be destroyed. The constant battle between life and death is too often lost, and only a man who has learned to look at the world with a jaundiced eye can go on to the next battle. This is why McCoy is a cynic on the surface—cynics expect the worst, and when it does come, then it doesn't hurt so very much. Or at least it isn't supposed to.

Except for Captain Kirk, no one aboard the *Enterprise* has more concern for the crew, as a whole and as individuals, than Dr. McCoy. His is the responsibility for the fitness and well-being of over 400 souls, and their consequent performance of their duties. It is an awesome responsibility, and one which in times of crisis can be almost overpowering. It says much for the inner strength of Leonard McCoy that he does the job so well, while still keeping those qualities of humor and humanity which endear him so much to us.

Much of his strength obviously comes from his background. A native of Earth, specifically the Southern part of the United States (Georgia?), McCoy was somewhat underprivileged as a child. True, in the time of Star Trek poverty and its accompanying ills have been eliminated, but there still remain "classes" of people. People will always be people, some faster, stronger, smarter, and richer than others; and the "middle class" will always exist. McCoy is a product of just such a middle class. Not rich, not poor, just a person who had to work his way through his schooling with a fair amount of difficulty.

As long and difficult a process as it is to become a doctor today, one can imagine what it must be like in Star Trek's time, with so much more to learn. Although he is highly intelligent and has the gifts of a natural-born healer, it still must have been a hard row to hoe for McCoy. The Protestant work ethic is clearly evident in his struggle through his present-day behavior. One of McCoy's favorite complaints is that man lets machines do too much of his work for him.

You can bet that the youthful Leonard McCoy paid for his education by working with his hands as well as his brains.

By this reasoning, it is an obvious assumption that McCoy did not marry until after he had become a full-fledged doctor. Not for him would be the road chosen by many medical students, who marry early and have their wives help support them while they finish their studies. There is, of course, nothing wrong with this, and many of these marriages are strengthened by the process. McCoy, however, with his "old-world" attitudes and basic self-sufficiency, would have considered the idea repugnant. He made his own way.

However, McCoy did marry, and judging by his present age and the age of his daughter, it was fairly soon after he had secured a position. He never speaks of his marriage, not even to Kirk, but it did not last long. More than likely, it suffered because of his work, which kept him away from home for long hours and left little time for an active social life. We can assume also that the marriage dissolved soon after the birth of the child, since McCoy seldom speaks of her and has not seen her in several years.

The breakup of his home is probably the primary reason why McCoy decided to join Starfleet, but judging by his nature, we can also see that his disillusionment with the type of society which had developed on Earth was also a factor. By his own gripes against the "system," we can tell that McCoy felt that there was a decreasing amount of personal challenges on Earth. So to escape his failed home life and to go where he felt he could do the most good, McCoy went into space.

During his further training in space medicine, McCoy saw that there was more for him in Starfleet than he ever could have found back on Earth. Here in space, where the treatment of illnesses and injuries was as much by instinct as procedure, his inborn skills as a healer could come to the fore. Perhaps Leonard McCoy was not a great doctor on Earth; he soon became one in Starfleet.

Little is known about the years McCoy spent in Starfleet before he joined the crew of the *Enterprise*. He had been decorated several times, both for bravery and in performance of his duties as surgeon. And it was revealed in "Albatross" that he headed up an inoculation team on Dramia II almost twenty years ago—which had to be fairly soon after he joined Starfleet, an indication of how rapidly he rose through the medical service ranks.

Contrary to what is stated by James Blish in his noveliza- tion of "Where No Man Has Gone Before," McCoy did not join the *Enterprise* until after the major reshuffling of the crew which was necessitated by that harrowing experience.

Upon joining the crew, he was put into close and constant contact with Captain Kirk by the nature of his duties, and being kindred souls, their friendship grew. As McCoy was responsible for the qualification of Kirk for duty, he also naturally became Kirk's confidant. His friendship with Spock also was due to the captain in great part, since Kirk and Spock were becoming closer with each shared experience, and McCoy was privy to Kirk's thoughts, as well as being in the middle of most of the adventures.

The idiosyncrasies which have always been a part of McCoy's makeup came strongly to the fore as he often found himself caught between two such strong and demand- ing personalities. They served him not only as a defense against having his individuality overwhelmed by Kirk and Spock, but they also gave him an outlet through which he could comment upon and sometimes influence the actions and opinions of the other two.

Aside from McCoy's wife, whom we never saw, and a few offhand mentions by Kirk of some casual flirtations, only three times do we see women that seem to break through McCoy's veneer of cynicism and become impor- tant to him.

The first, of course, is Nancy Crater. McCoy's "lost love," as the salt creature of M113 appears to be, causes him to become almost slushingly nostalgic, especially since she has not aged in his eyes.

From the way in which McCoy treated "Nancy Cra- ter," it is obvious that he was deeply in love with her when they were both young. Perhaps they were involved when he was still in training, which would account for their break- up. But it is even more likely that she and McCoy had an affair when they were a bit older, about the time he was leaving his wife.

The evidence supports this. McCoy's statements to Kirk would lead one to believe that they were both very young, but the way that he treats her suggests intimacy on an adult level. Also, the image of Nancy which the salt creature presents to McCoy is younger than the one which Kirk and others see, but it is hardly that of a young girl.

The breakup of their affair was most probably caused by two things: McCoy was still married to his wife when he was involved with Nancy—in fact, if not in spirit; and his disillusionment with his life would have led to tensions even more debilitating than those caused by a "normal" extramarital affair. McCoy probably did not love Nancy as much as she loved him, since it was she who broke off the affair; but he does feel a strong affection for her (and probably a fair amount of gratitude), since she provided love and comfort at a difficult time in his life.

In the adventure known as "For the World Is Hollow and I Have Touched the Sky," McCoy meets and falls in love with Natira, a high priestess of the planet-ship Yonada. What attracted McCoy to Natira so quickly is somewhat of a mystery, since there were no flights of passion, no classic signs of "love at first sight." Their relationship was more one of mutual respect, it seems, than affection. And it must not be forgotten that McCoy thought that he had only a year to live. The prospect of spending that time with a beautiful woman would certainly be more attractive than tending his duties aboard the *Enterprise*.

One thing which seems to have been forgotten by many Star Trek fans is that regardless of McCoy's recovery, he was still a married man. One can take for granted that McCoy was on hand to greet Natira when Yonada arrived at its destination. But what happened then? Since McCoy is back on the *Enterprise* without Natira; we can only assume that the marriage was either dissolved by mutual consent, or that Natira is a very understanding and undemanding wife. Most probably the marriage was dissolved, since the conditions which brought McCoy and Natira together had by that time changed radically. One hopes, though, that it was given at least a trial. We should hate to think that our good doctor and the high priestess were deprived of any fun.

McCoy also evidenced quite an affection and respect for the mute alien he named "Gem" on the threatened planet Minara. This was mostly subliminal, only becoming apparent in the gentle way in which he spoke to her and touched her when necessary. And when he tricks Spock into allowing him to be the subject of the Vians' experiments, we can feel that the sacrifice is not only for Spock but for Gem. As a trained physician, McCoy knows that an empath can help physical injuries, such as the ones he would experience, but little could be done for the mental damage which Spock would surely suffer.

Gem, being a natural empath, would try to help Spock. She too could suffer from the mental damage; or at the very least, by failing to help him, could condemn herself and her race to extinction. So McCoy's decision was not based only on Spock; there were other considerations, too.

That is yet another thing which many fans forget about McCoy. In his role as the "spokesman" for human values in his debates against Spock, it often seems that he rejects the course of being logical and thoughtful. This is not true, by any means. His profession itself demands the careful, deliberative collection of facts and then the making of a decision based solely on the information and training available.

In "The Empath," as cited above, it was Dr. McCoy's logical reasoning which was superior to Spock's on the question of who should go to meet the Vians. It was Spock who was more emotional about the whole thing, but McCoy showed the innate superiority of a human to a Vulcan. He made a logical decision, but when he found his judgment rejected, he emotionally took matters into his own hands.

McCoy often finds himself forced into more of an emotional, reactive stance than he would like by the simple presence of Spock and his cold Vulcan reasoning. As the captain's sounding board, McCoy must present the opposite side of any case with the same vehemence as Spock, so as to present Kirk with all of the necessary facts and information he requires. And in various episodes, we can see when McCoy is being sincere and when he is just being nettlesome. Again, the cynical facade is reinforced by this role McCoy must play. When he is not cynical, when he does make the impassioned plea, Kirk listens more readily. And probably so does Spock.

One must not forget, however, that McCoy is probably the greatest humanitarian aboard the *Enterprise*. His respect and admiration for the human species is mirrored in dozens of his statements, as is his belief that humans are not as good as they could be. He thinks that "a little suffering is good for the human condition—and the soul," but does all that he can to alleviate any suffering on the part of his patients. This is the main well from which McCoy's cynicism flows:

People, by his experience, are going to be just as bad as they can, so he expects them to be.

Only his faith in the innate goodness of humans, and the fact that he has fortunately found work and friends in which he takes comfort and satisfaction, keeps McCoy from being morose and spiteful.

Oh, sometimes he's a little moody or grouchy, but so are we all, and McCoy's far-famed "crusty exterior" makes it seem just a little worse. But it does bring up the question: Is Leonard McCoy really happy?

We know that his past has not been a particularly happy one. And although he is much liked and respected aboard ship, he seems to have no close friends besides Kirk, Spock, and perhaps Scotty. We are also pretty much in the dark about his hobbies and other spare-time interests. By implication, he buries himself in his work, except for brief and infrequent periods when he and Kirk go on shore leave and tie one on.

Although he and his daughter Joanna correspond as regularly as space mails permit, their relationship is not really a close one. Even if they were in constant contact with each other physically, it is unlikely that they would get along well, since they have grown too far apart to have a normal father-daughter relationship. This knowledge must also be distressing to McCoy.

However, we have to assume that McCoy is happy—at least as happy as he feels he can ever be—or he would take steps to change his circumstances.

His position is one of great responsibility, and to a person like McCoy, it must be immensely satisfying. The long hours and trying work would satiate the puritan in him, and helping those in need would satisfy the humanist in him.

But it is his unique position as part of the "ruling triumvirate" of the *Enterprise* which gives McCoy his greatest satisfaction, and probably his only moments of true happiness. Kirk and Spock not only need McCoy, they are true friends to him, and fill the void of emotional attachments.

Leonard McCoy is as essential to the smooth running of the *Enterprise* as a Dilythium crystal—more so. Without him, Kirk and Spock could not have the almost symbiotic relationship they share, since he is often the conduit through which their minds flow.

And while he is outside of that relationship, he still can

benefit from and take pleasure in it, since he helped to build it and constantly helps to maintain it. By being a friend to Kirk and a friend to Spock, he helps them to be more than friends to each other. It is a necessary function, and to him personally, it must be a supremely gratifying one.

The Starship *Enterprise*—and its captain and first officer —just wouldn't be the same without crusty, cynical, idiosyncratic old Leonard McCoy. And neither would Star Trek.

9. CHICAGO CON:
$100,000 FAN RIPOFF?
by Janet Smith-Bozarth

In 1975, the now-legendary Star Trek convention "Star Trek Chicago" was held. Janet Smith-Bozarth was one of the thousands of fans who attended the con, and she returned with mixed feelings. We encouraged her to try to express them in what amounted to both a convention review and a critique. Because we don't run con reviews as a matter of policy (they tend to be too similar), we asked her to keep the play-by-play as short as possible and concentrate on her observations. What Janet eventually emerged with is probably the perfect example of a person's feelings when they are having a simultaneously good and bad time. And we thought that that in itself was enough to merit space in the magazine, for the Chicago con reflected Star Trek fandom itself in a small way: good and bad, but always interesting.

Star Trek Chicago, billed as Chicago's first Star Trek con —and the biggest ever held! A reunion of the entire cast and many major science fiction writers were expected to draw over 15,000 fans.

And that is exactly what happened at the Conrad Hilton hotel in Chicago the weekend of August 22–24, 1975. Total attendance was over 16,000, making it the largest Star Trek con ever held.

Among the usual events, the con had an art show, which was sparsely attended, as it was hidden away in the basement of the hotel. This is truly unfortunate in that it contained a small but very good showing of artwork and was excellently run by Andy de Cyan and his staff.

There were numerous panel discussions; everything from writing sci-fi (conducted by Harlan Ellison, Robert Bloch, and Hal Clement) to a UFO discussion by Dr. J. Alan Hynek.

The main attraction was the panel entitled "The World of Star Trek," during which all of the cast of ST spoke from a mockup of the *Enterprise* bridge. This three-and-a-half-hour discussion allowed each member of the crew of the *Enterprise*—as well as Mark Lenard (Sarek) and Arlene Martel (T'Pring)—to express their views of Star Trek and answer questions from the 4,000-odd fans in attendance.

Each of the three panels featuring the Star Trek stars started with a group of Klingons capturing the bridge. This same group of Klingons (in authentic-looking costumes) served as the convention security force. And most efficiently, since who would want to cross a Klingon?

Then each star was escorted onto the bridge mockup by two of the Klingons.

First was Mark Lenard, who seemed somewhat out of place when asked questions like: "Why did you marry Spock's mother?" and "What is Vulcan like?"

Arlene Martel was next, and she seemed to be much more comfortable in the position of being identified as T'Pring.

The banality of the questions asked her and Mark Lenard wasn't unusual, as most of the questions asked of the actors were along the lines of "What are you doing now?" and "Was Spock really in love?" and "Did Dr. McCoy really like Spock?"

One question that was constantly asked was, "When is the movie going to be out?" The answer was unknown then; and is still not certain. (Roddenberry is working on the second draft.)

One highlight of the Chicago con was the costume ball. There were only forty or so entries, but most of the costumes were original and very well constructed. The winners were two teen-age members of the Klingon Auxiliary Corps. It was strangely appropriate that the second-place winners were a pair of oversize Tribbles.

Star Trek Chicago grossed $100,000 for its promoters, Lisa Boyton and the Tallos Four Group. These people supposedly put on trade shows for a living, but if Star Trek Chicago is any indication of their other shows, they must be pretty poor.

It was a fun con for many, since most of the people there had never been to a Star Trek con before. But to those of us who attend cons regularly, Chicago was a good example of disorganization and poor planning.

During the Saturday-afternoon panel, one irate fan (a convention member) was objecting to the $20 membership fee. David Gerrold and 3,998 other members silenced him by asking where he could see and hear all of the actors and speakers that were at this con for less money.

Granted, the events were numerous, but they overlapped so badly that it was impossible to see even one-quarter of what you wanted to see.

For example, the ever-present gofers were not even briefed on where anything was. Some did not even know what they were supposed to be doing.

If you can believe it, the costume ball, the main panel discussion, the art auction, and the Planet of the Apes movies were all scheduled at the *same* time!

The dealer's room was the greatest hoax of all. It was in a long corridor with six entrances, and only four security guards. Each night, all of the dealers had to pack up all of their merchandise and move it to their rooms to keep from being ripped off.

On a scale of 1 to 10 convention rating, Star Trek Chicago would rate a 4.5. And a rating this high is only because of the guest list.

10. AN EVENING WITH
GENE RODDENBERRY, 1974
by James Van Hise

*The following article first appeared in "Star Trek 1974," a
convention program book published by G. B. over three
years ago. Although the material is obviously dated, we decided to run it for several reasons. First, it is a concise look
at Star Trek when fandom was just beginning to take off
and assume the enormous proportions of today. Second, it
is interesting to compare the turmoil of the studio executive
processes in 1974 with exactly the same type of turmoil today. And last, it is one of the best articles featuring Roddenberry speaking on the difficulties of producing and "selling"
a television series. But most important to Star Trek fans, it
is always a pleasure to hear the words of the man who
created Star Trek. So here it is, about four years or so late
for most of you, but still an excellent article.*

Like Leonard Nimoy, Gene Roddenberry has also been
touring college campuses giving lectures. On September 24,
1974, he appeared in the gymnasium (of all places) of the
Miami-Dade Community College North Campus. It was a hot,
humid night and for some reason the powers that be had
switched Gene to this locale at the last minute, a poor decision since it was without air conditioning. Although Gene
arrived on time and gave a fine talk, the event was sur-
rounded by a maze of bad planning which only climaxed
with the non-air-conditioned room. Gene's appearance had
been very poorly publicized; and so no more than 200 people were there. It was so badly advertised that when a large
number of us from the local Star Trek groups showed up
and the university personnel realized that we were non-
students, they wanted to know, with great surprise, how we

found out about it. I found out due to the always active fandom grapevine in Miami which passes along anything to anyone interested in Star Trek. But enough of the shortcomings. The evening provided far more in the way of pluses.

The crowd waiting to see Gene started showing up over an hour before his talk, so that by the time he arrived everyone was tense with anticipation. As soon as he arrived, people started crowding around him, a figure tall and well tanned from California sun. For fifteen minutes before he got up on stage and began his talk, he allowed fans to corner him on one side of the room and ask him virtually any question they wished. The Star Trek movie was still up in the air at this stage, although negotiations were progressing. His series concept *Spectre* was being looked at by Warner Brothers but wouldn't be acted on unless *Kolchak* was a success. This was only some of the information garnered before the program started.

Gene began his talk by explaining how he broke into the writing field, and how very difficult it is to do so. He pointed out that there are 3,000,000 would-be writers, yet out of this number less than 4,000 succeed. In order to survive while he was trying to become a successful writer, he became a policeman on the Los Angeles Police Department. He explained that he wasn't very good because he hated writing tickets, and thus seldom did; then too, he was probably the only policeman in LA who was a card-carrying member of the American Civil Liberties Union. In order to get an agent to represent his work he hatched a clever scheme. A well-known writers' agent drove through his beat each day, so Gene just patiently waited until one day the man made a traffic violation. Instead of giving him a ticket, he got the man to arrange an interview for him at Four Star with the executives. He dressed casually for the interview, and as he became more involved in disclosing his concepts and ideas, he removed his sports coat. He found the executives hanging on every word he said. It was only after the interview that he realized they were so attentive because under his coat he'd been wearing his shoulder holster and .38-caliber pistol.

He went on to discuss television writing in general as well as Star Trek. He said that the previous year NBC had finally admitted it had been a mistake to cancel Star Trek.

Gene said that right after Star Trek was taken off, NBC had started employing demographics as part of the ratings system, and they had been informed that the show with the perfect demographics for success was Star Trek.

Gene explained that *Genesis II* was to have been a series until CBS decided that *Planet of the Apes* would be a surer bet. He said that the only way to save *Genesis II* would have been to change it drastically into a takeoff on *Apes*, which would have destroyed the entire series concept.

Questor had problems, Gene explained, even before it was filmed. A scene in the first draft script called for Questor to seduce a woman to gain information. The network executives balked at this and wouldn't allow it. Gene couldn't understand this in the light of much of what was being shown every night on the tube. He argued with them for hours, but to no avail. Finally it hit him what their real objection was. It was the old "Yes, but would you want your sister to marry one?" He went home and called his agent, for, as he explained, "It's not every day a writer creates a whole new area of intolerance."

This was just the beginning of *Questor*'s problems with the network. After NBC agreed to buy the series they decided they wanted to change its approach. They said "If ABC has *The Six Million Dollar Man*, we'll outdo them and have the *Hundred Million Dollar Robot!*" When the network made it clear that they were inflexible on this, Gene walked out on them and took the series with him. He'd rather there be no series at all than see it murdered in this way.

Gene talked about science fiction writing and stated that to be an SF writer, you must be a writer first, as SF is basically the events of today occurring on another planet. He said the network executives didn't understand this, which enabled them to get away with doing themes that wouldn't have been allowed in present-oriented shows.

Gene fielded questions from the audience ranging from the mundane ("What is Tom Snyder really like?") to the very serious. One young man asked, "If it's so difficult to do important themes on commercial television without tremendous interference, then why bother with television at all?" Gene found himself having to defend the medium he's often attacked for ineptness, stating, "You can't just abandon a powerful medium like television. It is the most powerful tool of communication we have. We can't just turn our backs on it because of the difficulties involved with it. We have to fight within it to change it."

Following this talk the films Gene always brings with him were shown, these being "The Cage" (the first Star Trek pilot as it was actually filmed) and the Star Trek bloopers from all three seasons. Gene referred to the scene in the bloopers where DeForest Kelley is grabbing Majel Barrett's—that is, Mrs. Gene Roddenberry's—bosom. "You'll notice she's enjoying it."

And thus the evening ended, an extremely enjoyable and entertaining evening with Star Trek's creator, Gene Roddenberry.

11. SHORTCUTS THROUGH SPACE IN STAR TREK
by Mark Andrew Golding

As Star Trek is a series which is primarily built around the someday-to-be-realized technology and hardware which will allow man to travel among the stars, our readers are always interested in any information which will help them to understand how the Enterprise *and its machinery works. Mark Golding is one of those not satisfied with pat explanations; he sat down and utilized the knowledge which we possess today to explain the wonders of the Star Trek universe. And then he backed up his conclusions with facts and figures —not wild and improbable theories. As you enjoy this article, reflect for a moment on the amount of thought, research, and sheer work Mark put into it. A perfect example of the dedication which Star Trek fans give to the ideas of the series, and to their fellow fans as well.*

It is obvious that when writing science fiction great care must be taken to ensure that the background is completely self-consistent. For the writers of the individual episodes of the Star Trek TV series, the Star Trek Writer's Guide gave some background information—but not nearly enough. Thus the writers were left with plenty of room—a whole galaxy, in fact—to contradict what was written in other episodes.

In addition, the staff of the series neglected to make certain that the speed of the *Enterprise* would be great enough to ensure that it could travel the enormous distances it was supposed to in any reasonable time. Although it was never explained on the show, we all have been told that each warp factor is the number cubed times the speed of light. Thus warp 2 is $2 \times 2 \times 2$ times the speed of light or 8 times the speed of light; warp 6 (the highest normal speed of the

Enterprise) is $6 \times 6 \times 6$ times the speed of light, or 216 light speeds; and warp 8 (the highest emergency speed of the *Enterprise*) is $8 \times 8 \times 8$ times the speed of light, or 512 times the speed of light.

At warp 8, it would take two years to travel 1,000 light-years, and at warp 6, about five years. The total distance traveled in all the seventy-nine shows, which could not have taken place over more than about a dozen years, would not have been more than 6,000 light-years if the *Enterprise* traveled constantly at warp 8; 2,500 light-years if the average speed (including times when the *Enterprise* wasn't moving at all) was warp 6; 1,450 light-years at an average speed of warp 5; 768 light-years at an average speed of warp 4; 324 light-years at an average speed of warp 3; 96 light-years at an average speed of warp 2; and 12 light-years at an average speed of warp 1.

Most episodes seemed to end with Captain Kirk telling Sulu to lay in a course for their next destination at warp 2. In "Friday's Child" it is stated that a freighter cannot go faster than warp 2. If the typical speed of interstellar travel is only warp 2, no person could travel more than 280 light-years from his home world and return in a human lifetime.

Yet in "Mudd's Women" the *Enterprise* visits Rigel XII, a planet of the star Rigel, which is 750 light-years from Earth. In later episodes such as "Tomorrow Is Yesterday," "Space Seed," "This Side of Paradise," "Amok Time," "Who Mourns for Adonis," "The Changeling," and "The Apple," the *Enterprise* visits worlds which are only a few hundred or a few dozen light-years from Earth's solar system, often in the opposite direction from Rigel.

In "The Doomsday Machine," the *Enterprise* is near Rigel again; then in "I Mudd" the ship finds itself orbiting the planet ruled by Harry Mudd, who has been to Deneb (1,200 light-years from Earth, in the direction opposite from that of Rigel) since the affair on Rigel.

In the next episode, "Metamorphosis," the crew of the *Enterprise* find themselves near Epsilon Canaris, less than 200 light-years from Earth, while the episode after that, "Journey to Babel," begins at the planet Vulcan, which is probably only 16 light-years from Earth.

Of the three main characters, Spock and McCoy have been to Rigel on earlier occasions, while Kirk has been to Deneb.

All this adds up to several thousand light-years of travel in the lifetimes of our heroes. But even worse, the *Enterprise* twice visited the edge of the galaxy.

Since the galaxy is three-dimensional, its edge must be a two-dimensional plane wrapped around the three-dimensional shape of the galaxy.

Our galaxy consists of a dense core of stars like a slightly flattened globe about 15,000 light-years across, a globe of very thinly scattered stars and star clusters about 100 000 light-years in diameter which surrounds the central core, and a disc of stars and gas which extends out from the central core as Saturn's rings would if they went down to the surface, and which is 100,000 light-years (or so) in diameter and a few thousand light-years thick.

Our solar system is in one of the spiral arms that form the disc of the galaxy, and is near to the galactic equatorial plane, about 30,000 light-years (give or take a few thousand) from the central point of the galaxy and about 20,000 light-years in from the outermost rim of the galactic disc.

Since we don't know whether the force field at the edge of the galaxy surrounds the entire sphere of halo stars, or instead surrounds only the core and the galactic disc, we cannot be sure just how close the nearest edge of the galaxy is. At least we can be sure that the force field does not surround only the core of the galaxy; in that case the *Enterprise* would not run into it while trying to cross the edge of the galaxy.

If the force field surrounds the halo stars, it must be a sphere with a diameter of 100,000 light-years, and the nearest spot on its surface would be at the edge of the galactic disc closest to Earth, 20,000 light-years away. The farthest point would also be on the galactic disc, on the opposite side of the galaxy, and would be 80,000 light-years away.

It is possible that the force field at the edge of the galaxy does not include the halo stars but only the core and the disc. In that case the nearest point on the galaxy's edge that could be reached without leaving the equatorial plane of the galaxy would be the same spot as before, 20,000 light-years from Earth. But there would be no reason why they shouldn't leave the equatorial plane and since the disc of the galaxy is no more than a few thousand light-years thick at Earth's neighborhood, that would shorten the journey to the edge of the galaxy considerably.

Unfortunately, since there is no well-defined edge to the galactic disc, the stars merely thinning out as the distance from the equatorial plane increases, there is no point at which the strange force field which surrounds the galaxy is most likely to be.

There is no way to say if the *Enterprise* would have to travel 500 light-years, 1,000 light-years, 1,500 light-years, 2,000 light-years, 3,000 light-years, or 4,000 light-years at right angles to the equatorial plane of the galaxy in order to reach the force field at the galaxy's edge.

In "Where No Man Has Gone Before," the *Enterprise* was disabled by the force field at the edge of the galaxy. The warp engines which propelled it faster than light were disabled and only the impulse engines were left. This meant that it would take centuries to reach places which would have been only days away on warp power.

But the *Enterprise* managed to get to Delta Vega, an uninhabited mining station just a few light-days away. There the warp drive was repaired and they returned to civilization, instead of spending the rest of their days crawling through space under impulse power.

But if Delta Vega is a planet of the star Vega, it seems strange that they didn't try to get any help from the colony on Vega IX. Besides, Vega is only 27 light-years from Earth, while the edge of the galaxy must be at least 500 or 1,000 light-years away. Vega could hardly have been much closer to the edge of the galaxy than Earth.

It is possible that Delta Vega is not a planet of the star Vega. It could have been named because it was the fourth planet discovered by the Vega Mining Company (delta is the fourth letter of the Greek alphabet) or it could be a short form of: "The Planet Claimed by the Delta Vega Company." In either case there would be no clue to the location of Delta Vega and of the place where the *Enterprise* reached the edge of the galaxy.

There is another possibility. Vega is a single star, but several times astronomers have mistakenly thought that stars which happen to look close to Vega are actually part of a double star system with Vega (when actually, though they are close to the line between Earth and Vega, they are dozens or hundreds of light-years farther away from Earth than Vega). Since the brightest star of a real multiple star system is known as —— A, the second brightest —— B, the third —— C, etc., it might make sense to refer to the widely-separated members of such illusory multiple-star systems as Alpha ——, Beta ——, Gamma ——, Delta ——, etc.

Thus Delta Vega would be on the line between Earth and Vega, but much farther away, and right at the edge of the galaxy. As seen from Earth, Vega is about 35° from the core of the galaxy and about 18° above the equatorial plane of the galaxy.

If one continues in that direction one will come to the edge of the galactic disc in about 1,500 light-years if the edge is 500 light-years from the equatorial plane; in about 3,000 light-years if the edge of the galaxy is 1,000 light-years from the equatorial plane; in about 4,500 light-years if the edge of the galaxy is 1,500 light-years from the equatorial plane; and in about 6,000 light-years if the edge of the galaxy is 2,000 light-years from the equatorial plane.

If the force field surrounds the halo stars as well as the disc stars, then Delta Vega would be about 75,000 light-years from Earth.

At warp 8, the maximum speed, the *Enterprise* would reach Delta Vega and return in twelve years if the total round trip was 6,000 light-years; in eighteen years if the round trip was 9,000 light-years; in twenty-four years if the round trip was 12,000 light-years; and in 300 years if the round trip was 150,000 light-years.

At warp 6, the fastest safe speed, it would take thirty years for a round trip of 6,000 light-years to Delta Vega; forty-five years if the total round trip was 9,000 light-years; sixty years if the total round trip was 12,000 light-years; and 750 years if the total round trip was 150,000 light-years.

At warp 2, the normal travel speed; it would take 750 years if the total trip to Delta Vega and back was 6,000 light-years; 1,125 years if the total trip to Delta Vega and back was 9,000 light-years; 1,500 years if the total trip to Delta Vega and back was 12,000 light-years; and 18,750 years if the total trip to Delta Vega and back to Earth was 150,000 light-years.

After the *Enterprise* visited the edge of the galaxy in "Where No Man Has Gone Before," after all the other trips I have mentioned, in "By Any Other Name," the *Enterprise* was lured to the edge of the galaxy by Kelvans, survivors of a ship from the Andromeda Galaxy which had been wrecked by the energy barrier at the edge of the galaxy.

As seen from Earth, the Andromeda Galaxy is 90° from the galactic core, and about 20° below the equatorial plane of the galaxy, thus being in a different direction from Vega, Delta Vega, and the place where the *Enterprise* ran into the energy barrier.

If a ship from Earth were to head straight for the Andromeda Galaxy, it would leave the galactic disc after about 1,500 light-years, or 3,000 light-years, or 4,500 light-years, or 6,000 light-years, etc., depending on the thickness of the galactic disc. If the force field is at the edge of the halo stars, then it would be reached in about 40,000 light-years by a ship heading from Earth to Andromeda.

But if the Kelvans were arriving from the Andromeda Galaxy, they would probably enter at the point of our galaxy which is closest to their galaxy. That would be on the rim of the galactic disc, at a point about 40,000 light-years from Earth.

The Kelvans captured the *Enterprise* and modified her engines to reach speeds of warp 11—1,331 times the speed of light. They began their return to the Andromeda Galaxy, saying it would take about 300 years. But the crew managed to make them return to our galaxy.

At warp 11, it would take 1,502.6 years to travel 2,000,000 light-years to the Andromeda Galaxy. But Spock, with his calculator brain, did not point out that discrepancy when the Kelvans said they would go to the Andromeda Galaxy in 300 years.

That can only be because it was no discrepancy. The Kelvans must have known of some method that would reduce the distance they would have to travel to about 400,000 light-years, and Spock must have known, without having to be told, that they knew of such a method.

In the episode "Obsession," Kirk chased a strange creature to a planet 1,000 light-years away, but signaled another starship that he would still meet them in just forty-eight hours. A detour of 1,000 to 2,000 light-years could not delay the *Enterprise* more than a day or two, though the top speed of the *Enterprise* was only 512 times the speed of light!

In "That Which Survives," Spock calculates that it will take just 11.33 hours to travel 990.7 light-years at warp 8.4.

But warp 8.4 is only 592.7 times the speed of light, and at warp 8.4 it would take about 14,652.4 hours to travel 990.7 light-years.

In "Obsession," the *Enterprise* was able to reduce the distance it would have to travel by about 1,000 times. In "That Which Survives," it was able to divide the distance it would have to travel by about 1,293.2 times. In "By Any Other Name," the Kelvans were able to divide the distance they would have to travel by about 5 times.

I postulate that there exist shortcuts through space, space warps which enable an object to disappear from one place and appear instantaneously in another place far away. That is a common enough concept in science fiction. That would explain many of the apparent historical contradictions in the various Star Trek episodes.

In "Balance of Terror," we are told that the Romulan War, fought a century before, had been fought with ships using impulse power only (and thus being slower than light). In "Whom Gods Destroy," mention is made of a Romulan ship destroyed near Tau Ceti, a star 11.87 light-years from Earth. In "The Deadly Years," part of the neutral zone between Romulan space and Federation space is near the star Gamma Hydra, which is 152 light-years from Earth and almost opposite in direction from Tau Ceti.

The Romulan War could not have taken more than a few decades, yet its battles seem to have been fought across more than a hundred light-years with ships slower than light! The *Enterprise* had gone to rescue the survivors of the SS *Columbia,* which had crashed eighteen years earlier, at a time thirteen years before the time of "The Menagerie." One of the crewmen said that the survivors wouldn't believe how fast the new time warp would get them home, implying that faster-than-light travel was a recent development.

But in "Metamorphosis," Zefrem Cochrane of Alpha Centauri, the inventor of the warp drive, was said to have disappeared at the age of eighty-seven, 150 years before the time of Star Trek. The invention of the warp drive must have taken place between 200 and 150 years before the voyages of the *Enterprise!*

And in "Where No Man Has Gone Before," the *Enterprise* finds that the galactic survey ship *Valiant* has been to the edge of the galaxy before them, about 200 years before. Since the episodes of Star Trek were supposed to be taking place only about 200 years in the future, the *Valiant* seems to have been rather an advanced model spaceship, to travel hundreds of thousands of light-years only a few decades in our future!

I believe that Zefrem Cochrane will invent the warp drive on a world of Alpha Centauri just a few decades into the future and explore many worlds without revealing himself openly to anyone. He will discover a tyrannical power which rules this part of the galaxy, crushing any world which develops warp drive before such a world can become a serious rival to its power. Cochrane wants to overthrow that power but doesn't dare give the secret to his own people for fear they will lead a revolt, be defeated, and be terribly punished.

So Cochrane comes to Earth and secretly contacts various governments, offering them the warp drive and the leadership in the revolt against the evil power. But not even the most freedom-loving, the most foolhardy, nor the most power-hungry leaders of our notoriously reckless race dare to snatch at the alluring prize of galactic leadership, so horrifying is the punishment for failure.

Instead, they build a fleet of warp-drive ships and man the ships with thousands and thousands of soldiers and scientists and send them deep into space. They travel through one space warp after another, hundreds and thousands of them, until none can remember the way back to Earth and Alpha Centauri. Then all their records of their course through the space warps are destroyed so that there is no possible way to trace their path.

They find inhabited planets and give all the secrets of Earth's technology to the natives, building up industrial power and especially space technology. Soon their new worlds are launching ship after ship. It is at this time that the *Valiant* is destroyed at the edge of the galaxy.

The secrets of warp drive and spaceship manufacture spread like wildfire among the civilizations they contact, and a vast alliance is built up. Finally, they make contact with the evil power which has tried to monopolize the secret of the warp drive, and soon a terrible war breaks out. Finally, the evil power is defeated.

Afterward there are many governments with warp drive, among whom the government of the colonists from Earth is the most powerful, with many planets under its rule. They begin a long search to find the way back to Earth, now that there is no danger of a victorious enemy tracing the location of the defenseless planet.

Meanwhile, Earth is developing without any knowledge of those events, gradually exploring the solar system. Finally ships begin to explore other solar systems, and the space warps are discovered. Using them, the Earthmen are able to discover far more worlds than they could have by crawling the entire distance from star to star.

The area that Earth has explored begins to look like a series of disconnected bubbles, as ships probe outward from each point of emergence from a space warp. Occasionally two of these spherical areas of exploration would grow into one another.

Meanwhile, the Romulan Empire is expanding through the same process. Eventually Romulan and Earth ships come into contact at at least two different points, near Tau Ceti and near Gamma Hydra. War breaks out, and finally a peace is made. Neutral zones are created at each of the points of contact between Romulan space and Earth space, and provisions are made for creating new neutral zones whenever Romulan and Earth zones of exploration come into contact in the future.

It was undoubtedly during the Romulan War that the planet Eden, in Romulan territory, was visited for the first time by humans. A ship must have landed and the beautiful scenery was viewed through the screens, but the crew could not have had time to go out and discover the deadly nature of the plants before having to take off to face a Romulan attack. Thus was born the legend of the beautiful and inaccessible planet Eden. The location was not recorded exactly, but there was enough information for Spock to be able to pinpoint it through its gravitational effects on nearby worlds.

Since the Romulan Star Empire consists of a series of segments of space, except where some have grown together or where there are boundaries with other powers, it is not surprising that details of the *Enterprise*'s journeys into and out of Romulan space in "The Deadly Years" and "The *Enterprise* Incident" suggest that Romulan space is like a sphere no more than a few dozen light-years, at the most, in diameter. By my theory, it is just a collection of dozens or hundreds of such spheres.

The *Columbia* crashed on Talos IV thirty-one years in the

past of Star Trek, while the battle of Donatu 5 with the Klingons took place about twenty-three years before the time of "The Trouble with Tribbles." It is not known if it was the Earthmen of the far colonies, with warp drive, or the Earthmen from Earth, without warp drive, who fought at Donatu 5.

It was at about the time that Kirk was in Star Fleet Academy that the war with Axanar broke out. Captain Garth won a great victory at Axanar. It is not known if that victory forced the enemy to make peace, or if they still had the power to fight on. Perhaps they even had the advantage. In any case, the Axanar Peace Mission seems to have had a difficult job and to have had far-reaching results—perhaps even the creation of the United Federation of Planets.

If Axanar did have the upper hand, then the appearance of ships from the colony worlds (which finally located Earth and its colonies and came to their aid) might have forced them to make peace. It is certain that it was at about this time that the distant worlds made contact with Earth and taught the secret of the warp drive to Earth scientists. It is impossible to deduce the order in which the events at this critical stage of galactic history took place.

The *Enterprise* was one of the first large Earth ships to be constructed with the warp drive. One of its first missions took it to Rigel and then to Talos IV.

It will be noted that the use of the space warps in "Obsession" and "That Which Survives" enabled the *Enterprise* to reduce the distance it had to travel by about a thousand times.

If the space-warp factor was applied in traveling from Andromeda to our galaxy and vice versa, it would be possible to actually have to travel only 2,000 light-years out of the 2,000,000 that separated the two galaxies.

The *Enterprise* can travel 2,000 light-years in four years at warp 8; ten years at warp 6; and 250 years at warp 2.

But Spock was amazed to hear of travel between the two galaxies in a mere 300 years. And that was at warp 11. At warp 8 it would take 779.882 years to travel the distance which could be traveled in 300 years at warp 11. At warp 6 it would take 1,848.6 years to travel the distance which could be traveled in 300 years at warp 11; and at warp 2 it would take 49,912.5 years to travel the distance that it would take 300 years to travel at warp 11.

As has been said, it would have taken 2,254 years to travel 2,000,000 light-years at warp 11. In the 300 years the Kelvans planned to make the trip in, they could travel only 400,000 light-years. That would be enough, for they would be passing through the space warps to avoid the necessity of traveling the other 1,600,000 light-years. Clearly Spock did not expect them to find even better shortcuts through space, for in that case there would be nothing amazing about traveling to Andromeda in just 300 years.

Clearly the cases, as in "Obsession" and "That Which Survives," in which a starship can reduce the distance it has to travel to a thousandth of what it would be without the space warps, must be extremely rare.

The Romulan War, when in a few years ships which could not travel as fast as light managed to travel distances that it would take light a hundred years to travel, was a case in which the space warps reduced the distance to be traveled by perhaps 99 percent.

I believe that the distances between the end points of the various space warps vary greatly. Sometimes a starship that emerges from a space warp may find an entrance to another space warp only a few million miles away. At other times the nearest space warp may be several light-years away.

The distance covered by the space warps must vary. A ship may enter one and emerge just half a light-year away. It may enter another and find itself 10 light-years away or 100, 1,000, or 10,000.

The arrangement is not systematic and not completely random. You will not find a space warp leading to the nearest star, and then a couple more leading to the other near neighbors of the second star; and in each that you visit two more leading to other near neighbors, and so on, so you can work your way in a straight line across the galaxy or explore all the stars within 10 light-years of your home world before going to explore all the stars within 20 light-years and then all the stars within 30 light-years, etc.

Nor will you find a space warp within our galaxy which will take you into the Andromeda Galaxy in one jump (at least none is known yet), though the system of space warps extends to the Andromeda Galaxy, perhaps throughout the universe.

And it is to be noted that even though the galaxy is 100,000 light-years across, a large proportion of the worlds mentioned in various episodes are within a thousand light-years, a few hundred light-years, or even a few dozen light-years of Earth.

There are dozens of stars from within an area of about 1/10,000 of the total volume of the galaxy mentioned in various Star Trek episodes, out of just a few hundred worlds that are mentioned.

As an example of what the organization of the space warps can lead to, take "Who Mourns for Adonis." While captured by Apollo on Pollux IV, Kirk says they can't expect any other ship to come that far out. Pollux is only 40 light-years from Earth. And it is only about 20 light-years from Capella, where Federation and Klingons struggled for mining rights in "Friday's Child," expecting that it would be an easy matter to transport their cargos back to civilization.

At warp 6, a starship could reach Pollux from Capella in 33.8 days, and could reach Pollux from Earth in 67.6 days. At warp 5, a starship could reach Pollux from Capella in 58.44 days, and from Earth in 116.88 days. At warp 4, a starship could reach Pollux from Capella in 114.14 days, and from Earth in 228.28 days. At warp 2, it is true, it would take 2.5 years to reach Pollux from Capella, and 5 years to reach Pollux from Earth.

I find it hard to believe that the *Enterprise* has never traveled more than 20, or even 40 light-years in the intervals between space warps during one of its voyages.

At any event, it is clear that nobody had ever discovered a space warp leading to Pollux before the *Enterprise* did. It is clear that they must have started from some distant world and passed through many space warps, often choosing between twenty or more that were equally close. Kirk obviously didn't think that when the *Enterprise* was missed the ships that would be sent to try to follow it from its last recorded position would be able to find them by trial and error, checking all the possible space warps they could have used.

Of course, Star Fleet isn't much concerned about missing ships. It is true that the *Enterprise* is ordered to find out what happened to the *Constellation* ("The Doomsday Machine"), the *Intrepid* ("The Immunity Syndrome"), and the *Defiant* ("The Tholian Web"), soon after they report trouble. But Kirk accidentally finds the *Exeter* ("The Omega

Glory") and wreckage of the *Beagle* ("Bread and Circuses").

The *Enterprise* is only sent to Eminiar 7 in order to negotiate a treaty now that one is needed, not to search for the *Valiant*, which disappeared fifty years before ("A Taste of Armageddon"). The *Enterprise* looks for the *Archon* (in "The Return of the Archeons") 100 years after it disappeared, and stumbles upon the recorder marker of the first *Valiant* 200 years after it had been destroyed, not a single ship having approached the edge of the galaxy since then.

Even so, I'm sure Star Fleet would send a ship on the comparatively long voyage from Earth to Pollux if they got a distress message. But if Apollo has knocked out the transmitter of the *Enterprise,* and Star Fleet is not informed of their location, they would certainly not think of sending a ship to Pollux on the one-in-a-billion chance that that particular star could be the location of the *Enterprise.*

There is no evidence as to whether the space warps are natural or artificial. About the only thing that can be said for certain about them is that they are large enough for a starship to pass through.

Because the galaxy is three-dimensional, two-dimensional maps often are very misleading concerning the relationships of various worlds. Since the galactic disc is very wide and flat, two-dimensional maps showing the location of worlds within it are fairly accurate as long as the worlds are separated by distances of at least 5,000 light-years or so from their neighbors.

If two political systems in the galactic disc are solid territories and extend over at least 10,000 light-years, it is fairly accurate to draw a line between them as their boundary. Because the galaxy is only 1,000 or 2,000 light-years thick in the disc, realms that large will be like nations on the surface of a world.

But because of the space warps, political bodies do not occupy solid volumes of space but consist of many separated volumes, all mixed in with the territories of other realms. Though the Klingon Empire might be 10,000 light-years long, it will occupy only a fraction of the total volume between the two farthest-flung sections of it. Much of the intervening volume will be occupied by areas that are part of the Federation and of the Romulan Empire.

The only correct map of the political structure would be

a transparent model of the galaxy, filled with thousands of tiny dots. Those colored red would indicate sections of one power, those colored blue sections of another, those colored green sections of a third, those colored yellow sections of a fourth, etc.

Furthermore, there is no indication that if all the realms of known space were put together (the Federation, the Klingon Empire, the Romulan Empire, the First Federation, the Gorns, the Tholians, the Orions, etc.) they would total more than 1 percent of the volume of the galaxy. Probably they would total a fraction of a percent.

Thus any map which shows the Romulan Empire, for example, covering a solid territory 10,000 light-years long and 10,000 light-years wide is inaccurate through making its volume thousands of times greater than it really is and showing it as a solid volume of space.

The remarkable thing about my theory of the space warps is that none of the crew members of the *Enterprise* ever mentioned them, even though on many occasions they must have been taken into account when calculating courses and arrival times. But people rarely talk about everyday things, or explain what they are doing to those who know perfectly well what is going on.

As Gene Roddenberry says, "A policeman doesn't need to explain how his gun works before he shoots it." And so it is with the crew of the *Enterprise*. They don't talk about space warps; they simply use them as another tool to get where they are going.

12. TREK INTERVIEW: JAMES DOOHAN

There's no doubt about it, Jimmy Doohan is Montgomery Scott. Just as you would expect Scotty to be cheerful, friendly, and outgoing, so too is James Doohan. The two following separate interviews were conducted by us with a time span of about a year between them, so (as in the Walter Koenig interviews) there is some overlap in the questions. However, Jimmy's answers are always so interesting and entertaining, we just couldn't bear to deprive you of even one of them. James Doohan is a wonderful man to be around, which is why he is among the most popular of Star Trek convention guests. He makes you feel good and full of life and fun—just as he is.

FIRST INTERVIEW WITH JAMES DOOHAN

Q: In retrospect, what is your opinion of the creative aspects of the Star Trek show?

A: I think Star Trek embodies as much as possible of Gene Roddenberry's original concept of what a space series should be. He wanted a vehicle in which something could be said—no easy task in modern TV. In a show hundreds of years in the future, no man would be ready to criticize ideas that were so far in the future. Whereas in the reality of Star Trek, much was said about present-day sociological problems and philosophies. His creation was enhanced by luck in putting together a cast of different ethnic backgrounds, then guiding those characters through their own part of the creation. He paid special attention to the scientific aspects of the show as well, and we know now that very little was too far-fetched. What he created had something for everybody, from the child to the most adult scientist.

Q: Was there any particular show you enjoyed doing more than others? That offered more of a challenge to you and your talents?

A: I was and am most interested in science—I don't like "monster" shows—so I have to say "The Doomsday Machine." But I don't think any show offered me much of a challenge.

Q: How did James Doohan land the role of Scotty on Star Trek?

A: You must believe that I have answered this question many, many times, but here goes again. About two weeks before the Star Trek pilot started, I read for James Golstone, who was to direct another series show. I didn't get that part, but about ten days later he called me and asked if I would read for a new series called Star Trek and do some accents for them. I met Gene, Bob Justman, Morris Chapnick, and Joe D. Agosta and voiced about five accents for them. They liked the Scottish accent, for which I was grateful, because I liked it so much. So Scotty was born and I named him myself and the writers liked him.

Q: How much research did you put into the role of Scotty? Did you do any research into engineering?

A: I have always been interested in science and engineering, so I was able to understand everything and even wrote explanations of how everything worked. I gave that to Gene Roddenberry and it is deep in his first-year files. I didn't keep a copy, but he promised to resurrect it.

Q: What was a typical—if the term applies—day's shooting on one of the shows?

A: Well, for me it was up at 6:00 a.m. . . . makeup at 7:00 a.m. . . . breakfast. Rehearse for lights and camera at 8:00 a.m. . . . shoot master shots, then two shots and closeups, each preceded by lighting breaks, rehearsals, etc. Break for lunch at 1:00 p.m.; 2:00 p.m. start work again until about 6:00 p.m. or 7:00 or 8:00 p.m.—until the day's work is completed. Home for a drink and dinner and right to bed. Leonard and Nichelle had to be there earlier in the morning for hair and makeup.

Q: Would you give one-word descriptions of your co-stars

on Star Trek, then elaborate briefly on your choice of words?

A: Shatner—Shorty: tough; good actor. Nimoy—Slim: great guy. Kelley—Doc: Mr. Conservative. Nichols: Booby; don't let her start talking; Takei—Hosato: stop that laugh; Koenig—Walter: cheer up; Roddenberry—Great Bird: don't cheat at pool.

Q: What is your response to the massive and unprecedented following Star Trek and its stars have received?

A: Unbelievable . . . but unbelievable!!

Q: Certainly this will vary, but how does James Doohan approach a new role?

A: That would be giving away all my secrets, but that really depends on the character and that takes a lot of examination first.

Q: Is there any difference between James Doohan the man and James Doohan the actor?

A: I don't think there is much difference. All the characters come from James Doohan the man in the first place, and James Doohan the actor knows it's all play-acting.

Q: How does your wife react to the fantastic following you and the other cast members have?

A: She doesn't mind as long as it doesn't invade our privacy.

Q: Has being associated with Star Trek helped or hindered your career?

A: It has limited some of us in some ways but has opened the doors to other things.

Q: What improvement would you have made on the series, looking at it with 20/20 hindsight?

A: I would have cut the "love affairs" in half and cut the monsters altogether—I do not consider the Horta a monster. I would have delved into science a little more.

Q: Do you feel that the series on its initial run had exhausted fresh new ideas and approaches? Would you have preferred more experimentation with plots, character interplay, etc.?

A: No, I don't think exhaustion set in, but when NBC showed disinterest it was natural that G. R. showed less interest in searching out new writers and new plots, etc.

Q: Initially, did you feel that Star Trek was anything more than just another job, and possibly a silly one at that?

A: I don't think of any job as "just another job," but after about four or five scripts, I think we all realized what a good show we had.

Q: Can you recall any of your reactions the first day on the set?

A: I remember examining everything very carefully and very enthusiastically. Savoir-faire turned to eagerness.

Q. Certainly Star Trek can't last forever. What do you wish to do after the following dies down? Do you have any projects you've always wanted to do?

A: I am really searching for a new series, preferably comedy. Then I want a farm.

Q: What are your feelings about a new series? Do you have any expectations or apprehensions about it?

A: If you mean a Star Trek series, I think it will be a series of motion pictures—not a TV series. Expectations, yes; apprehensions, no.

Q. How do you feel about Star Trek fans? Do you find some of them overbearing?

A: I would say that one in a thousand was "overbearing," but the rest have been most generous in their manners and they are a treat to be with.

Q: Have you always been interested in science fiction/ fantasy, or have you cultivated an interest since being on the show?

A: I am not much interested in fantasy, but science fiction I have always read and, I think, more before Star Trek than afterward.

Q: Does James Doohan have any thoughts—and this may sound a bit heavy—about man in the universe? I don't mean to be heavily intellectual, but surely a creative man such as yourself has thoughts on life after death, our purpose in life, etc.

A: You are flattering me, but I will take the bait anyway. I don't mean to be heavily intellectual either, but surely there is more. Man in the universe? Yes, I believe there are other people in the universe, but I also think they are not in our immediate area and it will take thousands of years for us to find each other. I don't think that is what you meant by man in the universe, but I think it had to be said first. We are absolute infants when it comes to the grand design. We have a purpose and I only can imagine what that purpose might be, but I think its manner of completion can only be accomplished with *love*. I think we will have very much more in the way of suffering before we realize that love is the only answer, not economic gain. Some of the thoughts I have belong to infinite heresies. But to round this out before I write a whole book—there isn't a philosopher dead or alive who has said, "Get yourself a lot of money and you will be safe and happy for the rest of your life." I believe that every human mind knows all there is to know. If you know how much of our minds we really use, you will realize how far we have to go.

SECOND INTERVIEW WITH JAMES DOOHAN
by G. B. Love

Q: How did you land the role of Scotty in Star Trek?

A: The man who directed the second pilot was going to direct another show about two weeks before Star Trek was to start. I read for him. He called me later and asked if I would come to Desilu on a Saturday morning to do some accents for the Star Trek people, none of whom I knew. I did and they picked the Scottish accent and I was delighted, as I like that accent very much.

Q: What was your opinion of the show then, when it was being made, and now, in retrospect?

A: It wasn't until we had done a few shows that we all began to realize that the good scripts weren't just flukes but were part and parcel of the real class that Gene Roddenberry had created. Now? I think it was, is, and will always be a classic and I am proud to have been a part of it.

Q: How much of the character of Scotty was James Doohan and how much was dictated by the script?

A: I think Scotty finally became somewhat more complete when the writers began to know me and therefore wrote a lot of me into it.

Q: Which of the Star Trek episodes is your favorite and why?

A: "The Doomsday Machine," because it was more scientific. I prefer science to science fiction—monsters, etc.

Q: Do you have any personal observations on your fellow

cast members and/or the production staff of the show? Have you remained close friends with any of them?

A: All of the members of the cast were great to work with and even better as we got to know each other well. The crew and production staff were terrific. I think it showed.

Q: What, besides the Star Trek animated series, have you been doing lately?

A: I did a play, a new one, in San Francisco for ten months and I am hoping to do it on tour in the East and South.

Q: Do you have any personal observations on your career or profession?

A: When you've been an actor as long as I have, most parts are just a job, because we get very little opportunity to do the parts we would really like to do.

Q: Do you like being associated with the Star Trek image? Has it hurt or helped your career?

A: I did like being associated with Star Trek but it has seemed to limit me, whereas before Star Trek, I did a great variety of parts. It's the old type-casting syndrome.

Q: What kind of person is James Doohan? What does he like?

A: He does like people to be honest with him because he likes people, but is disappointed, I think, a little too easily. However, he is trying to treat people as they are. He likes to keep busy with something just about all the time. He doesn't like being alone in hotel rooms unless he has a fascinating book to read. He just finished a convention in New York and bought three books that didn't impress him so he left them there.

Q: What is your reaction to the possibility of resurrecting Star Trek in a feature film?

A: I really hope they do a feature because Star Trek being the classic that it is, it deserves to be treated as well as possible.

Q: What is your impression of the Star Trek phenomenon, whereby more and more people have become interested in the show and its stars some six years after it left the network?

A: It is unbelievable but beautiful and is continuously amazing me.

Q: How much "boning up," if any, did you do on electronics and engineering to handle the role of Scotty?

A: I always was very interested in the sciences, so I knew

everything they wrote about or was able to imagine it without any difficulty.

Q: Did you ever have any suggestions in the way of changing or adding to the Scotty character that were never adopted?

A: Only to put him in more situations than the engine room. When I sat in the captain's chair and "in command," I felt really as if I was in command. A very comfortable feeling because I think James Doohan likes to be in command.

Q: Do you enjoy being a guest at the various Star Trek conventions, and what is your reaction/opinion of the fans in attendance?

A: Most conventions I have enjoyed, but I will not point out the ones I didn't enjoy. But the fans are just great with the most minute objections.

Q: What was your reaction to the fact that the show was almost always in jeopardy of being canceled, but was renewed due to the great demand of its following?

A: Having learned early to love the show so much and to see its great possibilities, when you heard it might be canceled, you began to doubt your own insight and question whether it was a good show or not, but along comes another terrific script and you felt much better. I think the movement to renew was probably the birth of what we see today in the ever-growing Star Trek conventions.

13. THE ANIMATED STAR TREK:
AN ANALYSIS
by Bill Norton

Bill Norton originally sent us his animation article for publication about a year and a half ago, but as we were unable to locate a good enough set of stills to accompany his excellent piece, we held it for several months before finally publishing it in Trek *No. 8. It was an immediate hit with our readers, and so we decided to include it in this collection. But when we informed Bill that we intended to do so, he pleaded with us to allow him to rewrite it, as several years had now passed since he originally wrote it, and he felt that an increase in his writing skills and the new information he had gathered warranted a rewrite. We agreed, on one condition: Bill had to do the rewrite in less than a week, in order to allow us enough time to meet our own deadline. After several days of backbreaking work and some sleepless nights (Bill had an impending deadline of his own—the start of college classes), he returned it to us in its present form. We think that you'll agree that all of Bill's trouble was worth it, as his is the most comprehensive animated Star Trek article from the viewpoint of story and character that we have ever seen.*

The animated film industry has slowly come into its own over the years, and has naturally gone where the money is—television. Unfortunately, the main thrust of TV animation has been in youthful cartoons, shown one after the other on Saturday mornings.

In the midst of one of its peculiar phases, cartoon producers in 1973 were resurrecting old live-action programs by adapting them to animation. Two examples of this type of adaptation were *My Favorite Martian* and *I Dream of Jeannie*. Star Trek, out of production for four years, was

96

extremely popular and had a large fan following that spent lots of money. The natural result of this combination was the production of a weekly half-hour Star Trek series, and many people wanted to do it. They contacted Paramount, and Paramount contacted Gene Roddenberry, the creator of the show. Gene was to have the privilege of choosing the lucky producer of a Star Trek weekly series.

Gene soon found that he had his work cut out for him. He was looking for an effort that would complement the original series and which adults could watch without having their intelligence insulted. He wanted something that the hard-core, serious fan could enjoy without ending up writhing and slobbering on the floor. Such was hard to find in the animation houses that released the standard Saturday-morning cartoon fare.

When Gene asked for examples, a large portion of the contenders' presentations were on a childish fantasy level, and usually not the least bit Star Trek in nature. For example: A planet is suffering from one malady or another. Naturally, the *Enterprise* arrives on the scene and quickly lands(!), and the faithful crew leaps out with their zap guns and promptly straightens things out.

Roddenberry knew that a successful show would require intelligent scripts with an acceptable science fiction premise, plus a working understanding of the Star Trek format. He was not about to destroy the appeal of his most successful creation with an effort which would address itself only to toddlers.

Finally, an end came to the dismal competition when Norm Prescott and Lou Scheimer, top executives at Filmation Studios, plus science fiction and Star Trek fans in their own right, offered their considerable talents.

Filmation already had some impressive credits to their record: *Batman, Superman, Aquaman, Fantastic Voyage,* and the animated film *Journey to the Center of the Earth.* Roddenberry was impressed, even commenting that Filmation was comparable to Walt Disney.

One thing that was suggested by Filmation and helped convince Roddenberry that these were the people that he had been looking for was their offer to allow him full creative control in the area of scripts. This would allow Gene, himself a television writer/producer, to keep his thumb on the most important component of an animated program. So the project was given the go-ahead, and NBC bought it.

Gene Roddenberry would act as executive consultant, and he assigned his story editor from the original series, Dorothy Fontana, back to her old post, with the additional duties of associate producer. As story editor, Fontana would be able to enlist the best writers she could locate.

Many writers that had written for the 1960s show returned to the fold: David Gerrold ("The Trouble with Tribbles"), Samuel Peeples ("Where No Man Has Gone Before"), Margaret Armen ("The Paradise Syndrome"), Stephen Kandel ("Mudd's Women"), David Harmon ("The Deadly Years"), Paul Schneider ("The Squire of Gothos"), and even D. C. Fontana herself ("The *Enterprise* Incident").

In addition, other notables also wrote for the animated show: Walter Koenig (Mr. Chekov on the original show, who because of budget did not work on the animated series), Marc Daniels (director of many of the original episodes), and well-known science fiction author Larry Niven. It seemed that many reputable writers had no qualms about having their name appear in the credits of a cartoon.

The major reason that Roddenberry felt an animated Star Trek was justified was the many new and creative things the medium would allow him to do. He was looking forward to the fantastic aliens and their cultures that could be displayed far more extensively than the budget of a live program would allow.

No longer would the production have to depend on mattes to depict large cities or landscapes. No longer would the size, number, or complexity of spacecraft have to be minimized because of the cost in supplies or the man-hours in constructing miniatures. And no longer would aliens have to be strictly humanoid to avoid the expense of producing complicated makeup appliances and costumes. Anything imaginable could be created on the drawing board.

The animation process is more involved than many people realize. Because it is so difficult to have believable emotions register on the faces of the animated characters, the script must provide nearly all the points of the story, with the moving action coming next. So the script is the first element which is secured before production can begin. Generally cartoons are written by people who are familiar with all phases of the animation production. Perhaps Star Trek was so different because they used regular television writers.

Animation has the longest preproduction of any type of film. A storyboard, which has drawings of every scene with notes on dialogue, music, and visual effects (much like a comic book), is made to outline the entire episode.

Backgrounds, over which the characters will move, are next painted on celluloid with opaque acrylic paints, often on several layers for depth. Star Trek averaged eighty backgrounds per episode, twice the normal number for the average weekly cartoon. Bob Kline, chief character and layout designer, was kept busy thinking up Star Trek's imaginative scenery and aliens, with commendable results.

The sound track is now meticulously mixed with voices, music, and sound effects. From this point on, the entire production will revolve around this track, expertly timed and regulated. Dialogue presented a unique problem for Star Trek. Generally the entire cast would read three to five scripts together in the studio, but with Star Trek's professional cast (the original actors having been signed to provide the voices for their characters), this was not always possible. The actors had to record their lines wherever they happened to be and send it in for mixing. Recordings would come in from all over the country.

The characters and their movements could now be drawn to coordinate with the sound track. This is first done on a glass-topped, illuminated table called an animation disc. The drawings are done on very thin paper, with each successive movement of the character done on a sheet placed over the previous one so that each corresponds exactly.

The drawings are then transferred to celluloid either by Xerox or hand inking. The moving arm, leg, head, etc. is often done on a separate celluloid sheet, which will simply be overlaid on the mass-produced common body. The figures and moving limbs are now painted in the same manner as the backgrounds, but with the paint applied to the side opposite the outline for definition.

The "cels" are then photographed moving over the background, and the sound track is added to complete the production. Full-scale movie animation is somewhat more involved and has many more drawings per foot of film. Television animators have a budget and a schedule to worry about. A single half-hour episode of Star Trek cost about $75,000, making it one of the most expensive cartoon TV series. Because the series was ordered late, Filmation was given only six months to get sixteen episodes ready for airing. With 5,000 to 7,000 drawings per show, and only a seventy-five-member staff (plus the high standards Roddenberry and Filmation themselves demanded), the pressure was tremendous.

The time squeeze forced Filmation to cheat a little and take some short cuts. The most readily apparent short cut to any regular viewer of the show is the use of stock cels. *Enterprise* fly-bys and bridge backgrounds are excusable, but the producers would repeatedly use several cels that the viewer soon became overly familiar with.

These included: Spock bending over scanner; Kirk in command chair; Uhura giving report from communications station; Sulu at helm; Spock looking at Kirk from science station; Scott operating transporter; and several others.

If you've noticed that nearly all of these are bridge scenes, then you've stumbled on the key to the short cut. Every episode has bridge sequences, so all that is needed is to add the correct movements and dialogue to existing cels, and hours of production time are saved. Unfortunately, it added a touch of boredom to the shows.

The pressure also had a rather humorous result at times. If the episodes are examined carefully, the observant viewer can spot a number of bloopers that made their elusive way into the final prints. Once I saw Scott operating the transporter, but when the scene changed to a shot over his shoulder, he suddenly had a mustache!

The biggest problem for the Star Trek team to overcome was the difficulty of fitting a meaningful and exciting story into the half-hour format. It was a unique problem, because although they were trying for a mature story and good science fiction, they were also playing to a predominantly young audience. This meant that sex had to be totally eliminated and violence toned down. As a result, much of the vocabulary and concepts was too far above the youngsters. Still, the producers had to satisfy the many Star Trek fans, who knew all too well what constituted an adequate episode of the immortal program.

As it turned out, what the television executives had been

saying all along about the first Star Trek pilot became true for the animated series. The cartoon was too cerebral for the time slot it was in.

The animated show introduced several new items to Star Trek's storehouse of futuristic equipment. This was done for the dual reasons of intrigue and expediency. The most remarkable of these new devices was the life support belt. This is a wide, pale-colored belt that, when activated, envelops the wearer in a lime-green aura. This aura acts as a shield and provides warmth and atmosphere to the occupant. It can be used in almost any environment, including water.

Also revealed was the automatic bridge defense system. This is a phaser array mounted on the ceiling of the bridge and activated during an intruder alert. Its fire can reach any point on the bridge.

A supplement to the shuttlecraft was added with the Aquashuttle. Larger than the normal shuttlecraft and opening in the rear, this vessel can maneuver and submerge in water. In the same episode, a Federation motorboat was shown.

Though I don't feel that Federation technology could have produced a device like the life support belt, the other items are reasonable when considering the *Enterprise*'s dual roles of diplomacy and scientific research.

But one new piece of equipment which I totally dislike is a recreation room that provides holographic illusions with odors and proper atmospheric conditions to simulate any setting. This would make the Starfleet seem too "luxury-minded." Besides, in the cartoon, crewmen are allowed to wear mustaches.

The animated series also added two new enemies to harass the Federation. Foremost is the Kzinti, a ferocious catlike race who have fought three wars with humankind, losing all three, but stubbornly persisting in their warlike ways. Star Trek fans finally get a look at the Orions, introduced in "Journey to Babel." They have their neutrality closely examined, and it is found somewhat lacking.

Two aliens are also added to the starship's command personnel. M'Ress is a female of a fellinoid species. She is covered with a golden fur and has a distinctive purr in her voice. She mans the communications panel in Uhura's absence. Next is a tripodal creature (three legs, and three arms with three fingers on each hand). His name is Arex and his post is navigation.

The budget and time restrictions, and perhaps the restriction of simply being a weekly television series, had some dismal effects on the cartoon. These may seem like small things, but remember that it was the small touches that made the original show seem like a true universe, believable and popular.

No longer does the viewer hear the confusion of voices reporting in over the intercom from every deck during an emergency. No longer can the fans depend on hearing a healthy variety of excellent musical compositions. Very few crewmen besides the regular characters can be seen aboard ship, even though the animators need not worry about paying extras.

The characters tended to lose their personalities because they always spoke and reacted in the same ways. They became painfully predictable. The characters were always drawn with the same clothing on (Uhura didn't even change earrings!), and this resulted in a further loss of individuality. These deficiencies tended to make the production, especially the scenes on the bridge, seem bland.

The freedom that animation allowed in creating awesome cities, landscapes, and collections of machinery worked well except when it was used on the *Enterprise*. Where before there were only tantalizing hints, now there are vast corridors of machinery and equipment.

Besides these looks at the technical side of the ship being somewhat disappointing, it has detracted from the mysticism and awe that the enormous starship had for many fans. It is not a good policy to examine a hero too closely, and that is precisely what the *Enterprise* is to many.

Another part of the production that I give poor ratings is the use of the regular actors to provide the voices for incidental characters and aliens that might appear in each episode.

James Doohan, an excellent dialectician, did the voice of Arex and almost every other important alien that popped up. George Takei also did a couple of fleeting characters. Nichelle Nichols did the computer dialogue, and Majel Barrett was the voice of M'Ress. These two women probably also provided the dialogue for the rest of the female parts in the show.

The use of paid actors to read other parts would normally be an acceptable expense saver, but with all the characters that Star Trek had, the doubling and even tripling of voices episode after episode became very distracting. And all too evident.

It would be difficult to evaluate the show's animation without taking into account the medium it was conceived in. Movements were jerky and characters' faces rather plain, but this can be attributed to the basic limitations of television animation, which is far less refined than theatrical productions. Actually, Star Trek's character concepts are among the best in the industry, and the backgrounds are the best.

In the realm of scripts, I found examples of things that could indicate a degree of lethargy. It is the fault of either the writers or the program's staff that an inexcusable literary offense was committed: the rehashing of plot concepts that appeared in the original show. By this I mean the shocking appearance in the animated scripts of elements of stories from the 1960s series. The serious Star Trek fan can pick these up without difficulty, but for the less knowledgeable, a few examples are in order.

In "Beyond the Farthest Star," the crew of the *Enterprise* battles a violent, murderous, mind-energy being which has infused itself into the ship's machinery. This concept bears a great resemblance to "Wolf in the Fold."

In "One of Our Planets Is Missing," the *Enterprise* battles an enormous, planet-eating cloud creature. It is interesting to note that the author of this script, Marc Daniels, also directed "The Doomsday Machine," in which a robot eats planets. It also resembles "The Immunity Syndrome," with the idea of a gigantic entity which travels through space.

In "The Lorelei Signal," a landing party is captured by a colony of women who absorb the very life forces of the men. This has the effect of aging the victims, so we are treated to the much overused trio of Kirk, Spock, and McCoy rapidly aging, as they did in "The Deadly Years."

In "How Sharper Than a Serpent's Tooth," the ancient Mayan/Aztec god Kulkukan intercepts the *Enterprise* and demands that the crew accept him as their master. Shades of "Who Mourns For Adonis?"

Other problems with the animated episodes were the thinly disguised messages (a plague of the original's third season), and a certain amount of childishness. The former ailment can probably be attributed to the half-hour format, which, all things considered, Filmation did a fine job of fitting Star Trek into. Childishness could be the result of sponsor pressure, front-office laziness, or a conscious effort on the staff's part to please their largest audience. Again, some examples:

In "More Tribbles, More Troubles" the wonderful Tribbles return, to the delight of all the toddlers. However, these Tribbles are different. Instead of multiplying at fantastic rates, these little darlings grow to enormous proportions. And one other major difference: These giant Tribbles are full of hundreds of little Tribbles! This episode is nothing but a simple milking of the Tribbles' popularity, and a cheap replay of the first episode that, I think, was meant to be funny.

I'll give you the plot, and you find the common points with "The Trouble with Tribbles." The *Enterprise* is escorting a shipment of quadro-triticale to the ailing Sherman's Planet when they come upon a small scout vessel being pursued by a Klingon cruiser. The scout ship turns out to contain Cyrano Jones and Tribbles; the Klingon ship is commanded by Kirk's old enemy, Captain Koloth. The *Enterprise* becomes infested with Tribbles, who eat the grain, Kirk is inundated with Tribbles, and in the end the fuzz balls are left in the care of the Klingons.

In "The Infinite Vulcan," an obsessed scientist, considering Spock some fantastic breed, kidnaps him so that he can create clone duplicates of him. These doppelgangers will patrol the galaxy and act as a police force to put down hostilities as required. The unusual thing about all this is that the scientist and the clone Spock are ten times normal size. Illogical? You bet! Exciting for the kiddies? You can count on it, and a shameful play on Spock's popularity.

In "The Ambergris Element," following an Aquashuttle accident, Kirk and Spock are rescued by an underwater civilization and injected with a drug which, in effect, turns them into fish so they can survive underwater. After conferring with the *Enterprise,* the two swim back down to find a cure for their peculiar malady.

In "Mudd's Passion," Harcourt Fenton Mudd is back, and this time he is peddling a love potion that is uncommonly powerful. Not only does it cause Mr. Spock to fall madly in love with Nurse Chapel, but it also affects a dinosaurlike creature that is about to eat a shuttlecraft.

Despite the pitfalls, the Star Trek staff obviously worked very hard and with the best of intentions. Star Trek was going to be the best, they insisted, and it certainly was. Every program has its good scripts and bad, and in the case of the animated Star Trek, the best efforts were the stories that most closely held to the original Star Trek format of action-adventure/science fiction.

In "Yesteryear," while utilizing the Guardian of Forever, Spock is somehow edited from existence. Time has been tampered with, and as a result Spock died as a child. He must therefore return through time to Vulcan and save himself so that he may again exist in the future. If the plot isn't intriguing enough, then one can certainly enjoy observing the point in Spock's early life when he had to choose the course his life would take, human or Vulcan. This is universally accepted as the most outstanding animated Star Trek script, and who could have been more qualified to write such a story than the Vulcan expert herself, Dorothy Fontana?

In "Jihad," a jihad (holy war) will sweep the galaxy if a stolen holy object is not recovered in a short while. A "Mission Impossible" type team is assembled from representatives of several races (including Kirk and Spock) to attempt the recovery. But there seems to be a traitor among the group. This episode has a great action-adventure plot and good character interplay. The show could easily have turned into a cheap space opera without experienced handling and care.

In "The Pirates of Orion," an Orion pirate ship is carrying stolen cargo that could save Spock from a deadly disease. Even though Kirk is anxious to save his friend, he attempts to use diplomatic means to obtain the drug. The script is well thought out and works very well.

In "Albatross," Dr. McCoy is held for possibly killing the inhabitants of a planet he gave medical treatment to nineteen years before. The *Enterprise* sets out to gather evidence in the doctor's behalf but runs into some serious trouble. Besides a very effective script, this episode is especially noteworthy for the exceptional rendering of aliens, spacecraft, and backgrounds. A fine example of a Star Trek show, live or animated.

The animated Star Trek is a good example of what concerned and determined people can accomplish in a medium that produces things like "Speed Buggy." The half-hour restrictions did affect many aspects of the production, but overall it is still Star Trek and good Star Trek. Despite this fact, the cartoon has largely been ignored by fandom. When the project was first announced, many fans were bitter, feeling that Paramount was slapping them in the face by answering their plea for a return of their beloved program with a kiddie show. They were in error, and I hope that many are now watching the cartoon in the syndicated reruns, which are shown in many cities in the early afternoon. And in some in prime time!

Material on the animated effort is available, as it is for the live show. Lincoln Enterprises (the official distributor of Star Trek merchandise) has been selling scripts and storyboards from the beginning, and also has biographies on the M'Ress and Arex characters.

Film clips from the show are difficult to come by but can be found. The next best thing to clips, perhaps even better, became available in early 1976. These are cels (the celluloid paintings), 14-18 inches, and exactly like those used in the production of the programs. Distributed by Tuttle and Bailey Galleries, these are true collector's items because only a limited number were made for sale. *The Star Trek Concordance* by Bjo Trimble has all the information on the contents of the scripts plus some great sketches.

Besides its existence, the most important contribution that the Star Trek animated series has made to fandom is the Star Trek Log series of books by the up-and-coming SF author Alan Dean Foster. He has taken the animated scripts and added the flesh needed to round them into acceptable material for publication. In the last few volumes in the series, he has managed to devote the entire book to just one of the short cartoon stories! He is to be commended on an excellent adaptation series that has given, and will give, many hours of enjoyable Star Trek stories to starving fans.

So, taking into account all the animated Star Trek's faults, pitfalls, and successes, one can easily conclude that Filmation's talents and deep concern for the show have added to Star Trek lore twenty-two (sixteen first-season and six second-season episodes) new and often excellent episodes. And Filmation has set a precedent in television animation with a beautiful and serious effort. Not only is this opinion shared by fans, but the Television Academy of Arts and Sciences also agrees. They gave Filmation an Emmy Award for the animated Star Trek.

14. THE ANIMATED STAR TREK INDEX
by the Trek Staff

*When we ran Bill Norton's excellent article on the animated
Star Trek series, we felt that we should include an index to
the animated shows for the benefit of our readers who did
not already have one or were dissatisfied with others they
had seen. And our readers have responded with many thanks
for the index, plus some excellent suggestions which we plan
to incorporate when we finally get around to doing our complete Star Trek index. However, that is in the future, so we
will leave you to enjoy this index with one final note: When
this index was originally printed, many fans got the impression that it was compiled by Bill Norton for his animation
article. Bill wanted us to correct that mistaken impression,
as he doesn't like the idea of "rating" individual episodes in
relation to each other. However, since we feel that the ratings should be included as a general guide for those fans who
haven't seen the episodes, we must make it clear that the
ratings are the opinions of the* Trek *staff only, and not those
of Bill Norton or any other individual.*

Below is a complete index of all the Star Trek animated
programs telecast on NBC-TV from September 1973 to
October 1974.

Included are title, major guest "voices" a short synopsis,
and a rating. The synopses and ratings have been compiled
by *Trek* editors Walter Irwin, G. B. Love, and Jim Houston.

Each rating is a total of the editors' ratings added together,
and should be interpreted in this way:

*****	Excellent
****	Very Good
***	Good
**	Fair
*	Poor

REGULAR CAST VOICE PERFORMERS

MAJEL BARRETT: Nurse Chapel/Lt. M'Ress
JAMES DOOHAN: Scotty/Lt. Arex
DeFOREST KELLEY: Dr. McCoy
NICHELLE NICHOLS: Lt. Uhura
LEONARD NIMOY: Mr. Spock
WILLIAM SHATNER: Capt. James T. Kirk
GEORGE TAKEI: Lt. Sulu

1. "Yesteryear" (9/15/73) by D. C. Fontana
Guests: Mark Lenard (Sarek), Billy Simpson (Young Spock)
Rating: ****
  Kirk and Spock return from a visit with the Guardian of Forever to find that Spock no longer exists, and Spock must travel back through time to correct history.
2. "One of Our Planets Is Missing" (9/22/73) by Marc Daniels
Guests: Majel Barrett (Cloud)
Rating: **
  A huge cosmic cloud, composed of antimatter, threatens several planets, and the *Enterprise* is drawn into it when trying to destory it.
3. "The Lorelei Signal" (9/29/73) by Margaret Armen
Guests: Majel Barrett (Theela), Nichelle Nichols (Dara)
Rating: ***
  The male members are tempted by life-stealing women with a signal only they can hear, and the female crewpersons must rescue them.
3. "More Tribbles, More Troubles" (10/6/73) by David Gerrold
Guests: James Doohan (Koloth), David Gerrold (Korax), Stanley Adams (Cyrano Jones)
Rating: ****
  A small scout ship rescued by the *Enterprise* contains Cyrano Jones and a new kind of Tribble: They grow to enormous proportions.
5. "The Survivor" (10/13/73) by James Schmerer
Guests: Ted Knight (Carter Winston/Alien), Nichelle Nichols (Lt. Anne Nored)
Rating: **

A long-missing philanthropist's identity is assumed by an alien, who disguises himself as Kirk and orders the *Enterprise* into the neutral zone.

6. **"The Infinite Vulcan"** (10/20/73) by Walter Koenig
Guests: James Doohan (Dr. Keniclius 5)
Rating: *

A warped scientist manufactures a giant clone of Spock to act as a galactic policeman, but leaves the real Spock near death.

7. **"The Magicks of Megas-Tu"** (10/27/73) by Larry Brody
Guests: James Doohan (Lucien), Ed Bishop (Prosecutor)
Rating: ***

The *Enterprise* enters an alternate universe where magic works, and because of their entry, they must defend one of the inhabitants in a trial.

8. **"Once Upon a Planet"** (11/3/73) by Len Jenson and Chuck Menville
Guests: James Doohan (Gabler), George Takei (Computer)
Rating: ***

Returning to the "shore leave" planet, the *Enterprise* crew finds that the Keeper is dead, and the computer which controls the planet has gone beserk.

9. **"Mudd's Passion"** (11/10/73) by Stephen Kandel
Guests: Roger C. Carmel (Harry Mudd)
Rating: ***

Harry Mudd is back once again, this time peddling a love potion which, to the surprise of everyone, causes Spock to fall madly in love with Christine Chapel.

10. **"The Terratin Incident"** (11/17/73) by Paul Schneider
Guests: James Doohan (Mendant)
Rating: **

An energy charge fires through the ship, causing everyone on board to begin to shrink in size.

11. **"Time Trap"** (11/24/73) by Joyce Perry
Guests: unknown
Rating: **

An ion storm sweeps the *Enterprise* and the Klingon ship commanded by Kor into a "Sargasso Sea of space," from which, according to the inhabitants, there is no escape.

12. **"The Ambergris Element"** (12/1/73) by Margaret Armen
Guests: unknown
Rating: **

After a shuttlecraft crash on a waterworld, Kirk and Spock find that they have been transformed into water-breathers.

13. **"Slaver Weapon"** (12/15/73) by Larry Niven
Guests: unknown
Rating: ****

Spock, Uhura, and Sulu are transporting a Slaver stasis box to Starbase 25, when they are captured by Kzin warriors who want to use the box to find a powerful weapon.

14. **"Beyond the Farthest Star"** (12/22/73) by Samuel A. Peeples
Guests: James Doohan (Kyle, Commander)
Rating: *

Escaping the pull of a dead star, the *Enterprise* finds that it has been invaded by an energy being which takes control of the ship.

15. **"The Eye of the Beholder"** (1/5/74) by David P. Harmon
Guests: James Doohan (Tom Markel), Majel Barrett (Randi Bryce)
Rating: ***

Kirk, Spock and McCoy are captured by a super-intelligent race of snail-like creatures who put them in a "zoo" for study.

16. **"Jihad"** (1/13/74) by Stephen Kandel
Guests: David Gerrold (Em/3/Green)
Rating: ***

Kirk, Spock, and a band of aliens must recover a sacred relic before a holy war breaks out throughout the universe.

17. **"The Pirates of Orion"** (9/7/74) by Howard Weinstein
Guests: unknown
Rating: **

Spock is dying of a rare disease, and the only available drug is stolen by Orion pirates.

18. **"BEM"** (9/14/74) by David Gerrold
Guests: James Doohan (Ari bn Bem)
Rating: **

Commander Ari bn Bem, an observer aboard the *Enterprise* from the planet Pandro, causes Kirk and Spock to be captured by aliens.

19. **"Practical Joker"** (9/21/74) by Chuck Menville
Guests: James Doohan (Romulan)
Rating: ****

An energy creature enters the ship's computers and plays pranks on the crew, but it becomes dangerous when it takes the ship into the neutral zone.

20. **"Albatross"** (9/28/74) by Dario Finelli
Guests: James Doohan (kol-tai, Prefect)
Rating: ***

The inhabitants of Dramia II put Dr. McCoy on trial for causing a mass epidemic nineteen years before, and the crew must clear him.

21. **"How Sharper Than a Serpent's Tooth"** (10/5/74) by Russell Bates and David Wise
Guests: James Doohan (Kulkukan)
Rating: *

A godlike alien appears in a ship that takes on the form of a feathered serpent and claims to be the ancient Mayan god Kulkukan.

22. **"The Counter-Clock Incident"** (10/12/74) by John Colver
Guests: unknown
Rating: ****

The *Enterprise,* carrying its first commander, Robert April and his wife, is drawn into an alternate universe by a small, powerful ship, and the crew soon discovers they are all growing younger at an ever-increasing rate.

15. A SAMPLING OF TREK ROUNDTABLE

*One of the greatest pleasures in editing a Star Trek maga-
zine is reading the comments of our readers. Not only do
we swell with pride at the compliments and cringe at the
complaints, but we never cease to be amazed at the thought
and effort that readers put into their letters to "Trek Roundtable." We are justifiably proud of the fact that many Star
Trek fans consider "Trek Roundtable" to be fandom's major
forum for expressing ideas about Star Trek, science fiction,
and related subjects, and the condition of the world in general. The high caliber of the mail we receive can be shown
by two simple facts: We never have nearly enough room to
print all of the letters we receive; and many of our letter
writers have gone on to expound on their ideas and write
articles for* Trek *and other magazines. The following letters
are selected from the past issues of* Trek, *and should give a
good idea of what goes on in a typical "Trek Roundtable."*

Teri Meyer, Omaha, Neb.

There seems to be a misunderstanding. I'm referring to
"Trek Roundtable" [No. 4] and my statement being classified
as support for *Space 1999.* I apologize for not being more
specific. I am *not* a supporter. . . . The show is boring, and
in my opinion, Barbara Bain only hastens the show's death!
I had merely answered the second half of your question . . .
this is my fault. . . . However, I still believe *1999*'s popularity (that's what I keep hearing) will improve the chances
to get science fiction back on TV. As for intelligent programming, I submit *1999,* with its poor writing, bad plots,
is better than falling bodies and flying bullets.

The most powerful attraction for a viewing audience is
good drama, such as *"City."* Fortunately, most of ST's epi-

sodes were dramatic with action-adventure scenes added
here and there.

It would be interesting to have original SF stories and
poetry in *Trek,* as long as your magazine devoted most of
its pages to ST. I am impressed with your new format—it's
a class ST magazine. Would like to see a special McCoy ish.

Trisha Ullman

First let me point out that this is not an entirely unbiased
view. I have a mental block against the moon galivanting
about in other star systems . . . I am strongly suspicious
that the moon idea was a desperate attempt to avoid using
a starship as transportation. . . . One of the most oft-cited
reasons for ST's poularity is the optimism and the hope for
the human race it offers. . . . In *1999* there is no background of peace, of the brotherhood not only of nations,
but of worlds. The people of Moon Base Alpha are not explorers and colonizers but helpless passengers . . . having no
desire to be where they are or doing what they are doing. . . .
And this is the main difference between the two shows, and
the reason why I do not think *1999* will ever have the sheer
power of feeling behind it that ST does.

There is an interesting thing I would like to mention here.
I have for some time felt that *Space 1999* is a pressure campaign. There were books on the stands before the pilot was
shown here . . . puzzles, games, etc. . . . most of this stuff
must have been in the works before the series came out. . . .
There could have been no fan reaction, no public demand.
. . . I think it is a deliberate effort to force the series on the
viewers. . . . And I have been itching to know, ever since it
started, how the fans would react. Recently I had a chance
to find at least a partial answer. I attended the first San An-
tonio ST con. . . . When the auctioneer came to a *Space
1999* book, it was booed off the stand. Loudly. Other
items . . . comics, movie posters . . . sold or went quietly
unbid. But the reaction to *1999* was like the response to the
villain when he ties the heroine to the railroad tracks. . . . I
think it is indicative to the overall reaction to *Space 1999.*

*This is sheer and simple merchandizing overkill, Trish.
Greed was the motivating factor here, not a plot to force
us to love 1999. But one must stop and think—would ST
fans have been so incensed over the deluge of 1999
material if it had turned out to be a great show?*

Larry Rew, Springfield, Va.

After having seen and read *Trek* No. 4, I just wanted to say what a fabulous issue I thought it was. You guys really did a *beautiful* job. . . . I eagerly look forward to the upcoming *Trek* No. 5. Keep up the good work!

Terry Whittier, Editor Altair and Stardate, 3809 Meramonte Way, No. Highlands, Cal. 95660

Thanks very much for sending a review copy of *Trek*. Out of all the fanzines in ST fandom, yours was the one I most wanted to get, and was the least expected when it arrived.

I will try to give it the best review it deserved. I'm terribly impressed by its polish and professional look. Overall, your written material is of a consistently high quality. It is informative and well-written prose. Although the piece by Leslie Thompson was a bit too "Gosh-Wow." You have an impressive use of photographs—assumption is correct that ST fans are primarily visually oriented. Hence your use of great amounts of beautifully reproduced phographs.

I applaud your effort to get some kind of letter column going in "Trek Roundtable." However, you and I are running into the same problem—out of the millions of ST fans, there are not that many letter writers out there. Only a small percentage are into correspondence.

Only one thing bothered me about this issue, though I don't intend to mention it in my review—I really don't think, considering the balance of the material devoted to, and not devoted to, Spock, that you should have called No. 4 your Special Spock issue. I think it was pushing it a bit. If you'd grouped all the Spock material together, and called attention to your Spock theme in the editorial, then it would have been more justifiable. Just a thought.

Leslie says she is gosh-wow for ST. However, she is far from shallow, and was writing from a simplistic viewpoint. Personal thoughts can become pompous very easily, and this was something she was trying to avoid. You are right, Terry, ST fans don't write much. That's something we are trying to change. We think that we had a good percentage of Spock in No. 4, which justifies our cover blurb. But don't forget, we can't put out Trek *unless we have readers, and the cover has to have something to attract them—Therefore, the*

"Special Spock" Catchphrase. (Every ST fan will be interested in Terry's zine. It is one of the best.)

James Caddell, Islip Terrace, N.Y.

I was curious as to why there are no subscriptions available, and if and when they will be available. I enjoyed *Trek* No. 3, although I felt it was too short, and I was curious as to why there was no letter column. . . .

(*On "The Omega Glory":*) . . . my own feeling is that "The Enterprise Incident" was the worst, not for what it was . . . but because of what it should have been. The original script by D. C. Fontana was fantastic, and would have stood out as the best of the third season . . . but the network was too paranoid to allow it on the air.

Perhaps a good article . . . would be the actual story as it was written by Fontana.

Unfortunately, we cannot judge a show by what it "could have been." All we have is the finished product. We agree, this discrepancy would make a great article. Do you, James (or anyone out there), have a spare copy of D.C. Fontana's original script you could send to us?

Brian Deslatte, Port Neches, Tex.

I have enjoyed the past three issues very much. I think you should start having articles on other sci-fi films, especially *2001: A Space Odyssey*. . . . I think *1999* is a very good show—but I prefer ST. I believe it will be picked up by a national network, which will help ST's revival, as the other networks will compete. . . .

A 2001 *article is in the works.*

Walter Turner, Athens, Ala.

I liked the content of *Trek* No. 4, since I think you should deal with one character in each issue. . . . I would like to see reviews of *2001, Silent Running,* ST cartoons, ST comics, and some of Roddenberry's other productions.

An ST con with Leonard Nimoy is being planned for Huntsville, Alabama.

Leslie is planning a story on the ST *comics. We have* Silent Running *scheduled for a few issues from now. We've been wanting to do a piece on the cartoon show for months, but lack enough solid material. Can anyone out there supply us with any?*

The *Enterprise* and the Klingon ship as made by Estes
Industries

"Amok Time" by Steve Fabian

Grace Lee Whitney as she appears today, lovelier than ever

"Kirk" by David Daniels

Walter Koenig today

"Uhura" by Monica Miller

Trek editor Walter Irwin in the shuttlecraft mockup at Houstoncon '77 with special guest George Takei

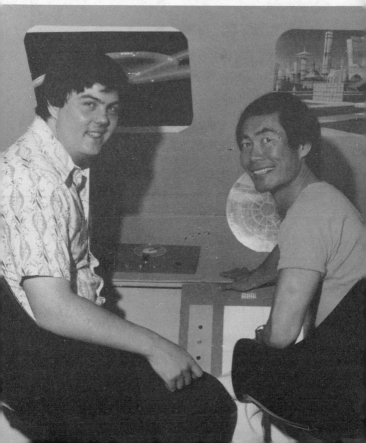

"McCoy" by Monica Miller

Dirk Pfeil, Milwaukee, Wisc.

I prefer thought-provoking episodes like "City" because the impact of the show lasts well after it ends. Like many other fans, though, I think "City" is the best episode. The combination of drama-romance that this episode achieved wasn't and probably never will be duplicated! It's rather unfair to say which kind of shows you prefer in general, because the variety of shows is one of the big assets of the series.

Carol Bush, Mt. Pleasant, Tex.

All ST episodes are good, but the best ones are the ones that have something to say. It is so hard to find a TV show that is good enough to have a "message." Most TV shows are just for action and laughs. They have no *meaning*. ST combines action with meaning and usually comes out with just the right amount of both.

I think it would be better to keep *Trek* just an ST magazine. To have SF stories and poems would be nice, but it could detract from *Trek's* Star Trek format.

Judy Lee Goldenberg, Kew Gardens, N.Y.

In your editorials (*Trek* No. 3), you urge fans to write to Paramount about the Trekfilm. Well, at the February committee con here in NYC, various people, including the Great Bird himself, told the audience *not* to write to Paramount. The film is definitely on schedule to be made, Paramount has committed $$$$ to the production and construction of sets, props and costumes are underway. (This was confirmed by Jimmy Doohan on May 9.) If people continue to write to Paramount asking dumb questions like "When are you going to make a Star Trek movie?" the bigshots will get mad and impatient at Gene to finish a script, and no one wants that, do we?

Judy, at this late date, it has become a question of us no longer just wanting a Star Trek film, it is now imperative that one be made if the momentum of Star Trek fandom be kept going. Jimmy Doohan told us in March that the film was scheduled for July. George Takei told us in June that it was scheduled for September, but had just been moved back to November. Are we going to be stalled back to the point where the bigshots can say that the audience isn't around any more, and scrap the project? We say keep writing. Let everyone concerned know that we, the fans, are beginning to get mad and impatient at them. Then maybe we will see our movie sometime before 1978.

Debbie Winkler, Clearwater, Fla.

I am new to *Trek,* and the first issue that I ever saw was No. 4, only because it had something on *Space 1999* in it. Because of this, I didn't get a chance to stick up for *Space 1999* in your "Trek Roundtable."

Anyone who has viewed *Space 1999*'s first season must agree that it could not and would never compare to Star Trek. But it has been one of the few SF series since Star Trek to try and be as great and as well known as Star Trek was and is.

Most of the people who have seen *Space 1999* and have dismissed it as junk probably don't know of all the radical changes and improvements that are being made for the second season.

Fred Frieburger, who handled Star Trek's third season, has taken over as script editor and line producer. The music, basic costumes, and even Moonbase Alpha will undergo changes. The characters have been rounded and will act more like people instead of like zombies. Some old characters will be dropped and new ones introduced this coming season. Even *Space 1999*'s huge budget will be increased!

Space 1999: Try it again, you'll like it! I wrote you this letter to prove that there is someone (myself) who will stick up for *Space 1999.* But believe me, I am not alone!

You weren't too late this time, Debbie; welcome aboard. We assume that just about everyone in Star Trek fandom has heard of the prospective changes in 1999, but from where we sit, the reaction has generally been "So what?" We have our opinions of Space 1999 (and they do not all agree!), but what we think and say is better left in our editorial columns. However, by a large majority, our readers have voted that we not devote any more space to Space 1999. However, the "Roundtable" is something else, so if you 1999 fans want to keep fighting, keep writing!

Pat Molnar, Carteret, N.J.

I just wanted to tell you how delighted I was to see and read about a painting of mine mentioned in your *Trek* No. 4

N.Y. con article. Since the problem of transport was brought up, I thought you'd be interested in hearing about how it was accomplished, along with a few other facts about the painting.

It was executed on two pieces of canvas (the seam is just to the right of Chekov along the vertical partition), and was stretched upon a collapsible frame. The top and bottom stretcher strips were hinged in the center, which enabled the picture to be folded once upon itself when the side strips were removed. The painting was then rolled into a four-foot by twelve-foot roll.

Other facts about the painting: Title, "Energize"; size, 8 × 8 feet; medium, acrylics; time involved in actual execution, 305 hours (worked on mostly on weekends over a nine-month period); awards, "Most Popular," N.Y. Star Trek Convention, 1975.

One funny thing which occurred during the painting of the "'Rod Squad." In order to keep myself sane, I would play the radio, and on several occasions, a song would come on that would be very appropriate to the character who was being painted. For example: when I working on Chekov, "Midnight in Moscow" came on; then, "Don't Mess Around with Jim" for Kirk; "Chapel of Love" for Nurse Chapel; and "Son of a Preacher Man" for McCoy. It got pretty freaky after a while.

Thanks for your comments, Pat, and congratulations on a beautiful job. All of us are looking forward to your next creation.

Russell Baker, Memphis, Tenn.

All of the Star Trek episodes affected me in some way and brought me closer to Star Trek fandom. But the thought-provoking episodes somehow seem to have affected me more. My favorite is "The Menagerie." It's the kind of show that, after it is over, makes you just sit there and think some more. Today, I'll watch an average television program, maybe enjoy it, but in a couple of minutes, it will be forgotten and never enter my mind again. But I'll watch "The Menagerie" and it will make me want to go write a book or a novel concerning that same subject because it stays in my mind. It makes me long for "a piece of the action."

No other show on television can really make me shiver

just to think about. Certainly episodes like "Arena" are good
and I like them very much, because nowadays in shows
there has to be action and violence or you lose interest, but
when a beautiful, thought-provoking episode like "The Menagerie" comes along, you don't need all that action. It's
there.

Jill Mielke, Peoria, Ill.

Although I have never had the pleasure (or displeasure) of
attending a Star Trek convention, I have read quite a few
articles regarding them, and most of them state that the
conventions are being very poorly coordinated and/or run.
That even the guest stars have been given IOU's instead of
being paid. The fans attending some of these cons may
have been bitterly diapppointed in many cases, but this
will not turn them against Star Trek altogether. The question to me in retrospect, seems to be: "Just because I went to
a bad con, should this turn me against Star Trek as a
whole?" Most of the followers of ST are quite intelligent
people. They know that these cons are sponsored by an individual, or group, who have no affiliation with ST in the
first place. Some of these people are out to make a fast
buck at the expense of the fan. When this happens, it doesn't
take very long for word to spread that they were ripped off,
and the fans will avoid the next con sponsored by these
people. I'm not placing all ST cons in this category, because
they aren't all run this way. A poorly held con will not affect
ST fandom, because the fan is more intelligent than to place
the blame on Star Trek, period. (*On ST magazines:*) I have
purchased several magazines in the past several months that
I wish I had looked at more closely while I was in the store,
before I wasted my money. One magazine in particular is
Media Spotlight, which is a big rip-off farce. Another magazine had an excellent article on ST, but I will not name it
as it is a left-wing radical publication, and the ST article
was a one-time thing. But I have also purchased some extremely good magazines like *Starlog* and *Enterprise Incidents.* Just like some of the cons, some of the magazines are
out to get one thing: Your hard-earned money.

*One thing about your letter impressed us, Jill. We are
glad to see someone finally admit that all ST fans are not
intelligent, charming, industrious, and so on. Just like anything else, there are a few bad eggs. And unfortunately,*

they seem to be the ones who get the most publicity. One word about Media Spotlight: *We talked with the editors, and they told us that they are planning to upgrade the quality of their book with typesetting, etc. By the time you read this, you should know whether or not they have succeeded.*

Linda Frankel, Jericho, N.Y.

I am basically SF, not Star Trek oriented. It took me a while to be convinced that I ought to watch ST. I only watched *Space 1999* this past week. It shall be the last time. There were a few passable ideas in the episode ("A Touch of Humanity"), but they were obviously stolen from a file of SF concepts. One might describe the plot as a hash of "I Mudd," "Requiem for Methuselah," and "The Wizard of Oz"; the method of transport used by the Vegan androids was as scientifically valid as Dorothy clicking her heels together and saying "There's no place like Vega." Three-quarters of the story line did not logically follow. The acting . . . well, they know their lines. Barbara Bain is either rigid and unexpressive, or overacts in a most embarrassing manner. One cannot expect *Space: 1999* to replace ST, of course. They seem to be too interested in presenting pleasing stock stories for the average viewer. Commander Koenig is of lesser stature than Kirk, Maya hasn't Spock's appeal as an alien, and Fred Freiberger is no Gene Roddenberry . . . as was long ago demonstrated.

(*On "Arena" vs. "City":*) I have nothing against action stories. They ought to be intelligent and original, however. The best of the genre in ST was "Balance of Terror"; "Arena" was unfortunate in its lack of originality. If I see another superior race (that demonstrates themselves as superior in nothing but obnoxiousness) once more, I shall probably junk my TV set. Many media persons seem not to have stumbled on the truth that mindless action is boring and undramatic. This is usually not the fault of ST, with a few exceptions. "Spectre of the Gun" is the most infamous example. "City" is a beautifully told story, but I really wouldn't describe it as thought-provoking. "Mirror, Mirror" or "The Alternative Factor" fall more into that category. "City," however, is a great acting script . . . a rare animal in TV-SF.

The performances were so effective that one forgets the time concept left so much to be desired. The purpose of SF is to present new ideas to set one thinking of possibilities. Yes, I do prefer to see thought-provoking episodes. Since I am also interested in philosophy, I like to see ST dealing very fundamentally with ideas and principles. Like "The Enemy Within," and *"Galileo* Seven." The nature of man, and the conflict of logic vs. emotion are explored in these episodes; they are certainly "thought-provoking."

Bob Craft, Boomer, N.D.

In five issues of *Trek,* I've learned as much, if not more, about the details of Star Trek as I have in the past ten years of filling my scrapbook, searching for bits and pieces on miniatures, animation, makeup (Spock), and other assorted goodies. The technical features alone were well worth the cover price, not to mention the photos. If I may suggest subjects for future articles, I would like to see a good photo-article on Spock's ears . . . detailing how they were actually molded, modeled, and made from the first rough pairs to fine later-season models, from liquid latex to finished products. Perhaps an interview with John Chambers would provide the necessary information and pictures. . . . How about a photo article on the phaser?

Sean Rockoff

I would like to voice an opinion against the popular "Grok Spock" button. After rereading *Stranger in a Strange Land,* I feel I have come to know the meaning of "grok" as closely as possible for a non-Martian, and I don't think anybody (besides Spock, a Martian, or a Vulcan) could grok Spock in the full meaning of the word. . . .

Executive Editor Walter Irwin has read Stranger *several times, so he answers you in this way: "As I see it, grokking is impossible for anyone who does not have access to full mental communication with another being. Literally, to "grok" is to understand fully, completely, and beyond question. Since as humans, we will never be able to understand the concept of a Spock in such a way, we cannot grok him. However, I do not object to the buttons, since they represent an effort by many to seek this understanding, not only of Spock, but all others and all things. This is healthy, good, and will hopefully wipe out one more little bit of prejudice. And that never hurts.*

Irene Cunningham, Charleston, Ill.

(*After informing us of the fact that WILL-TV in Urbana is among those public TV stations running ST, Irene goes on to say:*) It's clear that Star Trek has had a greater impact on society than any other TV show. Many people have made it and its ideas a part of their everyday life, whether consciously or unconsciously. For this reason, I call my generation the Star Trek Generation.

I believe that eventually those of us who watched and were influenced by Star Trek in our youth will be in positions of importance where we will be able to use Star Trek's ideas.

For example, ST fans will quite likely become network executives. At that time, more intelligent programming will be available on TV. ST's ideals could influence both future politicians and people all over the world. No one can say how far-reaching the effect could be.

Although many people will probably remain untouched by Star Trek, there may be enough others who are affected enough to get important things done. At any rate, the eventual impact of Star Trek will be greater than that of any other show.

Ann Tomek, West Covina, Cal.

I like Star Trek, but I'm also a general science fiction fan, and I appreciate the diversity of your magazine for including articles on *War of the Worlds* and *2001*. . . . despite everybody else's opinion, I happen to love "The Omega Glory." I see nothing wrong with a little flag waving. I love to hear Bill Shatner read the Constitution because he has such a wonderful speaking voice. We should be reminded from time to time that our most precious documents are not just words on a piece of paper, but have a meaning that can transcend 300 years, and many light-years, and are still worth fighting for. It doesn't matter that they came from the United States of America or the United Federation of Planets. It's the fact the words apply to all peoples and races on this planet as well as in other solar systems. Enough of that!

I'm a science fiction fan from way back. My favorite authors are Sturgeon, James Gunn, Asimov, and Clarke. I like most of all the science part of SF, and I like the vision of the future Star Trek reveals. And we'll get to that future one way or another. After all, we've heard the weather reports and seen the pictures of Mars live! From Mars!

Linda Quinlan, Peoria, Ill.

I've enjoyed every issue of *Trek,* and find it to be one of the most professional Star Trek magazines along with *Enterprise Incidents.*

When will the Star Trek Scrapbook for *Trek Special* be ready for sale? I always enjoy the "Spock Scrapbook" feature in *Trek,* and hope you have more.

I especially enjoyed the article by Fern Lynch. It's so nice to know that people of all ages enjoy Star Trek as much as I do.

I used to settle for an occasional article in movie magazines on Star Trek, but even then, they all used the same old photos, and not much of an article. I also enjoy the *Star Trek Poster Book, Starlog,* and *Star Trek Fan Clubs* magazines.

Will you ever do photo features on certain Star Trek episodes in future issues? I'd also like to see a feature on the so-called Spock-McCoy feuds. I also think *Trek* should have only articles on Star Trek. Keep up the good work on a great magazine.

Although we would like to do a Star Trek Scrapbook Trek Special, *we are going to be forced to wait until we get enough very, very good material to put in it. As for photo recaps of episodes, we feel that the only way to do justice to any episode is to allow it at least fifteen to twenty pages, and accompany it with discussions by both our regular staff and fans. So rather than pad out an issue of* Trek *with such a space-consuming article, we plan to present a couple of fans' favorite episodes in a special publication entitled* Starship Chronicles, *which we are planning later this year. Why not drop us a line and suggest episodes?*

Jeff Heine, Mound, N.M.

The vote on original fiction is 50-50? I can see that. I would like to see a fan story. But it must be good, well-written, and of course readable. I have no objection to the popular story line of a girl trying to reach Spock and driving him crazy as he battles with emotions "he has rarely felt before." As long as it has taste. I'd like to see an issue looking into Kraith. All I've heard about it was in "Star Trek Lives!"

Lynne Ann Morse, Madison, Wisc.

The demise of *Space: 1999* could be a severe blow to science fiction and possibly Star Trek. Even though there are some good SF films, any number of film studios could scrap their plans for any SF projects, saying that SF doesn't work, Star Trek was a (happy) accident, etc; and disbelieving all the evidence their eyes (and pocketbooks) give. Many an executive has done it before, and believe me, it will be done again.

Please, please keep writing Paramount. The more vocal we are, the better the chances are for getting Star Trek II started visibly, and the sooner we get it!

I'm glad there is more in *Trek* than Star Trek material. People who think of Star Trek fans as Trekkies (No! We're Trekkers or ST fans!) feel that all we do is eat, breathe, and sleep Star Trek. The variety of material I've seen in *Trek* proves that these people are wrong. I hope you keep publishing stories and articles outside of Star Trek's realm in your magazine. It's the best I've seen in a long, long time.

Abraham Rodriguez, Jr., Bronx, N.Y.

After buying your last two issues, I'm convinced that *Trek* is far above most Star Trek prozines in the market today, although the glossy pages are hard to read sometimes because they reflect the light so brilliantly! But that's a sacrifice I'm willing to make.

One question, though: I have pored through every fanzine/magazine in my collection, and still fail to see a pic of Nona, the Kanutu woman from "A Private Little War." I can't even find any stills with her in them! Could you print at least one in the future?

Why do so many Trekfans out there feel that any new SF show that comes along is a threat to Star Trek? Jeez, I've been to conventions where everything that isn't Star Trek is booed. Why? Why must fans be so piggish? Sure, there're people that stand up for Star Trek, but why put down everything, even good shows which openly admit their shortcomings and try to improve them?

Not all fans are like this, I know; but I've seen too many of these Star Trek-and-that's-all fans. I believe that Star

Trek will never be equaled anywhere, but you don't see me turning off to other kinds of SF, or trying to put it down without looking at the show with open eyes. Star Trek fans are supposed to be intelligent, right? So let's see if some of these narrow-minded people take a hint and stop calling every brand-new show "that SF garbage."

This is a problem which confronts us too. Many fans are down on other forms of SF not because they may not be as good as ST, but just because they are not ST. Which is why we run material other than Star Trek, to give our readers some diversity. Don't forget, just because Star Trek is the best thing, that doesn't mean that it is the only thing. There are thousands of other shows, films, books, and the like out there which we know even the most rabid ST fan can and will enjoy, and we think that it is part of our job to acquaint him with them.

Nancy Charpentier, Pomfret, Conn.

Why were episodes such as "Amok Time," "Journey to Babel," "The Naked Time," and "Mirror, Mirror" so high on everyone's list in your recent poll? The answer is obvious.

Who can ever forget the conversation between Spock and Kirk in "Amok Time" when Spock tells Kirk why he must return to Vulcan; Spock's desperate plea to T'Pau not to permit the combat between himself and Kirk; Kirk's willingness to risk his career and later his life for Spock; Spock's sadness at seeing his captain dead and his joy at finding him alive?

Who can ever forget Spock's agony in "Journey to Babel" when he must choose duty over his father's life; a badly wounded Kirk going to the bridge and convincing Spock that he was all right so Spock will give the blood his father needs to survive?

Who can ever forget a crying Mr. Spock in "The Naked Time" telling Kirk that he feels guilt about his friendship for him; and Kirk's confession of the loneliness of being the captain of a starship?

Who can ever forget in "Mirror, Mirror" the alternate Mr. Spock giving Kirk the chance to escape, and Kirk telling him that in every revolution there is one man with a dream and that he must be that man and save the friendly Halkons?

There is one common denominator in these episodes as

well as in "City on the Edge of Forever" and "The Enemy Within," and that denominator is the Kirk-Spock relationship. This relationship fascinated fans while the series was new and still does today.

Another reason for the popularity of these episodes is that they show us more of the characters of these two men. They are essentially people episodes, and Captain Kirk and Mr. Spock are two very special people.

Ken Janasz, Leavenworth, Kan.

I just finished "The Animated Star Trek" by Bill Norton, and I found it right up to par with the rest of your articles and the same quality that your magazine maintains with each issue. I, for the most part, agree with Mr. Norton's review. As animation, ST just couldn't make it. Perhaps if it had been an hour long, it wouldn't have been such a letdown.

But there is one important aspect to the animated series that doesn't seem to be mentioned very much. And that is what ST fandom got after this series: Alan Dean Foster.

Through his *Log* series (nine thus far), Mr. Foster has breathed life into animation; he has turned cartoon characters into living creatures. He has adapted all but "The Slaver Weapon," and in addition, gives us three new stories as well. It seems that Mr. Foster has used the animated shows as an outline for each of his adaptations and then expounded on them. He provides us with omitted explanations, filling in the gaps in the actions, and making the stories flow in a logical manner of cause and effect that the animation couldn't show. He has also injected the small, personal touches that were ever-present in the original shows.

In "Log One," in the very beginning, we find Kirk in his quarters relaxing, and we are exposed to the thoughts of that extra-special breed: the starship captain. And while Kirk is resting in his off-hours, he is interrupted by Mr. Spock, and we are immediately reminded of Spock's uncanny gift for understatement.

From then on we are exposed to the familiar personalities of the Star Trek universe. Scotty loved *his* Enterprise; Uhura showed her capabilities were good enough to take command; the McCoy-Spock feud was a good-natured clash of opposite personalities instead of something thrown in just because it should be there. We even saw Sulu fencing in "Albatross." In "The Ambergris Element," we learned a little of M'Ress' background and her decision to join Starfleet, as well as her promotion to the *Enterprise*.

In "The Survivor," we join in on the ship's Christmas party, something only hinted at way back in the live-action episode "The Dagger of the Mind."

It was things like this that brought back the flavor of Star Trek. From the revelations of ship's operations to Kirk's burping while making his log report, Alan Dean Foster deserves credit for his work. His detailed descriptions of alien landscapes and creatures, as well as his insights into the characters' thoughts, all made it seem as if we were really there on the bridge. Why, I swear I could hear those voices over the intercom and even the musical compositions that Mr. Norton noted were missing from the animation.

So we hope that Mr. Foster, if he hasn't already, will continue adapting Star Trek episodes (perhaps even the live-action shows that the late James Blish didn't do), and also writing his own original stories.

16. THE PSYCHOLOGY OF MR. SPOCK'S POPULARITY

by Gloria-Ann Rovelstad

Perhaps more has been written about Mr. Spock than any other Star Trek character; certainly most of the "character" articles we receive are about Spock. In fact, we get twice as many Spock articles as anything else. Because our magazine covers all of Star Trek and not just Spock, we are forced to reject most of these articles. However, once in a while one comes along that is so well written and has so much to say that we just can't turn it down. Gloria-Ann Rovelstad's article is one. It started out as a much, much shorter piece—it was, in fact, originally intended for our "Trek Roundtable" section. However, we felt that it showed such promise that we asked Gloria-Ann to expand it to a full-length article, and she happily did so. We think that it is just about as close to getting to the nub of Spock's popularity as possible in less than an entire series of articles—or a book!

He is above average in everything except emotional freedom, which prevents the full expression of his personality, yet at the same time makes him more interesting!

Although our society has come a long way from the inhibited Victorian era, some of that has still carried through to today, and we see Spock, in our way, as a victim of similar circumstances. (Although to those of Vulcan, it would seem just the opposite; they would lament his regrettable inheritance of human emotionalism.)

We would like to see him freed, as we also would like to have fewer emotional inhibitions. We admire him, yet we can feel sympathy for him. (Which makes for a good hero in any story or play.)

We, as humans, watch to see him show emotion.

In "This Side of Paradise," we see Spock as showing emotions caused by circumstances beyond his control—the flower pod spores on Omnicron Ceti III. After he has been cured by Kirk making him angry, he says that on the planet he was happy for the first time in his life. We think, as humans, "Poor guy!"

In most of the stories where Spock shows human emotions, it isn't through any fault of his own. In this way, the writers can show us glimpses of Spock's inner self yet not spoil the portrayal of the character, who is supposedly so logical and unemotional.

"Amok Time" is a popular show with Spock fans, both because it gives us our first glimpse of Vulcan society and customs, and because we learn more about Spock himself and how he differs from humans.

Because of Vulcan's hereditary cycle of *pon farr,* Spock is very emotional and irrational, changing the ship's course and getting annoyed at small things. Yet he is willing to proceed to the required destination of the mission—at the risk of his own life—rather than admit what is wrong with him. (This we can understand. If discussing sexual matters is embarrassing to humans, think what it must be to Vulcans!)

Down on Vulcan, he tries to avoid the fight with Kirk, even though he is strongly under the influence of *pon farr.* And when he believes he has killed his captain, he is very sad. (To say the least! If he were not, even a Vulcan would be angry at him, since Kirk is the main person to whom Spock has given his loyalty—and loyalty is an accepted emotion of Vulcans.) At the end of the show, we are touched to see Spock's happiness at finding Kirk unharmed.

When Kirk and McCoy are tortured by the Vians in "The Empath," Spock shows human feelings of sympathy and sadness for them. Next to Kirk, Spock seems to like and respect McCoy best, even though they are often at odds. There is a real bond between the two—just as between Spock and Kirk—which is evidenced by the banter between them; McCoy constantly baiting and Spock responding noncommittally, but sometimes sarcastically and sharply. Spock seems to enjoy these exchanges as much as anything.

When Spock has overruled McCoy and is preparing himself to be taken by the Vians, his statement that he is the "better" choice seems rather overdone; he actually sounds like he's almost happy about it rather than stoic, as one would expect under the circumstances.

Spock's loyalty to Kirk, over all others, is important to us. We all wish for such a loyal friend, and respect Spock for his loyalty to his commander. We feel a personification with the crewpersons of the *Enterprise,* since we too have met people whom we admire, yet who are inaccessible to us (as Spock is to them).

Since Spock's lack of expression is not due to a dislike of others, but is his own problem (as seen from a human viewpoint), we feel compassion and wish we could help him. This is like the wish of a very small child, who has his hero and dreams of doing him some great service, thereby gaining his liking and respect.

One of the foremost examples of Spock's loyalty to Kirk is displayed in "The Tholian Web," where Spock risks the safety of the entire ship on the chance he may be able to save Captain Kirk. This is quite a contradiction when compared to his actions in "Journey to Babel," where he refuses to risk the *Enterprise* to save Sarek's life.

It is clearly an emotional decision. Kirk is the one person that Spock can relate to and whom he likes more than anyone else; and we don't blame him for his choice. After all, where would the series be if he abandoned Kirk, even if it were a logical decision?

It is interesting to compare between the two stories. Kirk is a person who is known and valued by the audience much more than Sarek. Kirk and Spock get along with each other much better than Spock and his father, and they have much more empathy and compassion for each other.

If you stop to consider it, loyalty is an emotion, even in Vulcans, and this is even more true for Spock in regard to Kirk. Also, as the stories are laid out, Spock is expected to risk everything for his commanding officer, while Kirk, as the commanding officer, would more likely be excused for not taking risks for lower-ranking officers who are, unfortunately, considered expendable. (Although, to us, Spock isn't expendable, and Kirk does take chances to rescue him from quite a few situations.)

In "Journey to Babel," Spock's loyalty is to the survival of the ship, its numerous crew, and Captain Kirk (who is injured) over that to his father, who needs blood for a heart operation. His mother can't seem to understand and makes it hard on Spock by scolding and pleading with him, even though she knows his father and other Vulcans would agree his decision is the correct one. When he believes Kirk to be recovered enough to take over command of the ship, Spock is then free to help his father and cheerfully does so.

In "The Menagerie," Spock risks the death penalty to take his former commander, Captain Christopher Pike, to Talos IV, where he could live out the rest of his life in happiness rather than as a helpless cripple. A great deal of loyalty and compassion is shown by this act. If Spock were truly unemotional and strictly logical as he wants others to think, he never would have done it.

Spock's devotion to Kirk is also evident to others, even those who do not know them well. Edith Keeler puts this very well in "City on the Edge of Forever." When Spock asks her, ". . . and where would you say we belong?" Edith answers, "You, Mr. Spock, at his side, as if you had always been there and always will be . . ."

Spock represents by his repression of emotions a partial solution to one of mankind's most troubling traits: emotions that get in the way of logic. Anyone who has been emotionally upset and has been embarrassed by not trying to cry in front of others can appreciate the value of being able to control emotions or hide them as well as Spock.

And we agree that he does have them since he is half human, but he has been taught not to show them because of his upbringing on Vulcan. He certainly is logical enough for us, though perhaps not enough so for Vulcans.

In "The *Galileo* Seven," even though they are in a bad situation, Spock keeps cool as leader; so much, in fact, that the other, more emotional beings resent it.

But even his act of desperation—when he ignites the fuel of the shuttlecraft—is logical, as it gives them one last chance to be seen by the *Enterprise* and perhaps recovered. The alternative is a much slower but just as inevitable death. The ribbing Spock gets about this being an emotional act is really unnecessary, as it actually was the logical thing to do.

"Spectre of the Gun" shows McCoy getting angry at Mr. Spock for not showing emotion over Chekov's supposed death (as we know, it turns out to be an illusion). Even Kirk seems to doubt him for not reacting, yet Kirk and McCoy don't show all that much emotion themselves. People are strange creatures! At the climax, Spock protects Kirk,

McCoy, and Scotty from the illusion that would cause their deaths by using the Mind Meld. He is kind and shows enough understanding of their feelings to get through to them individually.

While humans may admire logic and control of emotions, they still are basically emotional beings; and when logic and lack of emotion are applied to them or their friends, they often resent it, especially if they are feeling strongly about something at the time.

In "The Naked Time," we again see Spock showing emotion by circumstances beyond his control when he and other crewmen are affected by an emotion-uninhibiting chemical. He tries to get out of sight so as not to show it affecting him. We all probably have experienced similar situations where we hide when we cannot control our emotions and don't want to show them.

Most of the time, though, Spock is a very calm, intelligent, and practical being whom others accuse of being more like a computer than a half-human entity. He is nevertheless respected for it, and by not being emotionally involved, he avoids a lot of the troubles that the other crewpersons get into!

As Leonard Nimoy himself has said, the alienness of the character appealed to him. There are more people today than we realize who feel alienated, who feel that they too, like Spock, are apart from conventional society.

Yet Spock, often misunderstood and mistrusted (even by some of his closest friends) and truly an alien to both human and Vulcan cultures, has adapted very well and learned to cope with the inconsistencies of behavior in his human friends. His aloofness and superiority come naturally to him, yet humans may find it a reinforcement to the ego to act the same way outwardly, even if they aren't so sure of themselves inside.

Captain Tracy in "The Omega Glory" is out and out prejudiced against Vulcans and won't even speak to Mr. Spock, despite his holding a high position in Star Fleet. Often people will pay less attention to differences of others if these nonconformists hold high positions, but not Captain Tracy!

One of the main reasons the other crewpersons are angry and nasty to Spock in "The *Galileo* Seven" (other than because he doesn't show emotion while giving his logical directions and decisions) is that he just looks different and thus is an alien to them.

If it were a human leader of theirs who was not showing emotion, they would probably be proud of him and think him brave and stoic. But because Spock both looks and acts differently than they (who have emotions), they show less understanding of his feelings than he (who supposedly doesn't feel) shows to them.

He lets them bury the dead crewman, even though it serves no practical purpose except fulfilling their traditions; and it endangers their takeoff from the planet by using up precious time and allowing the ape creatures to get closer to them. He goes along with it because he knows that they feel strongly about it, even though an emotional majority isn't necessarily right, and to a Vulcan it would certainly be illogical.

Yet they do make up for their lack of understanding and show their loyalty to him by rescuing him, even though he orders them off when the *Galileo* is attacked. So in that way, their emotions proved very valuable, for they save Spock's life (and ultimately the lives of the entire party). Had they behaved as logically as Spock, he would have been left behind to die.

That is the whole problem with emotion. It can work both ways, for good or bad; we can't really ignore it as Vulcans do. This is what so many Star Trek stories pointed out.

A last example of Spock's being a true alien is from "Journey to Babel." His mother, Amanda, tells us that even as a child Spock was never truly accepted by the other Vulcan children because of his human mother and inheritance. The same would be true of Vulcan adults, we assume, so we really can't blame him for leaving his home planet.

We can understand humans being prejudiced because of their illogical emotions, but why Vulcans? If they are so logical, why should they not treat him equally?

Well, because they are so logical, they would know that as a halfbreed he would have some human traits, and they would never trust him as they would one of their own people who had been conditioned over the centuries to inhibit their natural feelings. They would know that Spock might at some time break with their ideal of true logic and so would never give him as high a position as any true Vulcan, even if he was exceptionally intelligent.

By joining the Federation and serving on a primarily human-crewed ship (even though the people were totally different than those he had been raised with), Spock had a chance to rise to a high position, and perhaps be totally accepted by a few or at least one man—Captain Kirk.

Humans, by their very emotional and illogical nature, will at times accept someone who is alien or different from them and will treat him equally and be very devoted no matter what. With Vulcans this could not happen. Again, the advantages and disadvantages of emotions!

And as any alienated being has feelings of loneliness, when Spock joined the crew of the *Enterprise* he had more chance of alleviating this feeling than he ever would have had on Vulcan. Humans, with their feelings of love, anger, and sadness, would also be much more interesting to be with, even if he didn't participate in these emotions. Talk about infinite diversity in the universe!

If anything, Spock could be pleased with the gratefulness of his comrades when he rescues them or solves some ticklish problem, whereas on Vulcan such a result would be expected as the logical thing to do and taken for granted. (Although I suppose there could be an award for being the most logical, or something.) Fortunately for Spock, he does meet Kirk, who becomes his best friend; and one whom he can give his loyalty and devotion to and have it returned equally.

Emotions are an integral part of human life, and Spock's repression of his brings to our notice all the problems connected with "feelings."

For many young people, Spock's coolness and logic represent an ideal to follow in their dealings with parents or peers.

Others may sympathize with his inability to express emotions, just as they have a hard time expressing theirs appropriately. And they hope to see him express at least some of his human half's emotions.

Spock represents a truly intelligent, altruistic entity, whom we can count on to be kind, fair, and logical in the most trying of situations. He does seem a little bit sad. Yet, accepting all of the inconsistencies of life, that emotion is true of all humanitarians. We would wish to consider Spock among them.

17. THE STAR TREK COMIC BOOKS
by Leslie Thompson and Walter Irwin

The Star Trek comic books first appeared sometime during Star Trek's premiere season, and for that reason, fans who did not become involved with Star Trek until the boom of the early seventies were unable to find many of the early issues —or if they could, they were overpriced by dealers and used bookstores. But early in 1977, the Golden Press released a collection of the first ten or so issues in a thick collector's edition. As all of the early Star Trek comic issues were now readily available to the fans, we decided that it was time to run an article comparing the comics to the original. Leslie Thompson was assigned to write the article, and for assistance, she went to long-time comics fan Walter Irwin. The resulting article inspired many letters—more than almost any other article. And most of them simply said, "I agree." With what? Well, read the article and see if you agree also.

Any adaptation of one medium to another cannot, by its very nature, be just like the original. The various elements which make up an art form are unique to that particular genre and when adapted must be supplanted by another, often completely different set of elements. For example, a novel may become a best seller on the strength of its descriptive passages, and yet when translated into a film rouse the cry, "Why, this is nothing like the book!" And yet, the filmed version may be a far superior retelling of the basic story. The distinction is not made in the viewer's mind between film and literature.

The problem becomes even more complicated when reversing the process from film to literature. Film is visual shorthand; we can see an object or person—no time need be wasted in telling us about it. And when the original is a television series, with its need for a continuity of situations and characterizations, it becomes even more difficult to produce a workable adaptation.

Star Trek has been, in many instances, a notable exception to this quandary. The adaptations of series episodes by James Blish and (animated series) Alan Dean Foster are very well done, managing to fit nicely into the literary framework and still preserve the basic essentials of the program and the protagonists.

But these cited examples are fairly straightforward retellings of televised episodes. When an original story is called for, the requisite format becomes even more confining and difficult to work with. And again, Star Trek is a notable example.

All of the reasons why this is so are too numerous and complex to discuss in this article but they may be simply stated as follows:

The basic premise and characters of Star Trek are so deeply rooted in the minds of its fans that the adaptors, be they fan or professional, know and love the program, the people, and what they stand for.

Sadly, however, in the case of the Star Trek comic books, this is not the case. The creators of this medium of Star Trek are not fans; indeed, they seem to have only the scantiest knowledge of the show.

Star Trek is a very good television series. The novels are very good literature, as are fan stories. The animated series worked fairly well. Then why are the comic books so very, very bad?

The most obvious flaw with the Star Trek comics is the large number of inaccuracies contained in the stories. This is due to a simple lack of research on the part of the writers and artists of the strip, a lack which naturally stems from a "don't give a damn" attitude toward the series and the readers of the comics.

Gold Key, the publishers of the Star Trek comics, has been heavily into the movie and TV adaptation market for many years (many Gold Key properties are offshoots and takeovers of the now defunct Dell Comics line). To them, adaptation of a comic is simple: Buy the property, write and draw a story, and depend on the name to sell the book. A fairly simple process—and one which has accounted for many fine comic adaptations over the years. But when the writing and the drawing are done without the proper research of the property, you end up with a bad adaptation. And very often a bad comic.

Research for the Star Trek comic by Gold Key seems to have been no more than some brief character outlines and some stills. When reading the earlier books, it is almost impossible to tell if the writers and artists had ever seen the show. Probably not.

Questioning of comics fans and a letter to Gold Key both failed to turn up the name (or names) of the writers of the Star Trek comics. However, the names of the artists were revealed in the recent collection of Star Trek comics issued by the Golden Press. Nevio Zaccara drew the first two issues and Alberto Giolitti has been the artist ever since.

Since Giolitti lives and works in Rome, it is unlikely that he had ever viewed an episode of Star Trek at the time he took over the book. Therefore, only the exterior of the ship and the faces of some of the characters are drawn as they appear on the show.

Giolitti cannot be blamed for these inaccuracies, since it was the responsibility (and the failure) of Gold Key to provide him with the proper research and reference materials. Again, by assigning an artist who lives in a foreign country and does not (or did not) have access to the series and by giving him only the most basic facts to work with, Gold Key shows its lack of interest in turning out a quality product.

Since the writer of the Star Trek comics remains anonymous, we do not know whether or not he (or they) were at all familiar with the series. However, since most of Gold Key's work is done out of their editorial offices, we can assume that the writer lives and works in this country and should have been able to switch on his television once a week to see if he was keeping to the spirit of the series in his work.

Apparently this didn't happen. The stories abound in errors: the classification of the *Enterprise* as a slower-than-light ship; the size and crew complement of the ship are vastly underrated; characterizations are either wrong or stilted.

In reviewing the Star Trek comics, it would be not only a long and boring chore to go through each one and list the inaccuracies, it would be a fruitless one. Many comic adaptations have been entertaining without being mirror images of the originals. What the Star Trek comic book lacks is good and entertaining story lines. And while the errors are offensive to a Star Trek fan, it is the boring and trite stories which cause the book to be an unsuccessful adaptation. They do not capture the spirit of what Star Trek is and what the show was trying to say. The comic is space opera of the simplest kind, with people and things which just happen to be those on Star Trek.

The first Star Trek comic appeared on the stands in the summer of 1967. The cover was a dull mish-mosh of stills from the show, with an unimpressive logo. It was to set the style for every issue to come. The story "Planet of No Return" was a variation on the bug-eyed monster theme involving giant carnivorous plants. All of the classic and overworked elements of cheap sci-fi are present, including the capture of Janice Rand by the plants and an incredibly stupid and dull Kirk. It would have made a perfect fifties horror movie. Unfortunately, just as the cover set the style for following issues, so did the story.

"The Devil's Isle of Space," the second entry in the Star Trek comic series, turns on one of the oldest plots extant: "They are not what they seem" (destined to become a staple of the stories). Kirk and his "boys" (he calls them that in the story) beam down to a strange asteroid where the inhabitants claim to be shipwrecked. But it is soon revealed that they are (gasp!) criminals, and the asteroid is due to be blown up soon as their execution. Highlighting this tale is Spock joking with Kirk.

Each of the Star Trek comics is a variation of a classic science theme, as we have seen, and usually a not too imaginative variation at that. "Invasion of the City Builders" in issue number three retells the horrors which occur when machines overrun their creators. It amounts to a simple "chase" formula, with the *Enterprise* crew trying to find a way to stop the rampaging building machines before they pave over the last remaining ten thousand acres of planet Questionmark. A major plus in this story is a nice characterization of the alien leader, who feels his authority is being undermined by the saviors from the starship. This kind of touch is seldom seem in any of the comic stories.

The fourth issue was apparently written by someone who had been reading the trade papers, if not actually watching the show. It features Spock prominently and is a sharp reflection of the growing popularity of the Vulcan with fans of the series.

Spock is "possessed" by several alien beings as their only means of saving their planet, but one of them refuses to leave his body when the job is completed. He rids himself of the intruder by subjecting himself to both materialization and dematerialization in the transporter at the same time. A passable solution, since the show never stated that the transporter could not operate in this fashion.

The story returns to the "Not what they seem" formula in "The Ghost Planet." The twin leaders of Planet Numero Uno ask Kirk and crew to remove deadly rings of radiation from around their planet, but Kirk soon learns that they only wish to continue the war that the rings interrupted. In a flagrant violation of the Prime Directive, Kirk destroys all of their weapons and tricks them into making war no more.

The splash page of issue number six treats us to the spectacle of a meteor shower smashing through the bridge of the *Enterprise*. The story concerns two planets which are being irresistibly drawn toward each other, forcing the starship to ferry a white dwarf star to counteract the magnetic forces. It is the weight of the star which keeps the ship from avoiding the meteor shower, but luckily for our side, no one dies when the meteors penetrate the hull and let all of the air out of the ship. This issue also features a cutaway view of the *Enterprise*, which, to judge by this drawing, would be about the size of a 747 jet and hold about twenty people.

The seventh issue is entitled "The Voodoo Planet." Our crew finds a planet which is a complete replica of Earth, except that everything is made of papier-mâché. A mysterious laser beam destroys the Eiffel Tower on the doppelganger planet and the tower on Earth is destroyed as well. This is caused by one Count Dressler, who has fled and has discovered how to do voodoo. So Spock does Vulcan voodoo and does in the voodoo man.

This insipid story is probably the most typical example of the cursory treatment which Star Trek stories were given. Aside from the patent foolishness of an entire planet being reconstructed in papier-mâché, the scenes of Earth are very contemporary. If one were to assign a year to this story, it certainly would be no later than the 1990s. Add to this the spectacle of Spock researching through Vulcan textbooks for references to his ancestors practicing voodoo and then synthesizing a serum to give himself and Kirk voodoo "powers," and you have a perfect example of a story done without any regard for the original.

In issue number eight, Dr. McCoy and two of the engineers from the *Enterprise* are transformed into children via a ray, used by a power-seeking alien. This is "The Youth Trap" in which Kirk and crew find themselves. Once again, the two dozen or so intrepid officers of the starship are held at bay by a few aliens armed with little more than popguns. Kirk saves the day by reflecting the ray back at the villain with a shiny tin plate—again, a cliché so old it ought to have a long white beard.

It is really a shame that the Star Trek comic books were done as poorly as they were. They, like the Foster *Log* series, could have been a valuable addition to the Star Trek legend and mythos, but instead they must be relegated to the last place among Star Trek literature, fit only for children and rabid completists.

Plans are continually announced for the Star Trek series to move to another company; Marvel, D.C., and the now-defunct Charlton have all claimed the Star Trek prize at one time or another. Yet at Gold Key the series remains.

Perhaps another publisher will indeed obtain the rights someday, and the Star Trek comic books will have another chance.

18. THE TREK FAN OF THE MONTH

*In our eighth issue, we started a new column which would
appear in our magazine as often as we had space for it. "The
Trek Fan of the Month." We felt that the best way for our
readers to get to know one another was to occasionally
spotlight one of them briefly, and give our readers a look at
the thoughts, feelings, hobbies, lifestyles, and ambitions of a
typical Star Trek fan. The feature has been very successful
so far, not only in terms of reader popularity, but in terms
of response also. It seems that just about every reader we
have wants to be the Fan of the Month, and let the whole
world know about their loyalty to Star Trek. And if the Fan
of the Month feature can help in just the tiniest bit to
achieve the understanding and tolerance which the founda-
tions of the Star Trek philosophy are based on, then we will
consider all of our work on Trek to have been worth it.*

*Our first letter is from Mrs. Yvette Harley, P.O. Box 593,
Barnwell, S.C. 29812.*

There's no words to tell you what your magazine has done
for me. I'm stuck here in South Carolina in a small town
where most people are very narrow-minded. I work in a
plant and I've yet to find a Trekkie (by the way, TREKKIE
is my license plate) so I never have a chance to talk to some
other Trekkies and your magazine gives me that, with the
"Roundtable."

I would love to go to a con, but so far they have all been
too far away from where I live for me to afford it. Maybe if
there were to be one in Columbia, S.C., or Augusta, Ga. (I
live in between the two towns), I could afford it.

I'm a French war bride of twenty-seven years, and I'm

now fifty years old; so if my English or spelling is not correct, please excuse my ignorance.

Now, I want to know why everybody calls all those horrible monster stories ST. Where is the science? I hate them, I like to be entertained, not frightened to death. Space science fiction is my bag. I'm giving you my two cents worth about *Space: 1999:* I enjoy the books a lot better than the TV shows.

Could you tell me why Mr. Gene Roddenberry insists on having Paramount Studios do Star Trek II? After the way they acted in 1968, I would think he'd try somewhere else. Surely the other studios are not blind, deaf, and dumb? They should realize, with all the popularity Star Trek still enjoys, that there must be a gold mine if they knew how to exploit it. It should be soon, because unfortunately we're all getting old and so are the actors, and in a few years even the best makeup won't help.

For your magazine, I have a few ideas that might help.

For instance, why not ask your readers to rate all of the seventy-nine episodes of ST and give you and all of us an idea of the most popular on down to the least?

Also, why not have a serial novel? Maybe some of the oldies-but-goodies, or some that fans could write?

I have an SF collection of paperback books of about 400. My most favorites are Doc E. E. Smith (the *Lensman* series and *Skylarks*). I also have all 105 books of Perry Rhodan. (By the way, they try to say that P.R. is better than ST. That's not true.) I also have Cap Kennedy, the Avenger, most of the Doc Savage series, and *Space: 1999.*

I don't have to say that I have all of Star Trek by James Blish and all of the ST *Logs* series.

Since I see that you have fans from six to sixty-five, it would be nice to have a book review, where you could suggest the right kind of books for young readers, teenagers, etc. Since you are so busy and can't possibly read all the books, I suggest you ask your readers.

For instance, I thought that all of the Kenneth Robeson books are good for the young set. So are *The Ship Who Sang* by Anne McCaffery, *The Rolling Stones—David Starr* by Isaac Asimov, etc.

But the three Rack books by Laurence James and the four Hook books by Eully Zetford are a little more spicy and should be read by grown-ups first.

I watch ST twice a day every week, and I never get tired of them. I love most of them; the only one I don't like at all is "The Way to Eden." Maybe it's because I'm too old for the kind of thinking of those young people.

One more thing I want to tell you about me. I have made my den into a Star Trek museum. I have all the models I could find, and also the toys. Would you believe my children have given me ST toys for Xmas? No, I'm not in my second childhood, I never got out of my first one.

I'm sorry to have written such a long letter, but like I said, I don't have any Trekkies around me except for my daughter, and I'm training my four-year-old grandson to become a Trekkie, so forgive me.

It just occurred to me that sometime if you run short on your publications, you could ask your fans for pictures of their displays of ST and show them in your mag. It could give other fans some ideas. Not mine, of course, for I don't have the money or the room to do it in a big way.

Our next Fan of the Month is Christine Myers, 23712 TwinOaks Place, Hidden Hills, Cal. 91302.

First, I would like to say how pleased I am to belong to the "Federation" of Star Trek fans all over the world.

I guess I'm your average, everyday Trekkie! Mr. Spock, Captain Kirk, Dr. McCoy, and Scotty, and everyone else on the *Enterprise*, are my favorite people. I seem to learn something valuable from them with each show I see. The characters' personal and working relationships with one another is something special. I certainly have been more logical because of Mr. Spock. Logical? Is it logical for a twenty-nine-year-old modern-day career girl to have Star Trek dolls in her room? I think it is, although Mr. Spock might disagree!

Actually, buying the dolls and setting up the display was inexpensive, easy, and fun. All in all, a very enterprising project!

For anyone else who might be interested in setting up such a display, all that's required is clay (for the base), dried bark (eucalyptus trees provide super bark for weird effects), assorted dead twigs, and some imagination.

I am especially fond of the little "beastie" (as Scotty would say) that Dr. McCoy and the Keeper are discussing—he is actually a clump of dried festucca grass with hatpins for tusks!

My main ambition is (what else?) to see Star Trek on the movie screen and back as a weekly series. That is the Prime Directive!

In the meantime, thank you and the staff of *Trek* magazine for helping to fill the void. I look forward to every issue.

And now, here's our third Fan of the Month:

My name is Gamin Grigsby. I'm eighteen, just graduated from high school. I've been watching Star Trek since I was in seventh grade; actually, I realize now, I was watching it in '66-'67 . . . I was just too young to know what it was. I don't think I could have told you exactly what it was I liked about Star Trek, but I think I have figured it out now.

I like the idea of a show that has some philosophy behind it, and tries to say something about today's society; but at the same time manages to be funny sometimes, so that the situations seem real.

I also like the characters. They sometimes seem so real to me that if it didn't take place in the twenty-third century, I might mistake them for my next-door neighbors or friends.

I think my favorite aspect of Star Trek is the Kirk/Spock relationship, and the Kirk/Spock/McCoy relationship. I love the surface battle that goes on between Spock and McCoy. In fact, my three favorite characters are, in order, Spock, Kirk, and McCoy.

I also have a big Star Trek collection—the biggest in Oklahoma, I like to think. This includes over 100 posters, a dozen different magazines, and over fifty buttons! It was accumulated in eight months, since I just found out about the stuff this year. I'm also a member of the Leonard Nimoy Association of Fans. I just went to my first Star Trek convention, and I never had so much fun in my life.

Although my collection does include a pair of Spock ears, I am not a "Trekkie." I am a "Trekker," and don't you forget it! Although Star Trek is my main hobby and interest, I do have some others. These include art, writing, American history, and biology. In the summer, I also enjoy horseback riding and swimming.

I'm not sure what college I'm going to next year, but I plan to major in art, English (specifically writing), and maybe American history, depending on where I go. After college, I'll probably become an artist and have some job on the side.

19. GENE RODDENBERRY:
A SHORT PROFILE
by Adam Eisenberg

When dealing with an actual person (as opposed to a fictional character), we always prefer to have that person speak for himself. However, in the case of Star Trek creator Gene Roddenberry, his background is so important that we decided to commission a short, succinct biography of him to accompany our report on his "World of Star Trek" talk. Little did we realize that just the thing we were looking for had already been written—and by one of our most faithful readers and contributors, at that! Adam Eisenberg's article on Roddenberry had already appeared in his local hometown newspaper, but it suited our purposes so perfectly that we asked him if we could reprint it for our readers to enjoy. He graciously consented, and the following is what we consider one of the finest short personality profiles we have ever seen.

"Space, the final frontier. These are the voyages of the Starship *Enterprise*. Its five-year mission: to explore strange new worlds, to seek out new life and new civilizations, and to boldly go where no man has gone before."

Immediately following this introduction, the words "Star Trek" flash on the screen and the viewer knows he is watching one of the most successful series in television history. But what of its creator and producer, Gene Roddenberry? How does he feel about his science fiction series' success?

"I think the thing that interests me most in the Star Trek phenomenon is the fact that we reached out and touched the hearts and minds of millions of people. You can't go to the conventions (Star Trek conventions are held yearly in many areas across the U.S.) and see the fan mail and all that without accepting the fact that the show really got in-side people, inside their heads."

But its success is also haunting him, for Roddenberry has produced several unsuccessful pilots for possible television series in the past few years. Thus he has been forced back to Star Trek and is now preparing a full-length motion picture for a Christmas 1977 release. "I'd like to move on to other things, it's just that having done the TV show, I'd like to put the period on it and do something with a budget and op-portunities that the movie offers.

"As a writer, of course, I'd like some other things besides Star Trek carved on my tombstone. I'd hate to think my whole life could be summed up in those two words."

Roddenberry, fifty-five, first became interested in science fiction when he read many books on the subject in junior high and high school and was always disappointed in the movies and television items he had seen.

"It seemed to me, as a dramatic writer, they were making a major mistake. Once they got their hands on science fiction, they were treating it as if it were an entirely different form of writing. They were putting in cardboard characters and just not worrying too much about believability and all of those things. I thought, 'Hey, why not do a science fiction story, write it and produce it the same way you do a *Play-house 90*, where characters are important, believability is important and all of that?' And so that started me on think-ing of science fiction."

The producer became interested in television writing at a time when there were few openings in the field, so he joined the Los Angeles Police Department to supplement his hob-by. Roddenberry spent five and a half years on the force and is very happy he did. "It gave me a good look at life and death. Policemen see things that you just don't ordinarily run into during your life."

Eventually he reached the point where his hobby was bringing in more money than the police work and so he quit the force and became a full-time writer. As a result, Rodden-berry has sold scripts to many television series, including *Dragnet, Naked City, Goodyear Theatre, Four Star Theater, The Kaiser Aluminum Hour,* and *The Jane Wyman Theater,* and spent two years as head writer for the successful series *Have Gun Will Travel.* Then in 1963, he began his producing career with the television series *The Lieutenant,* starring

Garry Lockwood and Robert Vaughn in a story about the adventures of two marines.

Next, Roddenberry worked on the Star Trek series for five years (1965–69) and then moved on to other projects, including the motion picture *Pretty Maids All in a Row*, starring Rock Hudson, Angie Dickinson, and Telly Savalas, which he produced in 1971.

Returning to television, Roddenberry then produced several series pilots, including "Genesis II," a story about future Earth after the downfall of civilization; "The Questor Tapes," an exciting story of an artificial man who is searching for his creator; and a sequel to "Genesis II" called "Planet Earth." Presently he is working on the Star Trek motion picture and a new pilot film called "Spectre," dealing with horror and the supernatural.

Entering the field of television writing today is very difficult, and Roddenberry advises, "You've got to be ungodly stubborn. There will be so many times you will feel like giving up, when you think you've got something really good and it won't sell, and you think, 'Well, maybe I don't have it.' You really almost have to have an insane stubbornness to become a writer.

"Because of constant interference from the networks and production companies, television writing has become one of the hardest fields to work in.

"I guess that if I had my absolute choice, I'd like to end up writing only novels. It's the one type of writing in which you have about the greatest freedom. You can live anywhere, you don't have to live near Hollywood. You can work on your own time and schedule."

Gene Roddenberry summed up his career by saying, "I don't think of myself as a science fiction writer. If I have what I hope is a good science fiction idea, I'll write it. I love to write anthologies and I love to write movies. I'd also like to write some comedies. I'm a writer, I like to write."

20. AN EVENING WITH GENE RODDENBERRY, 1977
by G. B. Love

Early in 1977, the Great Bird of the Galaxy, Gene Rodden-berry, made a whirlwind tour of many cities in the United States with a show called "The World of Star Trek." The program consisted of the fabled "blooper reel," a showing of the original Star Trek pilot, "The Cage," and most exciting of all, a talk by Gene. When the show arrived in Houston, it was attended by over 6,000 enthusiastic fans, and Trek editor G. B. Love was among them. His report on Gene's remarks that night reveal a special insight into the mind of the man who created Star Trek—and, indirectly, a whole new genre of science fiction, Star Trek fandom, Trek magazine, and finally this book.

It was recently my pleasure to spend an evening with Gene Roddenberry. Oh, not alone, unfortunately. I had to share this event with 5,000 to 6,000 other Star Trek fans who attended Mr. Roddenberry's recent lecture here at the Houston Coliseum.

The whole *Trek* staff was there, Walter, Leslie, and myself; and it was a great pleasure to see the creator of Star Trek in person as he shared his ideas, views, and hopes for the future with those who have most responded to his message of peace and hope.

I came to the lecture not knowing what to expect. Some famous people who go on lecture tours are content to feed their audience an hour or two of meaningless pap. Mr. Roddenberry quickly proved to be a personable and able speaker.

One thing that quickly impressed me about him was his consideration for his fans. The weather was foul that night, and because of it he had arrived late, so the management had started the famous blooper reels to keep the crowd quiet. When they were half over, Roddenberry arrived. He told the audience that the rest of the bloopers would be shown later, and then at the end of the program they would be shown again for the benefit of those fans who had not yet arrived.

Roddenberry then set the stage with a joke or two. His humor was light and intended to invoke smiles, not gales of laughter.

Roddenberry began his talk with a comment on Star Trek fans, saying, "To understand Star Trek fandom you cannot generalize. They come in all shapes and ages. This includes presidents of large corporations, some U.S. Senators—these are what we call closet Trekkies—definitely the largest group." He then went on to say, "The thing that draws these fans together is more than just a television show. It has to do with ideas and ideals that go far beyond the adventures of a mythical starship."

Much of his talk was of his personal feelings toward Star Trek fans. I was especially touched by his remark, "We have a large number of people in Star Trek fandom that are handicapped. As many of you know, I was somewhat handicapped myself as a child. I had the good fortune to lose most of it. For me, and for those other fans, Star Trek represents a day when we'll be wise enough to look beyond the exterior of all people and find the beauty that is in all of us."

He then spoke about the history of Star Trek and about the movie. As most Star Trek fans know, Roddenberry had to fight the network executives most of the way in order to give us a show that was more than just another space opera.

One anecdote he told concerned the original personnel roster of the *Enterprise,* which was to include 50 percent men and 50 percent women. This plan drew a visit from a network executive who complained that if Star Trek were to go on the air with such a mixed crew, the viewing public would certainly be shocked by all the "fooling around" (as the network executive so delicately put it) that must surely be going on up there.

Though he fought long and hard for his half-and-half mix, Roddenberry was forced to agree on a ship composed of 70 percent men and 30 percent women.

This wasn't the only problem Roddenberry had with female crew members in the early days of Star Trek. When he agreed to do the second pilot, "Where No Man Has Gone Before," he was told that he would have to get rid of the character of Number One, the emotionless female first officer of the *Enterprise*.

At the same time he was told to "get rid of the guy with the ears too. No one's going to believe him either."

By now, Roddenberry knew he could never win both arguments with the network, so he decided to marry Majel Barrett and keep Nimoy on the show. "Obviously," he said, "I couldn't do it the other way around."

Though this led to a bigger part for Spock, it was kind of a disillusionment to Roddenberry's new wife. As he puts it, "All through her career my wife had heard of the advantages of sleeping with the producer. In the case of our marriage it has taken her from co-starring roles to a starship nurse with such great lines as 'Yes, doctor.' "

The subject that was of most interest to the fans was the status of the Star Trek feature. At the time the actual story line of the movie had not been decided upon.

This was due to the fact that: "We found it was harder to fit a story to a large-screen movie when we already have the characters and all of the conditions, and have to fit a story to them, than if we had done an original. I could have had a movie out by now if I had been willing to settle for something like 'Captain Kirk Meets Godzilla.' "

On the subject of the *Enterprise*, Roddenberry said, "We will keep the same basic configuration of the *Enterprise*. But science has jumped ahead ten years in time from when we originally started. We can promise a more sophisticated *Enterprise*, and are seeking the cooperation of every scientific lab in the country to be sure it is absolutely right."

This is perhaps one of the most fundamental reasons for the success of Star Trek. The care and planning that goes into even the smallest detail of the show is the kind of care that has to come from a man like Gene Roddenberry, whose first aim is the artistic, not the commercial success of the show.

Roddenberry has also concerned himself with the responsibility of television. He recognizes that the potential of television to harm is just as great as its potential to entertain or educate.

He reflects this concern in his own words. "We discovered that one of the greatest hungers in the world today is for heroes to admire and emulate. In our show we rejected the anti-hero and went with the old-fashioned heroes who believed that their word and their oath is their bond, and that there are some things in this universe worth a life of danger and discomfort, and, if necessary, dying for."

According to Roddenberry, what finally convinced the executives at Paramount that a Star Trek movie was a viable project was the letter-writing campaign that resulted in the NASA space shuttle being named after the *Enterprise.*

"Which," Roddenberry went on to say, "I was not for. I thought that Earth's first space ship should have a generic Earth name, not that it should be specifically *United States,* and certainly not a military name."

This same plea for the unity of man was part of the basic message of Star Trek. Yet this in no way meant that to be unified we must give up those basic and important ideas and customs that make up our cultural and ethnic backgrounds.

Roddenberry went on to support this by saying, "We tried to say that humanity will reach maturity on that day when we learn not merely to tolerate, but to look with actual delight on differences in ideas. If we cannot learn to take a positive delight in differences between our own kind on our own planet, then we do not deserve to go into space and meet the variety that almost certainly is there."

On the subject of man's future in space, Roddenberry said, "Do I and the people who wrote for Star Trek really believe that we are going to get out there and aim for the stars eventually? I must say that of course we do. We think that it is undoubtedly as likely and as necessary as it was for the first tribes to get over the next mountain and find out what is in the next valley. We do it for the same reason that we climb Mt. Everest, the famous Mallory statement, 'because it's there.' As long as the stars are there, we're going to get to them. A race that is tired of traveling, of taking risks, of learning and growing, is a race that is tired of living."

Roddenberry believes that mankind is not tired of living or of growing. His own vision of the future includes a development that may catapult mankind into the vastness of space sooner than any of us think.

The future of man was what Star Trek was most concerned with; therefore, it should be no surprise that the creator of Star Trek is also very concerned with the future of that strange and sometimes self-contradictory creature.

But what shape will man's venture to the stars take? Roddenberry believes, "It has to do with the evolutionary step that is happening to each and every one of us. I think that we are at the beginning, we humans, of a quantum leap forward that is going to take us beyond this speck of matter, this ancestral egg we call Planet Earth. I think that for those of us that want to go in that direction, it will take us out into the environment of the galaxy. That's a bold statement, to say we are evolving into something beyond what we already are. But I really believe that we are at the beginning of evolving beyond our present animal-human life form.

"To prove that point," Roddenberry continued, "I'm going to take a look at just one item that has happened in our lifetime, which is the computer. Computers have been around long enough so that we've grown kind of accustomed to seeing them. But you must understand that this device is in a very primitive state. Yet even in its very primitive state, this computer is capable of doing some things in one millionth of a second that take flesh-and-blood cells of our brains hours and sometimes days to perform. Now stop for a moment and consider how incredible that is. It is like frogs in a millpond have suddenly discovered a way of increasing their leaping power a thousandfold.

"In what is really one split-nth of time, we fragile human beings right now, within a whole lifetime, have discovered a way of increasing our thinking power a thousandfold, perhaps ultimately something on the order of a millionfold.

"Without getting into the semantic differences between memory, reason, creativity, and so on, it is a fact that within our lifetime man has begun to develop thinking machines. We are on the path to manipulating and supplementing the very creative intelligence that makes us unique in the first place."

But how would this affect man himself? Roddenberry goes on to say, "Scientists are now writing about things we science fiction writers have been writing about for years. It is very possible that in the future we will implant computers into our own bodies."

"I think it even more likely that we will implant some sort of a receptor device by which any computer anywhere can be linked, when we want it, directly into the chemical or electrical thought processes of our brains. I'm not saying that computers will control us, I'm saying rather that we will have access at a moment's notice, any time we want it, to greatly increased calculating ability, and to the equivalent of whole libraries of information."

This, Roddenberry believes, will bring about a future in which a portion of mankind will become part machine, and some of these people will be space explorers.

"I'm going even further than that," he went on to say, "I'm going to suggest that in the far-distant future, a segment of mankind may even become all machine.

"What I'm saying is that we humans have actually reached the point in our tool-making ability where we can begin to adapt our own bodies without waiting for the slow genetic process of changing.

"I'm also suggesting something even more than our present bodies, for us and for other civilizations, may be only an intermediate stage on to something else.

"That's difficult to consider," Roddenberry said, "because it's like asking a caterpillar to envision itself as a butterfly.

"But I think there's something very humorous about us humans running around this planet, proclaiming ourselves the supreme achievement of the universe.

"Scientists are beginning to realize that the possibilities of a machine form of life are almost infinite. This has to do with a question we have all asked: If aliens were to visit this planet, what would they look like? Well, it may interest you to know that some of the most advanced thinking on this subject, including a paper out of NASA, is that if we are visited, it seems to them very probable it will be just that, a machine form of life that thousands or hundreds of thousands of centuries before left their organic bodies behind.

"It is written nowhere that our conscious intelligence cannot somehow eventually be transferred to a machine life form, and that such machines will be so sophisticated that they can feel, can exult over beauty, and can reproduce in ways that are far lovelier than our own.

"When you think of machines like this, do not think of cogs and wheels or even transistors. We are talking about things that may be so sophisticated, so finely done, that they will be infinitely graceful and lovely even in our own eyesight. That is one road part of humanity may be taking."

Roddenberry then concluded his talk by opening the floor to questions from the audience. This section was rather disappointing, since most of the questions were about subjects most Star Trek fans know by heart.

One of the biggest treats of the evening was yet to come. This was a showing of the original, uncut version of "The Cage."

Though I have seen the "Menagerie" version of this episode many times, I was amazed to find how much depth and characterization was lost when it was recut for showing as "The Menagerie."

Roddenberry explained this as the fault of both too little time and too little tolerance on the part of the network executives.

I enjoyed watching "The Cage" almost as much as I had enjoyed the talk by Roddenberry. It was a grand evening spent with a warm and wonderful man.

21. A LOOK AT STAR TREK FANDOM
by Janet Smith-Bozarth

Without a doubt, Star Trek has the most diverse and interesting assemblage of fans of any type of hobby in the world. Trekkers range in age from toddlers to grandparents. They have jobs all the way from students to aerospace engineers. And, most important, they come in all sizes, colors, types, and backgrounds imaginable. If there was ever living proof that the spirit of Star Trek, the "beauty in diversity," is a real possibility, then Star Trek fans are it. But the question remains, what is a typical Star Trek fan? If they are all so different, then how can they be so much alike? These are questions which may be more suitable for a sociological thesis than a magazine article, but Janet Smith-Bozarth manages to give us an inkling of the answers in her article. And with her tongue tucked only a bit in her cheek.

LESSON NUMBER FORTY-SEVEN— ALIEN SUBCULTURES OF TERRA

There is a strange alternate world on Terra in which dwells a curious creature called a "Star Trek Fan." This creature, while mixing with other humanoid residents of Terra, is indistinguishable from the others of his species (i.e., the "Non Fan").

There are, however, certain rather obvious and easily identified traits of the Star Trek Fan, which even the untrained eye may readily discern:

When two (or more) fans meet, certain code signs are exchanged to identify one as "Fan" or "Non Fan." Usually, the right hand is held palm outward, thumb extended at a

45° angle, while the fingers are held rigidly together forming a "V" shape between the index and second, and the third and little fingers.

Upon this preliminary identification, a verbal communication is then issued, such as "Live Long and Prosper." A like response being voiced completes the ritual, and contact is completed.

One of the notable characteristics of the Star Trek Fan is his affinity for group activities.

A gathering of Fans is called a Con (i.e., Convention, a meticulously planned but curiously unstructured event). At these gatherings, a metamorphosis begins as the Fans speak of such obscure terms as Warp Drive and Impulse Engines, Tribbles and Gorns, Vulcans and Klingons, the Organian Peace Treaty, Interstellar Relations, and the Prime Directive.

Finally a physical transformation takes place: Some Fans' ears become pointed, others have their skin turn blue and grow antennae. Still others turn into nonhuman forms of fur and rock.

You scoff, ladies and gentlemen? Each and every case is fully documented, I assure you. But let us proceed to historical and personality observations.

What are these creatures called "Fans," and what is this subculture of theirs called "Fandom?"

The term "Fandom" is a popular corruption of the words "fan" and "domain," and is generally applied to science fiction, comics, films, fantasy, and other special interest groups, as well as to Star Trek. A simple definition would be, "Fandom refers to all activities that involve the devotees of any subject."

Although "Star Trek" (see Television, Earth, United States, Mid-20th Century, oth.) made its debut in 1966, Star Trek "Fandom" is a relatively recent development, which had its beginnings as a subunit of Science Fiction Fandom.

Between 1966 and 1969, a few clubs were formed and a few newsletters and fanzines were published, but most folded after the show was canceled by a national network. At science fiction conventions, a few of the hard-core Fans kept bringing the show up for discussion.

The seeds for an "organized" Star Trek Fandom were planted by an energetic science fiction fan named Bjo Trimble. In 1968, she organized the Save Star Trek letter-writing campaign that brought nearly a million pieces of mail to the National Broadcasting Company, and staved off cancellation of the show for another season (the third, and final, one).

Bjo Trimble also got the wheels rolling for Star Trek Enterprises (later Lincoln Enterprises), which was the first group to sell Star Trek memorabilia. Bjo and her husband, John Trimble, still run Equicon, a Star Trek convention held yearly on the West Coast of the United States.

In 1971, an organization called STAR (Star Trek Association for Revival) was formed to try to persuade a national network to bring the show back on television in new episodes.

Star Trek Fandom reappeared on the national scene in January of 1972, when the first major Star Trek Con was held in New York City. An article in *TV Guide* (see Publications, U.S., Mid-20th Century, oth.) on the Con literally brought Fans out of the woodwork. People began to realize that they were not alone in their affection for "a dead space opera."

In the summer of 1972, Jacqueline Lichtenberg, who had been answering Fan questions in her spare time and at personal expense, came up with the idea of a central group for collecting information and introducing new Fans into Fandom. Jeannie Haueisen became the first chairman of this Fan service organization, which was called the Star Trek Welcommittee.

The Welcommittee is still going strong, with another outgoing Fan, Helen Young, at the helm. But like most Fan organizations, they are volunteer-operated and run on a shoestring budget. So should you intend writing to them, enclose a self-addressed, stamped envelope or some extra stamps. This will save Welcommittee money and hasten your reply.

There are three major divisions of Fans: Trekkers, Trekkists, and Trekkies.

The Trekk*ist* is someone who watches the show periodically, may attend a Convention (if it is held in his immediate area), but is not actively involved in Fandom.

The Trekk*er* is the backbone of Fandom—the more mature Fans. Trekkers run the various organizations, and are the workers, the editors, and officers—the doers and movers of Fandom.

The Trekk*ies* are the obnoxious little creatures that are

forever underfoot at Cons and meetings: Running after the guests, demanding autographs and souvenirs in loud voices, and drooling at the sight of one of the show's stars.

Trekkers enjoy Star Trek for its dramatic impact, the interpersonal relationships and the ideas and ideals that compose it.

Trekkies (quoting Terry Whittier of STAR Sacremento Valley) "see Star Trek as just another exciting TV show, and the fandom associated with it simply as another 'in-group' they can try to join."

The typical Trekkie is an adolescent or pre-adolescent who has fallen in love with a character to the point of imitating that character constantly. That is, dressing up in Spock ears or zapping everyone with toy phasers for the entire three days of a convention.

Again quoting Terry Whittier: "Trekkers are responsible for most of the good things that are done in Star Trek Fandom. Trekkies, unfortunately, are responsible for the bad impression the general public has of Star Trek Fans."

(Writer's Note: Hence my badge that says, "Stamp out Trekkies . . . proud to be a Trekker!")

There are other thorns in Fandom's bed of roses besides Trekkies. Namely, the Opportunists and Ripoff artists whose only interest in fandom is a fast buck. They capitalize on Star Trek by selling high-priced junk, shoddy material, or "quickie-cons" in which the Fans are treated like cattle.

But the killing blow to Fandom may be dealt by the very people who brought it to life. The two main elements which are necessary to Cons and bringing Fans together are becoming harder to obtain: films and guests.

The price for renting Star Trek episodes has taken a geometric rise. It has been driven up not so much by Paramount, but by other groups who want to get onto the Wagon Train to the Stars (or maybe that's Gravy Train).

Recently, one group was charged $750 by the Screen Actor's Guild, $500 by the Screen Writer's Guild, and $1,000 by the Screen Director's Guild (over and above Paramount's rental fees) for the rental of several episodes. Part of the bill had to be paid in advance.

The Star Trek stars are now asking as much as $5,000 plus expenses for an appearance at a Con. Granted, the actors do deserve something for their time, talent, and energies, and do have to earn a living; but the Fans, who are the basis for the actors' present fame, deserve something too.

But despite all this, Star Trek Fandom will survive, for it is like a living organism. Old cells may die and fall away, but new ones are forming all the time. There is also a skeleton of hard-core fans who will always be there because Star Trek is more than just another TV show. It offered hope when it was needed. But above all, Star Trek is a universe of ideas.

Tomorrow's lecture will be on another alien subculture of Terra: Politics.

Class dismissed!

22. AN EVENING WITH GEORGE TAKEI
by Walter Irwin

It has been said of George Takei that when he enters a room he carries the sun in with him. We tend to agree, as of all the Star Trek personalities we have met personally, George has to be just about the most friendly, cheerful, and obliging of them all. And saying this in no way slights any other member of the Enterprise crew, as George is such a totally alive person that ordinary courtesy and friendliness seem to pale beside him. George is such an accomplished raconteur, it is almost as much of a pleasure to hear him speak as it is to watch him act. And we feel that almost all of the high spirits and vibrancy of George Takei comes alive in this transcription of his remarks at Houstoncon '77.

It was with a great deal of pleasure and expectation that we assembled in Screening Room B at Houstoncon to hear George Takei speak. The previous day, George had dropped in on the Star Trek panel discussion, and we found that he was just as much of a Star Trek and science fiction fan as all of us. And since his demeanor was so casual and friendly, we were looking forward that much more to his scheduled talk.

And in he came, smiling and waving; full of friendliness and good cheer as always. When Houstoncon chairman Marc Schooley introduced George, he slipped up and pronounced George's last name incorrectly. As many people do, Marc said "Tak-eye"; it should be pronounced "Tak-ay" (rhymes with "okay"). But George laughed louder than anyone.

"Well," he said, with a big smile, "it's all right Marc, because the way you pronounced it first, for your information, is a Japanese word. And it means 'expensive.' I'd be more than happy to comply with that."

Having immediately reestablished the casual rapport that he had with the fans the day before, George referred to the fact that the panel discussion had centered around something other than Star Trek.

"Thank you for your beautiful welcome. I really appreciate that, all you good *Star Wars* fans! And you've also presented me with a good opportunity to say that I did not play the Wookie."

Asking how many fans had seen the film, George pretended amazement when almost every hand went up. "Oh, well, then it is probably a *Star Wars* convention, isn't it?"

George praised *Star Wars* highly, particularly the special effects, which he termed "stunningly well done." From his viewpoint, he said, the film wasn't a projection into the future, but a flashback into the nostalgic past.

"Sort of a little bit of going back into my boyhood," said George, "when I went to the Saturday matinees. A lot of the sequences, for those of you who haven't seen the film, reminded me of the Errol Flynn swashbucklers, the Burt Lancaster *Crimson Pirate,* or the Flash Gordon type of thing.

"For example," said George, punctuating his words with exaggerated gestures, "the sequences with the walls closing in on you, or where you're caught on a ledge with the bad guys chasing you, and there's this bottomless pit between you and the other side; so you slip off this lasso thing, and with the damsel in distress, you swing across to the other side." By this time, the audience and George were both laughing so hard at his performance of these feats that he was unable to finish.

When things settled down a bit, George offered his critique of the film.

"I know that the filmmakers intended it to be pure fun, complete escape, but there were opportunities, I think, for the film to have some intelligence about it. And in that respect, it is different from Star Trek. Star Trek had a great deal of substance. I think that *Star Wars* could have been a classic if it really had that one little layer of awareness—and it doesn't have to be a heavy-handed, preachy message type of thing."

George then compared the destruction of the Death Star to the technology we have available to us today, specifically the neutron bomb. "And here is that terrifying sequence," he pointed out, "and it's just ha-ha-ha, the bad guys got it. I really regret that these and other opportunities weren't put into a little more intelligent context."

But then George chided himself for nitpicking, and urged everyone to see the film. He did reiterate his belief, however, that the film will not become an SF classic but will be remembered as simply the biggest money maker of its day.

George then moved on to Star Trek.

"Thank you for all the support you have given Star Trek. I think that is why Star Trek is different, say from *Star Wars* for example. It had a level of awareness and intelligence, some kind of commentary on our times and the human condition. And you people are a part of that. You played a very important part in the saga of the show, in its ups and downs since cancellation."

With a somewhat sly smile, George got onto the subject that was uppermost in everyone's mind. "As you probably know," he said, "the feature film project which Paramount has talked about for three years, and kept announcing starting dates for and pushing them back, has unfortunately been canceled. That project is dead.

"The latest press release suggests the return of Star Trek as a series, an hourly series, on a regular basis."

As some fans started to applaud, George raised a cautioning hand.

"That's a tantalizing prospect, but as those of you who know the history of Star Trek up to this point can agree, I'm sure we should not start cheering yet. Have your tongue placed very firmly in your cheek as you read those press releases."

George then revealed that he had talked with Gene Roddenberry the Wednesday morning before the convention, so as to get the latest "official word" to share with us.

"To quote his words," George said, "He said that Paramount might be interested in a television series. And I commented to him that that sounded very cautious and circumspect, and he answered that he means to be. So he is in discussion with Paramount, and apparently they're responding to him, which is refreshing for a change."

George also warned that although the news release stated that Star Trek would start shooting in the fall with a scheduled starting date in the spring of '78, we should wait for more definitive information. "At this point, there are no scripts, no writers assigned, no definitive evidence of any kind of progress in that direction, other than they are talking to Gene about it and have agreed to his playing the role of producer."

He then mentioned several people who were signed to work on the production side of the feature film, but that it was still canceled. However, George urged all of us to remain optimistic and mentioned the letter-writing campaign which saved the show in its second season.

"I think it's high time to renew that campaign, to inundate the Paramount executives with mail, saying, 'We're on to your game now.' This is a powerful tool you have, and if we can get it to multiply, I believe that this can lock it in. This will force Paramount to set a starting date and stick to it, and we will see Star Trek back on the air as a regular series again. But at this point, we are dependent upon your interest to make that become a reality."

George drew a big laugh when he inadvertently referred to the starting date as a "stardate." "Looking forward a bit, there," he chuckled.

Before opening the floor to questions, George spoke of his pleasure at being in Houston, revealing in the process that he is a modern-architecture buff, and referring to several buildings around the city which impressed him.

He then extended a general thanks for all of the kindness and hospitality which he had experienced during his stay, pointed out that while it was wonderful to be adored (here he mentioned New York conventions, and their "agressively expressive" fans), Houston's easygoing, casual type of love was much better.

George then drew another round of appreciative applause when he referred to the breakdown of the hotel's air-conditioning system by thanking the hotel for "Providing us all with a free sauna bath yesterday."

After opening it up for questions, George immediately got one which allowed him to register his respect and affection for some of his fellow actors.

When asked about being "tied down to a series," and the danger of type-casting, George answered that an SF format such as Star Trek's tended to tie an actor down less than a standard type of show, for instance a detective series.

"In a science fiction format, we are challenged in terms of acting opportunities, because strange things happen. In one episode ("The Deadly Years"), Dee, Bill, and I think it was

Jimmy, got to age rapidly, so they got a chance to play old men. And in many sequences, I was going crazy or affected by pongs or something like that. So I got to play somebody other than a normal Sulu . . . either a crazed Sulu or a spaced-out Sulu."

George compared a science fiction series with a repertory theater, where one often gets a chance to play a role completely different from his regular character. However, he said, there are hazards, and he pointed out one unique problem and his sympathy to it.

"Leonard played a very strong, unique, bizarre, but powerful character. A compelling, attention-grabbing type of character, and he was enormously successful at it. I think that one reason that Spock was so successful as a character is that Leonard is such a good, inventive actor."

George explained that many of the intriguing and interesting characteristics about Spock were contributed by Nimoy (he gave as an example the story behind the "Spock Pinch") to make the character fuller and remain consistent with what Spock would consider to be the easiest, safest, and most efficient solution to a problem.

"This kind of creative thinking made a tremendous impact on the audience. People remembered it. It's a compliment to Leonard as an actor but becomes a difficulty to him as a professional actor, whose stock in trade is to play as many different characters as possible. Because he made such an impact with one particular and freaky character, it is difficult for people to see Leonard in any other context.

"So Leonard's position has been, if he were to—" George paused for just a second and then went on—"and this is a big if. If he were to repeat as Mr. Spock, he knows that he will subsequently lose out on several other parts, since some producers would be reluctant to cast him in a different role when he is so strongly identified with Spock.

"So he feels that he should be fully and properly remunerated for playing Mr. Spock. I think that's fair and that's honest, since Paramount has got only one picture at stake, and Leonard has his whole career at stake. Their position is that Leonard wants them to pay for five or six pictures, while they are only going to use him in one. However, Leonard will probably lose five or six roles by playing Spock, and it is proper that with the kind of sacrifice that he would be making, Paramount should cover his losses there."

George stated that he didn't think that it was much of a problem for the rest of the Star Trek crew, as they have all had the opportunity to play other roles, and that Leonard's problem is a unique one.

When asked if he thought that a Star Trek movie could have made the money that *Star Wars* is making, George answered very emphatically, "That's right! They probably realize that now, and they probably realize that their decision to jettison the film was a dumb one, but I think that Paramount has been very consistent in this. They've been making a whole slew of dumb mistakes."

One fan referred to "The Naked Time," and George's use of a sword, and wanted to know if George was into martial arts.

"That was a lot of fun, one of my favorite episodes, but I must confess to you that a month before I shot that show, I knew nothing about fencing. The man who wrote that show, John D. F. Black, happened to be visiting the set and told me he was considering an idea for Sulu. He thought it would be interesting if we explored some of the physical-exercise things that Sulu might be interested in, and asked me how I was at fencing, and if I was any good, he would expand the role. When I heard that I said, 'Well, that's one of my favorite sports!' And when I got home that evening, I dragged out the yellow pages and started looking up fencing lessons!"

After the ensuing laughter subsided, George revealed that although he had had only two weeks of lessons when the episode was shot, he later took up the sport and stayed with it for almost two years.

Asked about how he felt about having worked with the Star Trek crew, George took off enthusiastically: "I think it was very, very good experience, and the fact that those three years were such a full, enriching experience was primarily due to Gene Roddenberry. Gene selected a cast of true professionals, people that brought not only a great deal of experience, but a great deal of themselves, and a great deal of integrity. All the members of the cast gave to the show."

However, George stated that his most valuable gain from Star Trek was the acting education he received. "Bill is a fine, subtle actor, and a very good technical actor, and I enjoyed watching his closeups. Some of the things he did technically were very educational to me. I learned a great deal watching Bill.

"Leonard, on the other hand, digs, probes much more deeply into it, for example that 'Spock pinch' type of thing. A very internalized actor. He rationally thinks out why he does do this or doesn't do this; and that type of analytical approach was a good education also."

George also explained his good friendship with Nimoy. "We were very much both political animals and found ourselves in the same campaigns, concerned about the same issues, supporting the same candidates, and our friendship cemented."

When asked if any of the crew had contacted him about being in the movie (before it was scrubbed) or the proposed television series, George replied:

"Gene, via Paramount, has touched bases with all of us on a quote, 'formal basis,' unquote. There has been no discussion of contracts, no definitive promises made, no discussion of money or anything. I have shared with Paramount 'my favorable inclination toward considering returning.' You know, you don't start jumping up and down, and saying that you're enthusiastic and eager—then they can get you for two cents. But we did it before, and we can do it again!"

This discussion of a new Star Trek brought up what is probably the hottest debating point in Star Trek fandom right now: whether or not the series should account for the passage of time. One fan commented to George that since the actors had progressed in their own lives, shouldn't the crew do so as well?

George wholeheartedly agreed. "Your comment is a very good one. As a matter of fact, as many of you already know, Gene Roddenberry was also one of those who wrote a script for the feature film project. This was rejected by Paramount, very consistent in character—again, stupid, dumb decision-making.

"In that script, Gene accounted for the passage of time. He begins his story three years after the return of the *Enterprise* from the completion of its five-year mission; and after it came back, all of us went our separate ways. Captain Kirk had become an admiral. Spock had gone back to Vulcan, to steep himself in its roots, to find something of himself in its history and its culture. And Sulu, in that version, had gone on to become captain of his own starship."

George interrupted himself with a grin. "As a matter of fact, I have a T-shirt that says 'Captain Sulu.' I was going to wear it for you, but in my haste in packing, I forgot to bring it." There were audible groans from the audience.

"Unfortunately," he continued, "in that script, Sulu's ship is hit by a disastrous explosion, and of course he plunges himself right into the middle of that, and he loses his leg. And for someone as physical and active as Sulu, that's really the end of his life.

"In the meantime, Dr. McCoy had returned to Earth—he never really did enjoy working with people—so he retires and becomes a veterinarian. But due to the insistence of Sulu, McCoy reluctantly agrees to return and work on human beings again and furnishes Sulu with what could be considered a bionic leg. So the leg that I lost is improved upon by the technology of that time, and the medical wizardry of Dr. McCoy!"

General cheers, laughter, and applause accompanied this short recap by George. When it subsided, he said, "Yes, I think that in any kind of return to Star Trek, the passage of time would have to be accounted for, and I hope that they account for it in the way that Gene Roddenberry did. He's the master!"

Another point brought up by a fan when discussing a return of Star Trek was whether or not George knew if a new *Enterprise* was planned.

"There's been many discussions," answered George, "but for the feature picture, they were talking in terms of a big, new, more impressive *Enterprise*. It would have been the basic set you all recognize, but modified a bit to fit in with the excellent suggestions that many experts in the field have made—such as engineers, astronauts, and various scientists. However, that was the feature film, which would have a larger budget, so now we will just have to wait and see."

Asked about how it felt to be a celebrity and constantly noticed by people everywhere, George told an amusing story about an incident which happened while he was in Germany recently.

As he was walking down a street in Germany, several teenagers passed by and stopped, came back, and passed again. When they finally worked up enough courage to speak to him, it turned out that none of them could speak English—and George cannot speak German! The only word which

George could recognize was the German equivalent of "Sulu," which is "Zulu." "So apparently," laughs George, "in Germany, I play an African character!"

The story brought up the question "Have you ever seen Star Trek dubbed into a foreign language?"

"Oh, yes," said George. "I've seen it in French, and I speak perfect French. And in Germany, you wouldn't believe how well I speak German! I told Paramount I do speak Spanish and Japanese, and I wanted to do the dubbing in those two languages, but apparently there are some union difficulties in the countries where it is aired, so they have to use actors from those countries. In Japan, I suppose that there is a little chauvanism, because Sulu is not a Japanese name, and they changed it to Na Kato, and they have a Japanese actor doing my dialogue, but I don't like it at all. It's all just whoo-wee-ha-soo-whee-la, and so forth."

After the boisterous laughter which followed this, George was asked if he enjoyed his role as a Japanese officer on a recent episode of *Baa Baa Black Sheep*.

George beamed when asked this, as it is one of his favorite roles. He explained that he was nominated for an Emmy award for it and unfortunately lost, but it was still great fun. For those of you who missed it, George played a Japanese major who masterminded a plot to capture General MacArthur. "Unfortunately," laughs George, "the best I could do was to kidnap Bob Conrad"—the series star—"and that's why we never did win the Second World War."

When a questioner asked George if he thought that Sulu should have a more important position aboard the *Enterprise*, George related an idea he had had which gave Gene Roddenberry a good chuckle.

"There is in television this thing called spinoffs—" He was interrupted by expectant laughter and applause. "So," George continued, "on Monday nights we could have a show with Captain Sulu on his own starship; on Tuesday a show which explores the women's aspect of space—*Star Women*—with Majel and Nichelle; and on Wednesday, we could have a medical show . . . and I believe we should know more about Vulcan, so on Thursday . . . and on Friday night, we have our familiar *Enterprise* crew. And on Saturday, we would have five hours of reruns! On Sunday, we rest."

When asked, "What kind of relationship did you carry on with the writers of Star Trek?" George brought the house down by asking innocently, "Male or female?" and giving a wide mock leer.

"Seriously," continued George, "there are some fine women writers, as well as men. The best of them you probably know; she labels herself D. C. Fontana, and her real name is Dorothy. I'm glad to see that the industry is opening up to women writers. At the time we were doing Star Trek, I guess that Dorothy felt she had to use her initials so that she was not especially identifiable, as some producers might have rejected her script just because she was a woman. So to have her script considered without prejudice, she had to have that kind of neutral name. David Gerrold is another fine writer. That was the first script that he sold; he was about twenty-one years old at the time. So again, this is an example of Gene Roddenberry's openmindedness. He wasn't prejudiced about whether or not this was a young and inexperienced writer or a woman writer; if it was a good script, it deserved to be produced."

George mentioned several other writers with whom he had gotten to be quite good friends, but pointed out that often the writers merely submitted their scripts and never got to be more than names to the actors.

George summed it up by saying, "Many of the writers are colorful and interesting people; sometimes I think that some of them are more interesting than the scripts they wrote!"

Sadly for all of us, time was up at this point. A convention official presented George with a beautiful plaque to commemorate his visit to Houstoncon. Obviously pleased and touched, George said to all of us:

"Whenever I see this, I'll think of the beautiful applause you gave me."

23. THE ROMULANS
by Leslie Thompson

After the great response to Leslie's Klingon article, we couldn't wait to have her take a look at the other Star Trek bad guys, the Romulans. But Leslie was hesitant. After repeated requests and turndowns, we discovered why: Leslie liked the Romulans too much! She just couldn't bring herself to write about them from the accepted Star Trek fan's viewpoint as villains. And here we were, asking her to do so quite insistently. After some thought, we agreed to let Leslie write the article from her own viewpoint. And it seems that after two years and more, time and Star Trek fandom is proving us wrong and Leslie right. Current fan writing, pro books, and fan beliefs in general are now reflecting the very conclusions which Leslie outlined in her article. Leslie is too modest to say so, but we think that she had a lot to do with this "second look" at a much-maligned foe and helped enrich the realm of Star Trek fandom.

The Romulans are a strange, mysterious race. They follow a code which rules almost every aspect of their lives; the code of *chirieta*, the code of the warrior. As to physical characteristics, the Romulans are an offshoot of the "seeding" of similar races throughout the galaxy by a superior race in the dawn of antiquity.

Similarities in the physical qualities of the Vulcans and Romulans are evident, and also in the makeup of their societies.

The Vulcans, of course, worship the beauty of diversity, and have suppressed their emotions in order to allow themselves to bring their intellectual pursuits to full flower. The Romulans, on the other hand, have developed a society where devotion to duty has been the overriding tenet. Historically, Romulans suffered from the same tearing and destructive forces that plagued the Vulcans for so long.

Constant warfare, their natural inclination for battle and rapine, and the need for a goal to serve caused the Vulcans to seek a desperate solution. The solution for the Romulan was a bit easier. A strong leader simply told them what to do.

The leaders, as most leaders do, came to power through war. But the power of these leaders was tempered, in many instances even controlled, by the influence of the Romulan priests.

The priests were followers of Mugeao, who preached the wisdom of tempering war with the finer parts of life: Art, poetry, song and dance, good food, and meditation.

As this was a religion which did not condemn war and conquest, it was quickly and gratefully snapped up by the Romulan leaders. However, as time passed, the leaders found to their chagrin that the priests of Mugeao were becoming more and more influential. Soon no leader dared make any important decision without first obtaining the spiritual advice of his Mugeao priest.

Mugeao (as the religion became commonly known) was adopted into the everyday life of the Romulans. Of course, this mass acceptance of the specifics of Mugeao caused it to change to a great extent.

The warriors, professional soldiers, had always held privileged positions just because of their value as fighters. Under the evolving Mugeao, they became a caste apart, and since they had the weapons, they became the upper caste.

No member of the warrior caste would demean himself by doing ordinary work, so the other, less fortunate members of Romulan society were relegated to these positions. Not to be outdone, they too formed themselves into castes, with the providers of food being the highest, the merchants next, the makers of weapons and goods below them, and the common laborer last.

The leaders of the diverging Romulan populace had to find a way to overcome this devotion to Mugeao. Since they were the leaders, and they had won their leadership through battle, why then shouldn't they be the chiefs of the Romulan caste as well? This view soon became very popular, since it was advocated under the persuasive auspices of the sword.

Once they had "convinced" their followers of the wisdom

of this policy, the leaders consolidated their position by further changing Mugeao.

They instituted the code of *chirieta*, which basically boiled down to fealty to your leader. Each Romulan simply bartered his services to one of the leaders in return for money and the protection that the leaders could supply. It was an especially good deal for the leaders, since they could increase their power by simply pointing out to potential recruits how much power they already had.

Among the warrior caste, which quickly usurped the name "Romulan" for their own, the teachings of Mugeao were practiced religiously. Each Romulan lived like a king, especially since he knew that at any time he could be called to war and meet sudden death. Too, death could come even in time of peace, as it was common knowledge that any member of any caste could kill a member of a lower cast for any indiscretion, however slight or imagined.

Since fighting for pay would attach the stigma of a "working man" to the Romulan caste, they fully accepted *chirieta* and made it a part of their daily lives, almost to the point of insanity in their devotion to duty and to their leige lords.

Thus the Romulans found the purpose which allowed them to give meaning to life, and with which to stabilize their society and advance their science.

Science advanced on Romula much as it did on Earth. In common with their Vulcan cousins, the Romulans had an insatiable curiosity about the unknown.

As science progressed and atomic power came along, war became the province of the scientists. So the warrior class became scientists or the politicians who told the scientists what to do.

But the racial ferocity was still there, without the suppression of emotion the Vulcans had adopted to restrain it. So Romulan advances were most often used for war and conquest—but soon it was war and conquest on other planets, since space travel was an inevitable result of Romulan science.

The other inhabited planets in the Romulan solar system found the combination of fighting skill, devotion to duty, and the overwhelming weaponry of the Romulan warriors to be unbeatable. They were soon part of the Romulan Star Empire (as the now federated Romulans were somewhat prematurely calling themselves).

About 100 years before the time of the *Enterprise,* the Romulans suffered their first setback.

Trying to expand their empire, which by this time covered several solar systems, they bumped heads with ships from the Federation.

The Romulans, who had thought themselves the sole possessors of space travel, were enraged and summarily rejected even the thought of peaceful communication. A Federation ship was destroyed without warning, and the war was on.

The war was long and brutal with many casualties on both sides. Due to the strange nature of space war, neither side ever got a glimpse of the other. Only the ships were seen, and then only over the sights of the respective weapons.

Finding that neither was stronger than the other to any conclusive degree, and desperate to disengage from a war which neither had really wanted, an overture of peace was made by the Federation, and to the surprise of many, it was accepted by the Romulans.

The treaty was negotiated by subspace radio, since illfeeling had reached such a degree on both sides that a faceto-face meeting might have triggered hostilities all over again.

A neutral zone was declared between the two factions, and this zone was not violated by either side for many years.

As this had been the first war in space for both sides (the Federation had yet to meet the Klingons), the respective sides made plans to prepare for another such confrontation. The Romulans threw even greater efforts than before into developing their weaponry; while the Federation set up a war college at the Academy manned by veterans of the Romulan conflict. The Federation also sent small emissary ships to every part of the galaxy to inform any other potentially dangerous races of their peaceful intentions.

No further contact took place between the Romulans and the Federation until the starship *Enterprise* encroached on the neutral zone and caused a balance of terror.

The Romulans remain the mystery foes of the Federation. Although not as much a threat to the security of the galaxy as the overbearing Klingons, the Romulans are held in high respect by the Federation and are watched as closely as possible.

One of the surprising facts which has been revealed about

the Romulans is that women hold an equal place in their society.

Of course, this fits in with the practice of *chirieta*, since warrior elite cannot be perpetuated except by allowing the women to be part of that elite (they bear the children). Romulan women were trained in the arts of warfare, but until the rise of push-button weapons and computerized war, they played a small part in Romulan battles.

But once the opportunity came to take an active part, the Romulan women seized it with a will, and now many of them are in high positions, some even commanding starships and fleets of starships.

To a Federation society where female equality came comparatively late, this practice among the warlike Romulans was something of a surprise.

The Romulans too encountered the Klingons, and by being the first to give them as good as they got, earned the respect and undying hate of the followers of Kling. Although the Klingons sneer at the peaceful overtures of the Federation, the Romulans impressed them highly with their ferociousness in battle and their don't-bother-us-and-we-won't-bother-you policy.

As usual, the crafty Klingons have tried to turn this to their advantage by supplying the Romulans with equipment and technology. So far, this policy hasn't been too successful, as the Romulans cheerfully accept all the Klingons offer while actually doing little to advance any but their own aims. Klingon stubbornness keeps the smiling "peace" going, but they have earmarked the Romulans as next in line after the Federation for destruction.

Surprisingly, as the code of the Romulan has become known to the Federation, more and more progress has been made in creating peace and cooperation between the two races.

The concepts of meditation and the love of art and beauty run deeply through many of the races who are Federation members. Knowing that these beliefs and practices are shared by the Romulans has helped the Federation in making overtures to them.

The Romulans are not unresponsive to these approaches. They realize that the immense wealth and power of the Federation can be valuable to them, and that their purposes would be better served by working with the Federation rather than against it.

Add to this the fact that both sides feel a greater affinity toward each other than either does to the berserker Klingons and an eventual meeting seems possible. An actual joining or treaty of cooperation in all matters is still far in the future, but most observers feel that the present "enforced peace" will soon become an actual one.

So while the Romulans remain a steadfast foe of the Federation for now, they are not a threat which hangs over the heads of everyone in the galaxy. The differences can be resolved between the two just as they were between nations here on Earth.

Foremost among the leaders who are working to overcome the enmity caused by the destructive war of almost a century before are the Vulcans.

The Vulcans' love of peace and their deep belief that all men are truly brothers, as well as the common ancestry between the two races, have caused them to take the forefront in the overtures for peace and cooperation.

One day they will succeed. And perhaps Mr. Spock will follow in the footsteps of his father and become the diplomat who brings about the greatest joining in the history of the universe: two great interstellar powers working together to advance the good of all.

24. TREK INTERVIEW:
GRACE LEE WHITNEY

For many years, Grace Lee Whitney was the "forgotten woman" of Star Trek fandom. While the other personalities were making con appearances, popping up here and there in movies and TV, doing voices for the Star Trek animated series, and generally keeping busy, Lee Whitney was at her home in Southern California, patiently working to perfect another facet of her talents—singing. However, in 1976, Lee decided that she would finally give in to the repeated requests of fans and convention planners and step forward to take her place in the spotlight of the adulation of thousands of fans. Trek was very fortunate to obtain the very first in-depth interview with Grace Lee Whitney after her long absence, and in it she reveals the answers to the questions that fans had been asking for years.

GLW: Since Star Trek, I have been staying home, raising my family and dogs, and getting back to my first career, my singing career.

TREK: How did you get the part of Yeoman Janice Rand?

GLW: I got the part after I did a pilot for Gene called "Police Story." The part I played got such a great reaction from the audience that Gene put me right on Star Trek.

TREK: Was your portrayal of Yeoman Rand influenced at all by the Women's Liberation Movement?

GLW: At the time of Star Trek, there was no large Women's Lib movement, so there was none of that in her character. But it did upset me that she had to shake, cry, and fear so much.

TREK: How much of Grace Lee Whitney was in Yeoman Rand?

GLW: I suppose the only part of me that was in the character of Rand was the innocent little girl part of me.

TREK: How did you feel about the show when you were working on it?

GLW: At the time, we all thought it was a little farfetched, but we trusted Gene, and it was well acted. We had no idea of the coming phenomenon then.

TREK: Which was your favorite episode? Your least favorite? Which episodes did you have the most (and least) fun working on?

GLW: My favorite episode was "Miri," basically because my kids were in it. The most fun was "The Enemy Within," for obvious reasons. The least fun, and my least favorite, was "Dagger of the Mind," as halfway through I was dropped, and it was rewritten for Dr. Helen Noel. *My part!*

TREK: Speaking of which, exactly why were you dropped from Star Trek?

GLW: The *official* reason given was that NBC felt Kirk needed a more varied romantic life—in other words, more sex for the captain!

TREK: How did you feel when you first heard you had been dropped?

GLW: To be honest, when I first learned I had been dropped, I felt shitty, even suicidal.

TREK: Were you, and are you now, bitter about being dropped?

GLW: Of course I was bitter toward Gene and the studio, but that doesn't exist any more.

TREK: When did you first realize that Star Trek had become so popular?

GLW: I first heard about the Star Trek phenomenon earlier this year, shortly before Equicon.

TREK: Why did you decide to involve yourself in this phenomenon?

GLW: What brought me back was a letter from Susan Sackett (*to the Screen Actor's Guild*), a meeting with D. C. Fontana and Gene, and then Richard Arnold and Equicon.

TREK: What is your reaction to Star Trek fandom, now that you are involved in it?

GLW: I was overwhelmed with the love and affection I was

getting from the fans. I've loved every con I've done and hope to do many more.

TREK: How do you feel about the fans?

GLW: I find the Star Trek fans to be the most loving, courteous, intelligent, and sensitive segment of fandom I've ever met.

TREK: Have you, like some other ST actors, had any bad experiences with fans?

GLW: So far, I've had no trouble from the fans, and hope not to, although we all occasionally get bad mail.

TREK: Did appearing on Star Trek have any lasting effect on your career?

GLW: The show had no great effect on my talent, it was just another role. But it had a profound effect on my ego, first up, then being shattered.

TREK: Would you appear on the Star Trek movie? Have you been contacted?

GLW: I don't think anyone but Bill and Len have been contacted about the movie yet. They can't afford to put any of us under contract until the last few months before the filming. I'm not that sure that I will play the role; we'll have to wait and see.

TREK: Would you have any reservations about working with Roddenberry and the crew again?

GLW: I would feel no different about working with Gene and the crew than I did ten years ago. I might even be better.

TREK: You mentioned your singing career. We understand that you've released a record. How's it doing?

GLW: The record is going great! Gathering momentum and picking up play. People love it, and I hope to have another out soon.

TREK: Have you and your backup group, Star, appeared in public yet?

GLW: Star has played a lot at Disneyland, private parties, bar-mitzvahs, political events, even schools. And cons, of course.

TREK: Why didn't you ever sing on Star Trek?

GLW: At the time of Star Trek, I was not singing as much as I was acting, and the role really had no time to develop.

TREK: And now you're concentrating on singing?

GLW: Yes, I've let film and TV work slide to concentrate on writing and recording.

TREK: Where will fans have a chance to see you perform?

GLW: My group will be appearing at cons around the country, including a rock concert in Philly in '77!

TREK: What else are you planning?

GLW: My plans at the moment are to continue recording, develop my personality, and write my book. (*A con book.*)

TREK: And where is Grace Lee Whitney going from here?

GLW: Where is Grace Lee Whitney going from here? Straight up, baby! Mars, then Saturn, then Venus! (*The title of Grace's album to be released this spring.*)

TREK: Thank you, Grace Lee.

GLW: Thank you and all of your wonderful readers. I send them my love.

25. STAR TREK TIME TRAVELS
by James Houston
with a rebuttal by Walter Irwin

*To be able to travel through time! Probably the most ex-
citing SF concept of them all, and one which Star Trek
explored several times. But as Jim Houston points out in the
following article, it did not always do so with complete success or even without inconsistency. Exploring these inconsistencies, Jim examines why they occurred—and more
important, what the consequences would have been if the
stories had all been consistent in their treatment of the subject of time travel.*

In an unprecedented move, Trek *editor Walter Irwin steps
in with a rebuttal to some of Jim's conclusions and statements. This action was prompted by a fan bull session in
which the time-travel paradox was heatedly discussed. One
of the fans finally said, "If you are going to publish Jim's
article, then do one speaking for our side!" Walter agreed
that this was only fair, but not wishing to devote yet another,
separate article to time travel, he expressed the opinions of
the "other side" in an addendum to Jim's article. But even
though both sides are represented here, the battle of differing
opinions will go on.*

Time travel has been a plot device used by science fiction
authors since the earliest days of the genre. Is it any wonder
then that Star Trek made such an extensive use of time
travel during the run of the series? Out of 101 stories
(seventy-nine live-action and twenty-two animated), six
stories feature the *Enterprise* or members of its crew traveling through time.

Unfortunately, Star Trek was only an hour long, and therefore limited by time and budget as to the amount of detail
which could be told of the various voyages through time. As

it was necessary to get on with the story, little or no time could be spent in explanations of the time-traveling process, or more importantly, of the physical, psychological, and existential ramifications of a journey through time.

The first temporal voyage of the *Enterprise* occurs at the end of "The Naked Time," when the starship is thrown three days back in time after being forced to mix matter-anti-matter "cold" to escape a crash. Happily, this somewhat extreme method of starting the warp engines did not blow our heroes to kingdom come. However, all physical evidence available to the crew shows that they have indeed traveled back three days in time, and they have "Three days to live over again." Fine.

Now we are forced to ask a question: Did the *Enterprise* appear at the same point in space that it occupied three days previous to warping back through time, or at some other point in space?

If the former is the case, then they are in big trouble. By all known laws of physics, two solid objects cannot occupy the same space at the same time; and by virtue of having gone back in time, and returned to its exact starting point, the *Enterprise* is now two solid objects.

Even though matter consists mainly of atomic and sub-atomic particles with relatively lots of space in between, it seems likely that whatever force binds these particles would tend to keep foreign matter out. After all, your hand didn't pass through the table when you sat down to eat breakfast this morning, did it?

If the universe was insistent on forcing two *Enterprises* into the same space, the atomic binding would probably break apart, scattering both sets of atoms all over the galaxy. Even if the bonding held, the least that would happen would be that everything aboard would instantly double in mass. Also, it's not very likely that the *Enterprise* would match each other exactly. A lot of crewmen are going to find themselves merging with equipment panels, bulkheads, and the like—with equally disastrous results.

But this need not happen. Perhaps the passage of time merely reversed itself for the *Enterprise* and crew only. This would mean that they would return to their former place in space, the starting point of three days before.

However, this would also mean that they (having reversed in time) would not remember what happened to them on Psi 2000. They would therefore go on to relive those next three days exactly as they did before, until the accident again occurs, and they are again thrown three days back in time. They would then be forced to repeat the cycle again and again, through a relative eternity, unless something happened to break it.

But since Kirk and crew do remember the events of "The Naked Time," we must assume that they appeared at a different point in space, and that they, personally, did not regress back in time. This by no means solves their problems. There are now two *Enterprises* in the universe, each identical to the other except for the point in space and time which they occupy.

In effect, the universe has made itself a mold, out of which it will continue to produce *Enterprises* until it runs out of time, matter, or energy. Seconds after "our" *Enterprise* goes back through time and appears in space, it will be followed by yet another *Enterprise*.

You see, while our *Enterprise* (let's call it *Enterprise A*) has just completed the mission to Psi 2000 and has traveled three days back in time; *Enterprise B* is at the same moment traveling to Psi 2000 to begin that mission. And as soon as *Enterprise B* completes the mission, and is thrown back through time, it will be hot on the heels of *Enterprise A*—as well as simultaneously co-existing with *Enterprise C*, which is on its way to Psi 2000 to begin its mission. And when *Enterprise C* finishes its mission, it will be thrown back through time . . . well, you get the picture. *Enterprises D, E, F,* and on far beyond the limits of our alphabet will continue to emerge from the time passage one after another, eventually filling the universe with *Enterprises* who have just completed the mission to Psi 2000, each of which is fully convinced that it is the one, the only, the original.

Or will this happen? There is a time lag of several seconds between the appearance of each additional *Enterprise*. This could crowd the *Enterprises* further and further into the future until two of them meet going in opposite directions along the time line.

God only knows what the resulting explosion would do. It might even break the cycle. Or it might start a chain reaction which would destroy all of the *Enterprises*. If the latter is true, then their troubles are certainly over.

If, however, the former is true, they still have to contend

with the problem of what to do with the remaining *Enterprises,* which would number into the hundreds, perhaps into the thousands. And this is certainly not a minor consideration.

After all, how would you like to have several thousand nearly exact duplicates of yourself running around loose? And how would anyone be able to determine which is the original *Enterprise* and crew? Each crew would believe that it was the original (it would be, but let's not get that deep; just consider the first one out of the cycle to be the "original"), so it would be a pretty problem indeed for Starfleet. They certainly can't have thousands of *Enterprises* warping around the galaxy, each representing itself to be the real McCoy (sorry).

One hell of a mess.

As everyone knows, none of these possibilities came into being at the end of "The Naked Time." Instead, the *Enterprise* simply went merrily on its way to its next mission— something it should not have been able to do. It seems obvious that the effect of having them thrown back through time was added at the last minute. Possibly to demonstrate that time travel was within the realm of the *Enterprise*'s abilities, or more likely to add some excitement to the end of a show which was, for all intents and purposes, over. What a thrill it was to watch all the pretty little chronometers go backwards while the crew bounced around the bridge!

"Tomorrow Is Yesterday" marked the second voyage of the *Enterprise* through time. This trip was considerably longer than three days, however, since the crew found themselves in the second half of the twentieth century.

It seems while returning to Earth, the *Enterprise* was caught in the gravitational pull of a black star. When they pulled away at great speed, a "slingshot effect" threw them back into time.

Winding up in Earth's atmosphere, America's radar spots them, and fighter planes are scrambled to intercept the UFO. One of the aircraft's pilots, a Captain Christopher, is beamed aboard when one of the *Enterprise*'s tractor beams accidentally destroys his ship. Kirk will not allow the hapless pilot to return to Earth, saying that Christopher's now sure knowledge of the future could eventually get into the wrong hands and possibly affect the flow of time.

This is rather puzzling on reflection. All Christopher knows about the future is that one day man will reach the stars, and that we will encounter at least one alien race, the Vulcans. How could this relatively meager knowledge of coming events ultimately affect the existence of these events? It's not as if he'd learned the results of the next Kentucky Derby, or who the next president will be.

During the course of the episode, our boys manage to shanghai an Air Force sergeant too, and finally decide that they will put the two men back on Earth where they found them.

Scotty and Spock figure out a way to recreate the accident, enabling them to return to their own time. Kirk decides that the best way to return his guests to Earth is to beam them back down as the *Enterprise* begins its journey back home. Each is to be placed exactly where and when they first found him.

There seem to be several small problems with that plan.

First, when you beam Captain Christopher back down into the cockpit of his jet, where are you going to put him? Remember, as the *Enterprise* is going back to when Christopher first saw it, there is already a Christopher in that cockpit. The Christopher beamed down by the *Enterprise* might rematerialize up to the point where the bond between atoms would shatter, but then he would merely explode.

Perhaps "merely" isn't the word to describe it, as when the atomic bonds break, all that matter would be instantly converted to energy. And when two lumps of material the size of a man are converted into energy, the resulting explosion would tear away about half the western hemisphere.

Even if this doesn't happen, even if the good Captain only becomes twice as heavy and massive as before, why should this prevent him from remembering what happened to him? And why should the *Enterprise* simply vanish from sight? They return to the future from a point well after they first encounter Christopher. Just the act of returning from the future can't wipe out those events.

If Kirk was afraid that Christopher might change the past, imagine how he must have felt about what McCoy did in "The City on the Edge of Forever."

As we all know, in "City," McCoy travels to Earth's past, where he changes history by saving the life of Edith Keeler. Kirk and Spock must repair his damage by the same method he used, traveling back through history via the Guardian of Forever.

They succeed, with both happy and tragic results.

Only one thing is wrong with this premise: Whatever McCoy does in the past can indeed change it, but not to the extent where the entire future will be changed. If he were to do that, then he would never have been born, much less made his way to the Guardian Planet on the now nonexistent *Enterprise*. Thus, how can he (who hasn't been born and can't get to the Guardian) change the past?

But he did change the past, so he must have been born, which means that the past hasn't been changed, so he can go through the Guardian and change the past. . . .

It's a never-ending circle without resolution. But it does show that the time lines would realign themselves so that McCoy could exist.

In this case, the influence of the Guardian of Forever may preclude that law. It's possible that anything within the influence of the Guardian may be immune to such changes. That would explain why Kirk and the others were unaffected when McCoy changed the past.

"Assignment: Earth" marks the next journey to the past. The *Enterprise* uses the trick of traveling towards a black star, then breaking away at tremendous speeds in order to throw itself back in time. This seems to be a rather drastic method of time travel.

For one thing, how could you be sure where you would end up? And what if you can't pull away in time? Their mission, to do historical research, hardly seems worth the risk involved. And on top of everything else, all of that lurching around must be awfully hard on ship and crew.

Though they can't manage to keep out of trouble, they do manage to keep from violating the laws of space and physics this time around.

In "All Our Yesterdays," Kirk, Spock, and McCoy are sent into the past of the planet Sarpeidon through a "time portal." Unfortunately, they have not been prepared by the atavachron, which adjusts the psychology and physiology of an individual to the particular period to which he is going. To remain in that time without being prepared is death. To leave that time having been prepared also means death. Kirk, in a period resembling seventeenth-century England, uses his quick wits and cool head to immediately have himself arrested as a witch. McCoy and Spock wind up in an ice age, where Spock develops a rather strong attachment for Zarabeth, another time traveler who saves them from frostbite.

Kirk and McCoy seem unaffected by their respective environments, but Spock is reverting to the thinking of his ancestors. Discovering that they cannot remain, they help Kirk, and all (except Zarabeth) return to the present.

But why did Spock revert back to the thinking of his ancestors? It can't be that he was somehow prepared; if that were the case, he would have died upon returning to his own time.

Possibly, he was the only one affected because of his Vulcan structure; or perhaps once he realized he was trapped in the past, he no longer felt the need to subconsciously suppress his emotions. This is supported by his statement "I am back in every way" when he returns to the present.

The final time anyone from the *Enterprise* took a journey to the past was in the animated episode "Yesteryear."

Kirk and Spock return from a historical-research mission to discover that no one has ever heard of Spock. Research shows that Spock was killed at the age of seven during a Vulcan maturity test. Spock recalls the incident, but remembers that a cousin of his had been visiting at the time and had saved him.

Using the Guardian to return to Vulcan's past, Spock discovers that he was the cousin, and sets things right with only several small details altered.

Apparently, Spock's trip with Kirk to the past of Orion prevented him from being on Vulcan at the proper time to save himself, but how and why is never explained. And when Spock and Kirk return to the present from past Orion, no one there at the Guardian remembers Spock either. McCoy and the others should have retained their memory of Spock while under the influence of the Guardian.

Strange that a series which is famous for its attention to detail should be so lax when it came to time travel. It is possible, though, to construct several rules for time travel using information provided in these episodes. When *Star Trek* returns, we can only hope that shows dealing with time travel will pay a little more attention to detail and stay within these rules.

1. One object can exist in two places at one time.

2. It is possible to alter the past, but unless there is some outside influence, such as the Guardian, the time lines will repair themselves, at least to a limited degree.

3. It is possible to travel through time by using faster than light speeds, by using the Guardian of Forever, by mixing matter and antimatter "cold," or by using a device similar to the "doorway" in "All Our Yesterdays." There are probably others which the Enterprise crew has not yet discovered.

Even though the shows mentioned contain several deviations from the rules stated above, they all remain fine examples of the imaginative world of Star Trek. We must remember that the main purpose of any television show is to tell a story and entertain. Sometimes you have to allow for poetic license.

A REBUTTAL
by Walter Irwin

As Jim Houston is one of the Trek *staff, we were all present during the development of his ideas for the preceding article, "Star Trek Time Travels." And, just like Star Trek, there was "harmonious diversity" among our staff as to the validity of some of Jim's conclusions. Normally, an editor will run an article without comment—much less rebuttal— but this is a special case, as Jim is on the* Trek *staff and is a close personal friend. So editor Walter Irwin is trying something different in beating you readers to the punch in the way of comments and disagreements with the author of an article. If you like the idea, write and let us know. And then when one of the staff's articles doesn't reflect the majority opinion of the rest of us, we will give you both sides.*

In Jim Houston's time-travel discussion, he ignores several salient points, knowledge of which leads to a reasonable explanation of the processes of time travel, and smooths away the difficulties and inconsistencies arising from that form of travel.

In "The Naked Time," Jim wonders why the *Enterprise* can travel back in time three days and then continue on as if nothing had happened. He postulates that, at best, there would be a literal plethora of *Enterprises* emerging from the "time circle."

Here he ignores the revered time-travel postulation that states that no two identical things can exist at the same time in the same place. When the *Enterprise* emerged from the time warp, it was still the same *Enterprise* which went into the warp; there cannot be nor were there two (or more) of it. And as it became the *Enterprise* of three days ago, it was the only *Enterprise* which could exist in that space and time under the laws of time travel. There are no others merging into the start of the cycle, no others emerging from it.

There is only one *Enterprise*, whenever in space or time it is. The flow of time, which Jim quotes as being enough to repair McCoy's damage in "City," simply adjusts itself to a position where there is an *Enterprise* which did not go to Psi 2000—yet did go (the crew and chronometers providing ample evidence of the journey).

The same explanation can be given for McCoy's actions in "City." He caused a history to take place in which he did not exist—yet he did, in order to have caused the change. His action was at one of the important cusps of time, where seemingly small actions may have great effects. Any one of you readers can quickly think of several more examples and there are probably thousands of them.

When an action in past time is taken, a divergent flow is caused in the time stream. This diversion causes an alternate dimension to be created, one in which certain things happened which did not happen in the "real" dimension. Real history is not changed, only the time traveler (and those involved with him, such as the crew in "City") can be affected, and now exist in the alternate dimension.

In "City," Kirk and Spock caused the divergent dimension McCoy created to be nullified, throwing all of them back into the real dimension. In "Naked Time," the opposite happened, as the *Enterprise* flew on into the divergent dimension which remained exactly the same except for the fact of the experiences of the ship and crew. Yes, there was a difference, but as Spock says, "A difference which makes no difference is no difference."

As for the Captain Christopher problem, the act of beaming him and the guard down was a changing of the time flow, creating an alternate dimension in which Christopher did not see the *Enterprise* (it was elsewhere, so could not exist within his range of vision), and the guard could not walk in on Kirk and Sulu (they were somewhere else, see?).

And as for the transporter being able to work in this fashion, it is reasonable to assume that the transporter, along with everything else, performs two necessary functions: It scans the beaming-down point to see if it is occupied by any matter. If so, the person beaming down would instantly be sent back to the ship so that he would not suffer injury. The transporter would also make a scan of the entire molecular structure of the person beaming down, so as to reassemble him properly.

So when the transporter was focused on Christopher and the guard and they were beamed down, a sort of short circuit took place in the system. The fail-safe mechanism told the transporter that the space was already occupied, while the molecular scan told the transporter that the person beaming down was already there. Since they were already there, they could not materialize. Yet they could not return to the ship because they had already "beamed down." So they just disappeared. They didn't die in the normal sense, as they still existed on Earth. It was just a mechanical way of creating a divergent dimension for each of the men, one in which their stay on the *Enterprise* never happened.

A divergent dimension also explains why Spock "died" and had to go save himself. In the real dimension, Spock did not travel back to Vulcan; it was not necessary. In the alternate dimension, he did not travel back and died. In the third, he did travel back, but his pet died. So again, we have a case where the crew (and the historians present) continued their existence in an alternate dimension, but again, it made no difference.

As to those around the Guardian not remembering Spock, this was obviously a slip-up on the story writer's part or intentionally done to heighten the suspense. Also, Spock seemingly violated the rule that no two persons can exist in the same place at the same time by meeting his boyhood self. However, it is ridiculous to assume that two people are the same when separated by over thirty years. The child Spock bore no relation to the adult Spock, save in the memories of the adult.

So in this author's opinion, Jim's rules must be amended to read:

1. No object or person can exist in two places at the same time.

2. When time is changed, an alternate dimension is created, but the original still exists and a series of corrective procedures can get the traveler and those involved with him back into the proper dimension.

3. Remains the same, except that the transporter can be used in certain circumstances to change the time dimension of individuals when the ship is traveling through time.

26. A SAMPLING OF TREK TRIVIA

Whenever two or more Star Trek fans get together, inevitably they will start to play Star Trek trivia. It is the single most popular word game played by ST fans, and entire books have been published on the subject, both by fans and even by Signet in their very successful The Trekkie Trivia Quiz Book. *And just about every Star Trek magazine has a trivia section—including ours. We publish "Trek Trivia" whenever we have the space, as it is both a popular feature with readers and fun for us to create as well. As a rule, our questions are a bit easier than most, as we have such a mixed audience, but we occasionally slip in a real puzzler for the more adroit fans. We only have room for a few questions in this collection, but we think they will give you a good idea of how much fun playing "Trek Trivia" can be!*

QUESTIONS

1. What is Charlie X's real name?
2. What is the name of the ship Charlie X destroys?
3. What does Charlie X cause to disappear that destroys this ship?
4. In "Elaan of Troyius," name the Troyian who betrays the *Enterprise* to the Klingons.
5. What was the name of Captain Merik's vessel in "Bread and Circuses?"
6. What substance reverses the aging disease?
7. What is the name of Harry Mudd's wife?
8. What part of the tractor does the Horta steal in "Devil in the Dark"?
9. What is the name of the Federation ambassador to Eminar VII?
10. What is the name of the planet Eminar VII is at war with?

11. Name the two episodes that feature Bruce Hyde as Lieutenant Kevin Riley.

12. What stolen object threatens to set off a holy war in "Jihad"?

13. Who is the traitor in "Jihad"?

14. Name the shuttlecraft used in "Slaver Weapon."

15. How do you find a stasis box?

16. What eats Tribbles?

17. What is Spock's home town on Vulcan?

18. Name the Capellian who leads a revolution to become Teer.

19. What is the secret of the evil Kirk in "Mirror, Mirror"?

20. Who commands the Fesarius?

21. What is the true secret of corbomite?

22. What is "Jack the Ripper" in "Wolf in the Fold"?

23. Who does Kirk wrest the title of medicine chief from in "The Paradise Syndrome"?

24. What substance gives the Platonians their powers in "Plato's Stepchildren"?

25. What planet does Ari bn Bem hail from?

Match each famous science fiction author with the story he wrote for Star Trek:

1. Frederic Brown   A. "Mirror, Mirror"
2. Jerry Sohl   B. "Catspaw"
3. Richard Matheson   C. "The Corbomite Maneuver"
4. Jerome Bixby   D. "Arena"
5. Robert Bloch   E. "The Enemy Within"

Match each planet with the episode it appears in.

1. "The Apple"   A. Gamma Hydra IV
2. "Obsession"   B. Iotia
3. "The Deadly Years"   C. Cheron
4. "Wolf in the Fold"   D. Arret
5. "A Piece of the Action"   E. Gamma Traianguli VI
6. "Patterns of Force"   F. Argelius II
7. "Return to Tomorrow"   G. Tycho IV
8. "The Omega Glory"   H. Mantilles
9. "Let That Be Your Last   I. Omega IV
   Battlefield"
10. "One of Our Planets Is   J. Zeon
    Missing"

Unscramble these episode titles:
1. DDOGHA RT EGE FIMN
2. CFE NHKNCNHOIG TT SEI COEE
3. TORONLF AE BACRER
4. NTI KHDEM ETAÉ
5. WRU TTTILH ERHB OBBLSIEE
6. ULNN ANOP O ECTAPE
7. POSDS MAIUDNS
8. OSTE YRHW DDSOGOM
9. ADFRCN RE NREOY
10. SUF GOHIRT ST HOEOEO

ANSWERS

1. Evans 2. Antarees 3. A reactor babble plate 4. Dryton 5. The S.S. Beagle 6. Adrenalin 7. Stella 8. The reactor pump 9. Robert Fox 10. Vendikar 11. The Naked Time, Conscience of the King 12. The Soul of Skorr 13. Tchar, Prince of Skorr 14. Copernicus 15. With another stasis box 16. Glommers 17. Shi Kahr 18. Maab 19. The Tantalas Field 20. Balok 21. That it doesn't exist 22. A Phantom entity that feeds on fear. 23. Salish 24. Kironide 25. Pandro

Matching Authors:
1.D 2.C 3.E 4.A 5.B

Planets:
1.E 2.G 3.A 4.F 5.B 6.J 7.D 8.I 9.C 10.H

Scramble:
1. Dagger of the Mind 2. The Conscience of the King 3. Balance of Terror 4. The Naked Times 5. The Trouble with Tribbles 6. Once Upon a Planet 7. Mudd's Passion 8. Whom The Gods Destory 9. Errand of Mercy 10. The Squire of Gothos

MORE TREK TRIVIA

QUESTIONS
1. Name the first ship to visit Iotia.
2. How long ago did they leave?
3. Why was the game Fizzbin invented?
4. What is Kirk's nickname for Spock?
5. What are the names of the two most powerful Bosses on Iotia?
6. What is the name of the book that the Iotians have modeled their rather peculiar culture after?

7. How many times are Kirk and Spock captured in this episode?
8. What does McCoy leave behind that may change the whole of Iotian culture?
9. What is Iotian slang for "phaser"?
10. What finally convinces the Iotians that Kirk means business?
11. Why was the *Galileo* transporting Nancy Hedford to the *Enterprise?*
12. What accomplishment was Zefrem Cochrane famous for?
13. What crisis was Nancy Hedford attempting to solve?
14. Why does the Companion want to keep Zefrem trapped on the asteroid?
15. Why are the *Enterprise* crewmembers held?
16. What is Zefrem Cochrane's true age?
17. Why has he remained young?
18. How does the Companion save Nancy's life?
19. Why does the Companion do this?
20. Why does Zefrem decide to remain on the asteroid?

ANSWERS

1. U.S.S. *Horizon*
2. 100 years
3. To help him escape from kidnappers
4. Spock-o
5. Bela Oxmyx and Jojo Krako
6. *Chicago Mobs of the Twenties*
7. Four
8. His communicator
9. "Fancy Heater"
10. Kirk has the *Enterprise* phasers stun a block full of Iotians
11. To treat her for a major illness
12. He invented the warp drive
13. To prevent a war on Epsilon Canaris III
14. Because she loves him
15. To keep Zefrem company
16. 237
17. The Companion prevents his aging
18. By merging with her body
19. So that Zefrem will love her
20. Because he now loves the Companion, who cannot leave the asteroid for more than a few days.

27. AN EVENING WITH
LEONARD NIMOY
by James Van Hise

*As with the report on Gene Roddenberry's talk, this article
was originally published in 1974. The same reasons for the
validity of its publication still hold; however, in this instance
there is an added element to consider. And in a way, it is a
sad one. At the time this article was written, Leonard Nimoy
could still appear in public without literally fearing for his
life and safety at the hands of overenthusiastic fans. And the
freewheeling type of discussion and give-and-take which appears in this article between Leonard and the fans may never
come about again. As this is one of the very last pieces published before the advent of the "big con" and the subsequent
difficulties of personal contact between stars and fans, it is
an invaluable look at how Leonard Nimoy and his admirers
were once able to meet on a common ground. It may never
happen again.*

When Leonard Nimoy appeared at Palm Beach Junior
College to give a talk, I wondered just what he would really
be like. There have been many conflicting stories about how
he looks back on Star Trek and his role of Mr. Spock, although all sources have always credited him with being a
very personable and friendly individual. Nor were they
wrong.

When Leonard first appeared on the stage he was smiling
and holding up his right hand with fingers spread in the
Vulcan peace sign. He was greeted with thunderous applause from the packed, standing-room-only auditorium, and
he set the relaxed atmosphere of the evening in responding
to the ovation by saying, "You humans have really got to
learn to control your emotions."

Leonard is a very articulate and interesting individual who is involved in many ideas beyond the sphere of theatrics.

He began his informal talk by discussing the science fiction society we live in. How things we take for granted were science fiction fifty years ago.

To give examples, he read and discussed headlines from a newspaper he had picked up at the airport. He pointed to a headline and said, "Look—here's an article about the energy crisis, the biggest science fiction story of the century."

Another article he pointed out concerned a scientist who had been developing anti-aggression pills to prevent national leaders from abusing their powers. "A good science fiction writer," he remarked, "could pick that up and really make a great episode of Star Trek. Who says Star Trek is unbelievable?"

On the subject of Star Trek, he discussed what it was like playing Mr. Spock five days a week, twelve hours a day. "All week long I'd have to think like Mr. Spock and talk like Mr. Spock. When the weekend came, it would take me until Sunday to start thinking like I used to think, and talking like I used to talk. I think that philosophically I was affected by the character of Mr. Spock. I think from playing Spock I learned how to think more rationally and logically in my own life."

When asked if Star Trek would ever return, he stated, "I'd say the odds are 76.24 to one against. Paramount is afraid that a new series would severely reduce the profitable syndication of the reruns. There was more than one time, though, when I was sure that it would return as the studio had contacted me to see if I would be available."

Although he said that NBC was trying to get Star Trek back on the air, he said of the network: "I don't think they really understood it. I don't think they really understood what the market was for the show. They did not think it interesting or worthwhile to have a lead character with pointed ears. NBC underestimated the potential of Star Trek all along. Last week I was at the Star Trek convention in New York. Fifteen thousand fans turned out. NBC was there to cover the event, and I'm sure they are aware of it now."

On the animated Star Trek show, Nimoy said that he'd done sixteen episodes and doubted that it would be renewed.

While discussing science fiction, he mentioned that he didn't care for the nuts-and-bolts type of SF; the type which described all sorts of rockets and gadgets and explained how they worked.

One fan remarked, "Like *Zombies of the Stratosphere?*"

Leonard cringed. He turned his face partially aside with a grin expressing both humor and embarrassment. Turning back to the audience, he said, "What he was talking about is that in the 1950s I made a serial called *Zombies of the Stratosphere*. You must forgive me, I needed the money."

Leonard mentioned that since anyone who appears on a tour usually has something to plug, he'd brought his book, *You and I*, with him.

The book is poetry written over the years on his evolving feelings about love. It's illustrated with various photographs he's taken over the years as well.

He said that he really hadn't expected anything to come of it, so he took it to a small publisher in California, one which specializes in print runs of only a few thousand. That publisher in turn sold the paperback rights to Avon, and his book has already sold over 300,000 paperback copies.

The passage he read from was so hauntingly beautiful that the entire audience was rapt with attention. I usually don't care that much for poetry, but this was good.

It was very probing, very emotive, showing a facet of him that one is seldom in touch with because it is so much inside, in his thoughts and his feelings. It revealed a whole new side of Leonard Nimoy as a person and a talent.

That is one thing about Leonard that few people seem to understand. Leonard Nimoy is talented. His characterization of Mr. Spock brought him recognition, but that is not the only reason he is admired.

Leonard's talents include singing, as he proved with some very well-done songs on his albums; and writing, as he has proved in his books.

The press fosters this tunnel vision of him as well by invariably making Mr. Spock jokes in every article they do on him. This is the same press mentality which spawned the word "Trekkie," and don't think they meant it to sound any more complimentary than it does. This typical newspaper mentality reared its obnoxious head at the press conference prior to his talk.

Area fan Joyce Huser, who is a fine artist as well as a member of Star Trek Fans United, was talking with Leonard when a writer by the name of Tom Van Howe (of the Palm

Beach edition of the Miami *Herald*) walked up to them, and barging into their conversation, asked Joyce if she was a Trekkie, and if Leonard Nimoy was her idol. Joyce felt about two inches tall, as Leonard was still standing there next to her.

She managed to recover her composure, though, and put the reporter in his place by stating that she didn't think she'd qualify for his definition of a Trekkie since her club didn't have a mob of fans waiting to meet Nimoy at the airport; and her admiration for Leonard Nimoy was not just based on Star Trek, as he had also done many plays, and was an accomplished singer and writer. The reporter didn't know what to say.

Leonard congratulated Joyce on her response to the reporter. He understood the situation all too well.

Not to be stymied, said reporter went on to do an all too typical article that appeared the following day and began, "Sorry to have to break the news, Trekkies—but Mr. Spock doesn't really have pointed ears." Some people never learn.

A week later I met another reporter from the same paper, and I discussed the very low image of his readers that Van Howe projected in that article and in others I'd seen by him.

The other article that appeared on Leonard's talk was much better, but it centered solely on Star Trek and ignored the many other things that he had discussed.

Many of the subjects that Leonard covered were topics that he finds particularly fascinating.

One such discussion concerned plants. This was just not a simple horticultural interest, but rather one which delved into the recent scientific tests and discoveries that bear out some long unproved theories: that plants not only react to human emotions but have emotions themselves!

The specific studies about which he talked at length were those conducted by Cleve Backster in 1966. Backster is one of America's foremost lie-detector experts, and as Leonard put it, his experiments began like this: "One day he was in his office and he decided just for the heck of it to see what the polygraph would register if he attached the electrodes to the plant on his desk. He was astonished to discover that it gave off a pattern that was very close to that of a human under emotional stimulation."

Backster further experimented by first dropping brine shrimp and then other simple animals into boiling water in the presence of the plants. The polygraph registered a very violent reaction in each case as if some sort of extrasensory broadcast was being transmitted to the plants by the dying cells communicating danger. Thus Backster concluded that, like animals, plants stake out a territory and react to phenomena occurring in that immediate vicinity. Backster even concluded that plants develop relationships with their masters.

He tested this with automated equipment and synchronized stopwatch, leaving the plants and keeping notes of the times certain things occurred to him, when he felt certain emotions, as well as the time when he decided to return to the laboratory from fifteen miles distant. The plants registered specific reactions at all these junctures, thus showing that they had an extrasensory link with their master!

Leonard was obviously very excited by these discoveries because of the whole new vistas of science they had opened up to exploration, especially those which demonstrated positive extrasensory links.

Leonard also brought up the subject of UFOs. To lead into it, he read a quote which was quite obviously a description of an extraterrestrial vehicle from which beings disembarked. Most people recognized it as the much publicized section of the book Ezekiel from the Bible.

Leonard said that he does indeed believe in UFOs, and mentioned that the methods that UFOs employ are quite similar to those our astronauts would use should they reach an alien, but inhabited world: to avoid mass observation and study the planet and its inhabitants in order to learn as much as possible before attempting any sort of contact with them.

Leonard discussed other subjects as well, every once in a while returning to Star Trek when some aspect of his talk touched on it to some degree. He mentioned in passing that although Star Trek opened many doors for him, it also cost him jobs as some directors feel that he is typecast as Spock. But that hasn't been that much of a problem as he now gets enough offers so he can pick out what he wants to do.

Leonard's talk was one stop of a ten-day tour of colleges around the country, and those of us who were there that night undoubtedly saw more of him than any of the fans who have seen him at any of the major Star Trek conventions were able to. Aren't we glad we did!

28. STAR TREK MINIATURES: THE OTHER SPACESHIPS
by Richard Van Treuren

Following the enthusiastic response to Richard's Starship Enterprise *miniature article, we asked him to do a follow-up covering the other Federation and alien vessels that appeared on Star Trek. He responded with this article, which is just as entertaining and maybe even more informative than the previous one. One fan singled out Richard's efforts when he stated that* Trek *had told him more about Star Trek in four issues than he had been able to learn on his own in ten years! As of this writing, Richard's work hasn't appeared in* Trek *again, but we are constantly making efforts to have him do another of his excellent articles. And with a new Star Trek in the works, well . . .*

The sale of Star Trek to the network in May 1966 found the production crew with but one spaceship chiseled out in miniature, and the first production episode calling for another vessel.

How does one go about designing an alien craft when the possibilities are limited to what can be practically assembled, illuminated, and properly photographed? Many video science fiction projects have solved the problem by using a point of light; using the viable arguments of visibility vs. speed, distance, reflectivity, and so on. Had it not been overworked, a light ball would have been an acceptable way of leaving the design up to the viewer, à la old radio shows.

As called for in "The Corbomite Maneuver," the First Federation Flagship *Fesarius* would be too important to pass off. A miniature said to have been made of Ping-Pong balls and the like was created, achieving an excellent vague and indefinite appearance. Coupled with striking optical effects and good music, the ship made the first episode click.

The next show, the best example of the near anthology the series was actually supposed to be, called for a "small Class J cargo ship." This was an excellent opportunity to use the license number prefix hastily added to the nacelles of the *Enterprise*, but since it was not a key element, the point-of-light idea was substituted. "Charlie X" afforded the opportunity of seeing both a Federation and an alien craft, but again these nonessential items were deleted.

The Romulan spaceship for "Balance of Terror" was the focal point of the episode. A well-detailed miniature about a yard across was assembled and the photography was accomplished at Film Effects in Hollywood. Detailed photographs of this ship are rare, and those available somehow contradict themselves. What happened to the model is a mystery. Stock footage was later used in "The Deadly Years," but the terrible weapon of the Romulans had lost its destructive power.

Roddenberry's first Star Trek concepts called for a small "shuttle rocket," the obvious way of transporting people from an orbiting ship to the surface. Considerable thought went into the project, even to a docking sequence being planned; the lack of funds forced the magic transporter machine instead.

A hangar bay was still planned in the ship when the show finally sold, and the models were so modified as it entered production. Money for the shuttle was not available until the second half of the first year.

The final shuttle design reflected the use of optical effects rather than miniature stages, since it had but three windows; some have compared the design to a butter dish. A foot-long miniature was constructed, along with a miniature hangar deck on the same scale.

The most imposing creation ever made for the series was hammered out in September 1966, and was a full-size shuttlecraft mockup constructed of plywood, pine, Masonite, and steel.

Although it contained several chairs for the actors to sit in while awaiting their cues, the interior possessed little more than the bulky framework which allowed the top parts of the door to slide in and back. The door mechanism was operated with a single handle from the inside, about where the red "fuel modulator" panel can be seen from the port side.

The rear strut, modified from an aircraft nosegear, could be swung up and the entire craft tilted up and pushed about on two removable steel wheels mounted just aft of the jack pads. The mockup was finished on both sides, but the starboard side was never seen on the screen.

The shuttlecraft interior set was built about one-third larger to allow headroom and free movement; the complicated door movement was not duplicated. Unfortunately, actors were directed to enter and exit from the rear of the ship, where no door had ever been planned in the mockup. (A door-opening-and-closing effect was added in spite of this fact!)

The set, like the starship interior sets, was changed whenever and however a script demanded. The craft was seen a couple of times each season, although the series eventually disagreed with itself about how many shuttlecraft were carried on each starship.

"The Alternative Factor" called for a space-time ship, but since no spaceflight scenes were desired, a miniature was not created. The full-size mockup was hauled out on location and also filmed on a stage, but was never seen again. The top plastic bubble was resurrected to become the case for the brainy gamblers of "The Gamesters of Triskelion."

The Gorns of "Arena" were left shipless. But late in the production year, "Space Seed" was accepted and an old *Enterprise* design was finalized to make the DY-100 Class sleeper ship. The resulting miniature, about four feet long, was not lighted but was very well detailed.

This is a good example of how an art director can develop an excellent design, the crew can produce a striking miniature, and still the whole thing can go unnoticed. So little good footage of the model was included in the final cut that it came off as a simple redressing of a submarine. A halfway plausible explanation was dreamt up to explain why stock footage of the ship was included in the second season's "The Ultimate Computer."

Though introduced in that year, the Klingons were left shipless, even though "Errand of Mercy" called for a battle between two space fleets.

Discounting the questionable fiberglass-looking cigar that went about devouring planets in "The Doomsday Machine," ship miniatures went the way of the magnificent matte paintings during the second year—someone decided that none were necessary.

Focusing on the (in)famous second-season show "The Trouble with Tribbles," there were two ships called for, Cyrano Jones' scout ship and a Klingon ship. The author, David Gerrold, mentioned in a book he later wrote that his agent recommended that he leave out anything that would force the studio to build expensive miniatures. Oddly enough, the only model made that year was that show's K-7 space station, seen again later in the season.

The miniature situation got off to a good start in the third year even before production started. Walter M. Jefferies designed the new Klingon ship, and an excellent twenty-nine-inch miniature was made of balsa wood and plastic.

It was given long exposure in the second episode made that year, and AMT Modeling Corporation bought the rights to manufacture a model kit version. The kit was actually tooled from the professional miniature and remains the most accurate Star Trek kit any company has ever made. The kit was on the stands before the ship was even seen on television.

As with other show elements, the Klingon ship was used to return more on its investment by inventing a truce between Romulans and Klingons. Unfortunately, NBC decided to air "The *Enterprise* Incident" right after the season premiere, so when the Klingon ship was first seen by the viewing public, it was not manned by Klingons! When the Klingons finally did appear, they did not have the Romulans' invisibility cloak. Much to the chagrin of AMT, the ship appeared only briefly in one more episode. The kit did not sell.

If the same effect of alien vagueness used for the *Fesarius* was supposed to be seen in the ion-powered ship in "Spock's Brain," it failed as miserably as did the episode as a whole.

The excellent show "The Tholian Web" featured a clever little miniature made out of balsa and plastic, decorated with the same stick-on reflective metal fabric seen on many of the hand props. This same model had pieces added to it to simulate the *Aurora* in "The Way to Eden."

Things were really going downhill by the time that "Let This Be Your Last Battlefield" was produced. The script called for two ships. The final cut shouted cheapness, since one ship was simply invisible, while the other was only stock footage from "The *Galileo* Seven."

Upon cancellation, Paramount elected to get rid of as much Star Trek material as possible. The shuttlecraft mockup was donated to a local chapter of the foundation for the blind. The shuttle miniature and Romulan miniature were lost, but Roddenberry managed to hang on to the yard-long *Enterprise*, and Jefferies got the Klingon ship.

While a Japanese company had made miniatures in kit form while Star Trek was run there, nothing other than the starship was manufactured. Aurora Plastics of the United Kingdom manufactured a kit of the most popular character, Mr. Spock.

As the years passed, Star Trek gained popularity in syndication and AMT gambled that an updated version of the Klingon ship kit would sell. They retouched out the attention-grabbing planet from the box illustration and re-released the kit with the words "as seen on NBC-TV" removed.

In a tool-trading deal, they got rights to manufacture the Spock kit in this country. It was packaged in a box of AMT's design and offered with the two older kits in the 1973 AMT catalog.

As the program moved into the animated format, AMT finally decided to manufacture a shuttlecraft kit, in spite of the fact that the shuttlecraft had been changed in the cartoon. Unhappily, the people who worked with Jefferies on the earlier kit were not involved.

At the same time, they decided to make a kit of the hand props, which were about equally accurate. AMT artist Steve Wlanzo did a fair rendering of the shuttlecraft for the box cover, while the illustration (and kit) of the hand props was done with a strong influence from the animated series by one Judy Savic. AMT's 1974 catalog offered the two new kits along with the older three.

With the number of suitable subjects diminishing, the next logical choice for a kit was the Romulan ship. In an honest effort to gain information on this elusive design, AMT's model development staff, headed by Richard L. Wardorf, dug into available sources, including this writer's collection. The wooden tool-cutting miniatures were finished in the fall of 1974.

In October 1974 a new dimension was added to Star Trek modeling when Estes Industries, the largest model rocket firm in the world, acquired the rights to manufacture flying rockets in the shape of the show's spaceships.

This writer was interrogated for two days by Wayne Kellner and the model development staff out in Penrose, Colorado. After almost a year of development, flying kits of the *Enterprise* and Klingon ships were introduced in the spring of 1975.

The Smithsonian Institution expressed a desire to obtain a representative collection of science-fiction-oriented models in 1974. Jefferies was kind enough to donate the Klingon ship, and others, including myself, donated miniatures.

AMT revised their boxing size and released new versions of their old kits as they introduced the new Romulan "Bird of Prey." The finished kit shows the less than rabid desire for quality on their part. Like almost everything associated with the program of late, it sold in great numbers, giving birth to yet another kit, the K-7 space station, which was released in the spring of 1976.

If one desires to build accurate versions of the show miniatures with these kits, the best idea is to study available film clippings and publicity pictures. The Klingon kit is nearly correct as it comes in the box; a few decals from the Estes kit can be used to make it perfect.

The Romulan ship is not shaped correctly, and pictures of it are rare. If desired, an accurate version can be built by discarding the oversized fin and making one out of sheet plastic.

Add material to ship's rear and cut severely forward, matching the fin's angle. Discard the incorrect nacelle caps and simply round off what remains. Small eyelets should be added to the front to simulate the surface detail; a chip of balsa can be shaped to form the nose piece.

Remember that available plans are based on extrapolation rather than examination of actual miniatures. Also bear in mind that heated tools can be used to create damage and other effects.

Let's hope that the new Star Trek, whether it be the movie or a new series, is made with some new spaceship miniatures and that model companies make accurate kit versions of them.

29. STAR TREK MYSTERIES—SOLVED!
by Leslie Thompson

One of the favorite pastimes for Star Trek fans is to sit down and play "knowledge" games with one another. Trivia is probably the most popular of these, but many fans also like to speculate on the "why" of many facets of the series— especially those which the scriptwriters left vague or unexplained. Leslie Thompson summed up the feelings of many of these fans when she said that those loose ends were "quite annoying." It was an understatement if we ever heard one, so we asked Leslie to do an article mentioning some of the more bothersome ones. "Wouldn't it be better," she answered, "if they were explained too?" And coincidentally enough, Leslie just happened to have some explanations handy for some of those questions. Leslie has told us that this article was one of the most fun to write she's ever done, and our readers told us that it was one of the most fun to read. We think you'll agree.

Did you ever find yourself rising from your fifth, sixth, or even twentieth viewing of a Star Trek episode with the vague feeling that you've missed something, or that something about the show wasn't quite explained? This has happened to me several times, and if you are as much of a stickler for accuracy and explanations as I am, then it drives you just crazy. So you run to your Concordance and your zines and your correspondence. You search and search, but nowhere can you find the answer to what is bothering you. And when you are just about to scream, you do one of two things:

You rush to your typewriter and write your own story tying up all the loose ends of that blankety-blank episode.

Or you sit down and logically find a way to fit the inconsistency into the framework of the episode, so that it changes nothing but still makes things nice and neat, and satisfies your aesthetic sense. Until next time, that is.

The sheer volume and necessary speed with which the episodes were filmed are the major cause of inconsistencies in character and plot in any television program; and it is primarily due to the superb efforts of Gene Roddenberry and his staff that more of them didn't occur in the entirely new universe they had to create and work with each week. However, many of these "What the?" clinkers showed up in individual shows, and they are the ones that drive a person crazy. And once you think about it, a small and seemingly simple unexplained occurrence could conceivably affect the direction of the series much later in its run.

Here at *Trek*, whenever we get a few minutes to spare (which isn't often), we like to challenge each other to come up with an explanation for one of these inconsistencies. We think it is a much more enjoyable pastime than trivia, since it involves not only a working knowledge of the show but also exercises the creative juices. And let me tell you, as the game goes on, the questions posed get harder and harder! Because we have so much fun with this, and because I receive an occasional letter asking me about one of these bloopers, the editors have asked me to tell you about some of our favorites in this article. Some of these have probably already popped up in your thoughts and discussions about Star Trek, so let us know if your explanation differs from ours.

In "Where No Man Has Gone Before," the plot revolves around Lieutenant Commander Gary Mitchell, who receives psychic powers from the radiation at the edge of the galaxy and then threatens the ship. But even more important to the drama of the plot is the fact that he is Kirk's best friend and holds a high position aboard the *Enterprise*. The nagging point is: Just what position did Gary Mitchell hold?

Well, we are told in the script that Mitchell is chief navigator, that his rank is lieutenant commander, and that Kirk asked for him on his first command. But he is also one of the few people who call Kirk "Jim" in front of fellow officers, and his rank is the same as that of Mr. Spock (who was still a lieutenant commander at the time of WNMHGB). So now the question boils down to: Who was Kirk's second in command at this time? Was it Gary Mitchell or Spock?

Answer: Gary Mitchell.

Look at the facts. Mitchell and Spock both had the same rank, and both served as chiefs of their respective sections. However, Spock has mentioned many times that he has no desire to command, whereas the outgoing Mitchell would certainly long to captain his own ship. Too, Mitchell was Kirk's best friend. Even in our services today, a ship's captain is given a certain amount of freedom in choosing his executive officer, if the person he wants has the necessary experience and rank. And this would be even more true in Starfleet, where things are a bit more casual, and the autonomy that a starship captain has can only be enhanced by his having a first officer whom he can both trust and get along with. Given this, Kirk would have definitely chosen Mitchell to be his second in command.

Spock may have had more seniority than Mitchell, even with their equal rank. However, in the military world this does not always bring power or position. Scotty was also a lieutenant commander at that time and remained so, while Spock did not become a full commander until after the events of WNMHGB. It makes sense that he would be promoted after assuming the duties of second in command left vacant by Mitchell's death, as the position of science officer is much more of a "full-time job" than chief navigator. Spock received a higher rank commensurate with his increased responsibilities.

One more bit of evidence: Kirk did not become good friends with Spock until Spock became his second officer. It follows that the increased time he would have to spend with Spock after he gained his promotion would form a bond between them; one which did not begin to grow when Mitchell was alive, and had both the second command and Kirk's best-friendship.

There you have it. An explanation which is logical in light of all the given information, that remains true to the series concept, and even manages to heighten the dramatic conflict of the show.

That's really the trick in forming your own hypothesis for an inconsistency in any episode; they have to fit, and fit well. If the reasoning doesn't fit into the framework of the events as given, then it cannot apply no matter how logical or detailed it may be.

For example: Sulu was ship's physicist-astrobiologist in the second pilot. Why? A case can be made stating that he felt himself uncomfortable in this position; that he was needed more at the helm; that he was rewarded with a more responsible position because of some heroics; and so on. All very logical and well thought out. But it ignores one fact about Starfleet officers: They serve in every section of the ship in order to gain the necessary experience for command. Therefore, it is much more logical and in keeping with the framework of the series to simply assume Sulu was taking a short term of duty in the physics section during the events of WNMHGB.

So it gets tougher. But even more difficult is extrapolating past events with the given information of the series. Whenever you give a reason why one of the Star Trek characters did something in the past, you must make his action fit logically with his present character. Let's look at one of the most-often-discussed problems: Why does Mr. Spock smile and show other emotions during the events of "The Menagerie"?

Knowing as we do the traumas which Spock suffered in his early life and the social stresses he went through daily on Vulcan, it is easy to understand why he chose to leave the planet and join Starfleet. But we are also told (by Spock himself and by his mother) that Spock considers himself a Vulcan. So why then would he abandon his training as a Vulcan and show any amount of emotion, for any reason?

He had a very good reason, indeed. He was exploring the human side of himself, its capabilities and its responsibilities.

Remember that Spock was still rather young during his service with Captain Pike. It follows that his rise through Starfleet was a rather rapid one; a supposition which his great intelligence and native courage would help to enforce. And his close experience with humans would have been stilted, since to move so quickly through the ranks, he would have had to spend almost all of his time working and studying.

But once he had attained a position of fairly high rank and responsibility, Spock would begin to have enough time on his hands to do some introspective thinking. His career, up to this point, had provided challenge and satisfaction enough, but he still was not content. The ever-logical Spock would decide that if living the life of a Vulcan did not make him happy, then he should try living the life of a human for a while.

Luckily, in Christopher Pike, Spock had a commander that he both had great respect and affection for (later events prove this beyond a shadow of a doubt). Planning to change his lifestyle would naturally be embarrassing to Spock, but he instinctively knew that Pike would understand the change and not make an issue of it. So he proceeded to "emotionalize."

He was not successful. We obviously know this from the Spock of today, but it is also evident in the small bit of him we have seen from that time in "The Menagerie."

The emotions which Spock displays (most notably the smiling at the vibrating alien plant, and the shout of "The women!" when they transport down without him) seem to be very forced, almost as if he were acting out the way he should feel in these situations.

Spock can experience emotions, as we know, but they have to be very strong and sudden to overcome the training he received for suppressing them. And when he tried to act human he found his training too strong. He had to battle not to suppress emotion but to show it, and this created a half-hearted, strained effect.

So that mystery is solved. Spock was merely experimenting. It was not successful, and the question remains open as to how long he attempted it, and what effect it had on his personality. However, that is something that requires yet another bit of theorizing. Try it yourself.

And speaking of "The Menagerie," why do the enigmatic Number One and our own Christine Chapel resemble each other so closely? (Majel Barrett played both parts, of course, but we're speculating on the Star Trek universe here.)

This is really easy. They are sisters. An explanation which needs no involved reasoning but still satisfies all of the requirements to fit into the established format of the show.

An interesting case could be made as to why they are so different, and what were the causes of Number One's "cold-fish" personality. However, there is not enough information available on either of the women to begin to speculate. A shame, since both are such potentially exciting character studies.

Once in a while there is something which is of primary importance to the believability of an episode and that doesn't quite jibe with the established facts of the series. It is then the job of the person offering the explanation to form one which does not invalidate the events of the episode, while still having a logical basis which fits into the framework of the series.

A perfect example of this is in "Turnabout Intruder," where the psychosis of Janice Lester is based on the refusal of Starfleet Command to consider women qualified as starship captains. But the series format has established the full equality of the sexes and has shown women acting in almost every position. How can this discrepancy be explained without wrecking the entire story line of "Turnabout Intruder"?

Janice Lester is mentally ill, and has been so for some time. Her irrational actions and beliefs drive her and Kirk apart, and that separation causes yet more damage to her mind.

Now no responsible service in the universe is going to allow a mentally disturbed person to rise to a position of responsibility if it can be prevented, and the difficult Starfleet is no exception. So there is little question that Lester was either refused admittance to the Academy or removed from it when her aberration was discovered. And in her twisted way, she would have perceived this not as a protective measure but as persecution of herself by the powers-that-be.

Like most psychotics, Janice would have been unable to recognize her own illness, so she would have to rationalize her dismissal by pinning the cause on something else. The most obvious choice was her sex.

When Kirk, refusing to abandon his own goals and dreams, did not also quit the Academy, Janice began to see him as being involved in the "conspiracy" against her and all women. Of course, this led directly to the breakup of an already stormy relationship.

Once again, in her mind abandoned, Janice soon enlarged her hatred of Starfleet to encompass Kirk, all other men, and eventually her own sex. She was hated, she felt, simply because she was a woman. So she, too, hated women, and her burning life's ambition became the desire to be not only a starship captain but a man as well.

So Janice Lester's contention that women could not be starship captains was only in her mind, fueled by the rejection and inadequacies of her life. And since it was a mistaken belief, the events of "Turnabout Intruder" can go on logically and well within the established framework of the series.

So, as you can see, all it takes is a little imagination and a working knowledge of the Star Trek universe to fill in those irritating gaps left by lazy scriptwriters and rushed production.

Solving the many Star Trek Mysteries is fun, but only one person can solve the greatest mystery of them all: Why isn't Star Trek back now? So how about it, Gene?

30. HOW THE TIME WARP DRIVE WORKS
by Mark Andrew Golding

Mark Golding's article on the space warps which the Enterprise *utilizes to travel vast distances through space drew such a great number of comments that we asked him to do a follow up giving his explanation of how the warp engines themselves work. As usual, Mark responded with a superbly thought-out and detailed article, which is firmly based in both known and projected scientific fact. Mark is planning an entire series of these articles which will explain the technology of the Star Trek universe (most of which we hope will be published in* Trek), *and when completed, it will be the most ambitious and comprehensive look at the physics, mechanics, and esoterica of the Star Trek universe ever written.*

When I first saw the Star Trek episode "The Changeling," I was struck by what seemed a colossal scientific blunder—one which, no doubt, any Star Trek fan interested in science has wondered about.

As we all know, a given warp speed equals the speed of light times the warp factor cubed. When the *Enterprise* detected energy bolts headed for it at warp 15 (equal to $15 \times 15 \times 15$ times light speed), the alien vessel was reported to be about 90,000 kilometers away.

Since the speed of light is 183,000 miles per second, or 299,793 kilometers per second, and warp 15 equals 3,375 times the speed of light, the time it took the energy bolts fired by Nomad to reach the *Enterprise* should have been only 90,000 divided by 299,793, and then divided by 3,375, or 0.0000889 second.

Instead, the bolts took several seconds to reach the *Enterprise*. If memory serves me right, the energy bolt which was fired at the moment closest to the one in which Nomad's distance was said to be 90,000 kilometers took about five seconds to reach the *Enterprise*.

That, of course, is thousands of times as long as it should have taken—56,242.969 times to be precise. Considering the probable inaccuracies, it would be safer to say within the range of 45,000 to 67,000 times as long as it should have taken.

In "The Menagerie," when the crew of the *Enterprise* had found what seemed to be the crew of the U.S.S. *Columbia* (which had crashed on Talos IV, thirty-one years before the time of most Star Trek voyages), one of the crewmembers told the survivors about the new "time warp" which would get them back to Earth much faster than they expected.

Thus it seems safe to assume that the reason why Nomad's energy bolts seemed to take 50,000 times as long as they should have was that the time rate aboard the *Enterprise* was speeded up 50,000 times the normal time rate. To the outside world the bolts would have seemed to take only 0.0000889 seconds to reach the *Enterprise,* but to Kirk, Spock, and the others on board, the bolts seemed to take five seconds or so to reach the starship.

Thus we see that the way a starship manages to travel faster than light is to travel at a rate slower than light, while at the same time a warp field speeds up the rate at which time passes aboard the ship. In the accelerated-time-rate bubble of space which surrounds the ship, the ship is traveling at only a fraction of the speed of light, and so violates no laws of nature. But at the same time it appears to outside observers to be traveling faster than light and will arrive at its destination far sooner than light could travel such distances.

It is not known what kind of drive propels the *Enterprise* and other starships when they are traveling in time warp. We know that they have impulse engines, which seem to work on the reaction principle and to be highly advanced rockets.

But if such engines were used, the *Enterprise* would accelerate and decelerate like a rocketship. It would gain speed as long as the engines were working and would not lose speed until the thrust was reversed. If it took an hour to build up speed from zero to warp 8, then in order to reverse course, the *Enterprise* would have to turn around and fire its engines for an hour to slow down to zero speed. Then when warp 8 was again required, it would require another hour to build back up to it.

Yet the *Enterprise* can simply change course, and in seconds it is proceeding at the same speed as before. Perhaps it simply can accelerate to maximum speed in a fraction of a second.

If at maximum speed time is speeded up by 56,000 times or so, then the actual speed at warp 8 would only be 0.0091428 of C (light speed), or 1,673.1324 miles per second, or 2,740.9474 kilometers per second.

If it takes a second to accelerate from zero to 1,673.1324 miles per second, it will take an acceleration, and an artificial feeling of weight, of 276,061.846 gravities!

Twenty-five gravities is the highest G-force endured for seconds in a dry capsule. Thirty-one G has been survived for five seconds in liquid suspension. A force of 82.6 G has been endured for 0.04 seconds, while a man who survived a fall off a 185-foot tower endured a G-force of 209 for an even tinier split-second!

Clearly no human can survive forces thousands of times as intense. Of course the *Enterprise* has an artifical gravity field which can compensate for acceleration and provide a steady one-G feeling of weight—but there must be limitations to the effectiveness of such a field.

The crewmembers are rarely seen to be affected by even a slight fraction of one gravity's force when the starship accelerates and decelerates. That indicates that the internal gravity field can neutralize accelerations of up to 276,000 G. And yet that internal gravity field is unable to compensate as well when it strives to neutralize the joltings the ship receives from enemy phaser blasts. And certainly it is illogical to assume that a jolt from a phaser beam could give a ship greater acceleration than the full power of its own engines!

Thus we must assume that the drive which is used during the warp travel must be some kind of what Poul Anderson calls a "field drive"; one which affects all the particles in an object equally, so there is no feeling of gravity when being moved. In known science we see such an effect in the feeling of weightlessness felt by those who fall freely in a gravitational field.

It is well known that all normal objects are capable of moving at any speed less than that of light. Light photons and a few other particles such as neutrinos, etc., can and must travel at the speed of light. They cannot travel at any speed less than light, nor stop without changing into other kinds of particles.

When they hit objects, either they are merged with other particles or they are reflected off on an entirely different course. It would take an infinite amount of energy to accelerate any ordinary particle to the speed of light, but photons can reverse course instantly, the equivalent of deceleration from the speed of light and reacceleration back to that speed instantly!

I believe that the space drive used by the *Enterprise* during warp travel changes the nature of the particles aboard the *Enterprise,* so that they no longer behave like normal particles. Instead, they behave much like light particles and must always travel at a constant speed—in this case, about 0.0091428 C.

The warping of time around the ship makes the speed of 0.0091428 C appear to be dozens or hundreds of times the speed of light to those who observe the ship from outside.

I find it rather hard to understand how the crewmembers could walk around while that field drive was on. Their movements would make them travel a tiny fraction faster or slower than the ship as a whole—but it would be impossible to travel even 0.00000001 percent faster or slower than the speed at which it would be their nature to travel while the drive was on.

Probably the field drive is switched on and off thousands of times a second. The thoughts, movements, actions, and words of the crewmembers would occur during the intervals in which the field drive was switched off. If you could see and think that fast, and if you were immune to the effects of the field drive, you would see the persons aboard the *Enterprise* stop as still as statues many times a second, and then resume movement. Falling objects would stop, fall, stop, fall, stop, fall . . . until they reached the deck.

Dr. McCoy hates having his molecules "scrambled up and beamed all over the universe" by the transporter. I wonder how he feels about having his life and consciousness switched on and off many times a second!

When the *Enterprise* is going full speed, the conditions aboard are certainly different from normal conditions. There is the field drive changing the nature of the matter aboard so that it can only travel at 0.0091428 C; the time warp speeding up time 56,000 times so that the speed of 0.0091428 C seems to be 512 light speeds; and the internal acceleration compensator, an artificial gravity field creating a force of one G (in a direction at right angles to that of any acceleration which might be felt due to the ship's changes in speed.)

In addition, when the *Enterprise* passes through one of the space warps I mentioned in my previous article (which offer instant transition from one place to another), still a fourth distortion of normal laws is superimposed upon those already altering the condition of the crewmembers!

Another reason for supposing that the impulse drive is not used with the time warp is the way the engines can be reversed to change course without turning the ship. If the drive used with the warp was the impulse drive, it would have to reverse thrust by firing its rockets forward through the main saucer section of the *Enterprise*—which would not be very safe.

I do not know if there is any reason why the impulse engines cannot be used with the time warp. The field drive that is used seems to be better for maneuverability than rockets. It is not known if Zefrem Cochrane invented the field drive when he invented the time warp, or if the first warp-drive ships used the impulse engines for propulsion.

Though gravity control is used throughout the Federation to neutralize weights (as seen in "The Changeling" and "Obsession"), to float massive objects ("The Cloud Minders"), and to provide internal gravity fields for starships, apparently it cannot be used for propulsion.

The Tholians, however, may be able to use gravity for propulsion. In the book version of "The Tholian Web," Sulu was astounded when the Tholian ship decelerated from 0.51 C to zero in a second or so. (*Enterprise* time. If the time warp was on, the actual speed would have been much greater and the time much shorter.)

It seems to me that the *Enterprise* has had a pseudo-acceleration—not a real one—as great as this whenever it accelerated to a higher warp speed. Thus Sulu must have been surprised because there was no known way to decelerate that fast from a real speed, instead of switching off a time warp.

This indicates that the Tholians have gravity control and

can use it to propel their starships. In order to decelerate a ship from a real speed of 0.51 C, it is necessary to use all the power resulting from the total conversion into energy of an enormous amount of matter. The mass needed to provide the energy for the initial acceleration, and then the deceleration at the end of the journey, would equal 1.33 times the total mass of the rest of the ship.

The mass needed for the initial acceleration, the deceleration at the end of the trip, the acceleration for the return journey, and the deceleration on the return home would total 3.0989 the mass of the ship's payload. And that's merely the mass needed if the ship's drive is 100 percent efficient! The Tholians probably contain their matter and antimatter fuel in super-compressed form, held in place by force fields.

In any case, if the Tholians accelerated a ship to 0.5 C, and then turned on a time warp with strength sufficient to speed up time 56,000 times, they would appear to outside observers to be traveling at a speed of 28,560 times the speed of light, or warp 30.5!

Thus it would seem to be advantageous to discover a method of using gravity control to propel a spaceship, especially while the time warp is turned on.

It is hard to decide how the *Enterprise* changes from one warp speed to another. Is the field drive changed to give a different speed, while the time warp remains constant? Or is the time warp changed, while the speed produced by the field drive remains 0.0091428 C? Or are both changed?

The following chart is based on the first assumption.

Warp factor	Speed to outside observers	Speed of field drive
1	1^3 or 1 C	0.0000178 C
2	2^3C or 8 C	0.0001428 C
3	3^3C or 27 C	0.0004821 C
4	4^3C or 64 C	0.0011428 C
5	5^3C or 125 C	0.0022321 C
6	6^3C or 216 C	0.0038571 C
7	7^3C or 343 C	0.0061250 C
8	8^3C or 512 C	0.0091428 C

The next table is based on the assumption that the field drive must always produce a speed of 0.0091428 C but the ratio of internal time to external time can be changed.

Warp factor	Speed to outside observers	Ratio of internal time over external
1	1^3 C or 1 C	109.37568
2	2^3 C or 8 C	875.00546
3	3^3 C or 27 C	2953.14340
4	4^3 C or 64 C	7000.04370
5	5^3 C or 125 C	13671.96000
6	6^3 C or 216 C	23625.14700
7	7^3 C or 343 C	37515.85900
8	8^3 C or 512 C	56000.35000

If the third possibility is assumed, there will be an infinite number of possible systems by which the speed of the field drive and the time warp can be changed to give different combinations, with a result of different warp speeds.

In the case of the second assumption, you will notice that the number times the time rate the *Enterprise* is increased over that of the outside universe always equals the warp factor cubed times 109.37568. In the first case, the speed of the field drive would equal the warp factor cubed divided by 56,000. Neither mathematical relationship is particularly handy.

It is not known if the warp drive is used to travel slower than light to orbit planets, etc. In one episode, I remember Kirk telling Scotty to use impulse power if necessary to break out of orbit, implying that its use is strictly related to emergencies.

If the speed produced by the field drive is always 0.0091428 C, then in order to slow down the ship for orbital speeds, the time warp would have to slow down on board the ship (instead of speeding it up) to a speed of 3,048.8 times as slow as normal, which would be warp factor 0.0143.

On the other hand, if the field drive can be adjusted for different speeds, it might be able to produce a speed on the order of a few miles per second, and there would be no need to use the time warp to slow down time aboard the ship.

If the field drive can produce varying speeds, it might

often be used apart from the time warp to travel slower than light. If it can only produce a speed of 0.0091428 C, then the time warp would probably be used to speed up or slow down time to produce the desired rate of travel.

It is to be noticed that warp factor 1 is exactly the speed of light. That is more surprising than speeds faster than light, for relativity does not forbid faster-than-light travel; it merely states that it is impossible to accelerate an object which is traveling slower than the speed of light up to exactly the speed of light. The difficulty with faster-than-light travel is how to get past the speed of light.

Of course, if my time-warp theory is correct, there is no problem, for the real speed of a starship traveling at warp 1 would be much less than that of light in relation to the space immediately surrounding it.

If the rate of the time warp remains the same, while the speed of the field drive is changed, the actual speed of the *Enterprise* at warp 1 is merely 0.0000178 times that of light; while if the field drive constantly provides a speed of 0.0091428 C, that will actually be the speed at warp 1.

So far, I have explained how the *Enterprise* is able to achieve its speeds of from 1 to 512 times the speed of light— as seen by outside observers. Such speeds, combined with the space warps mentioned in my previous article, explain how the *Enterprise* is able to travel thousands of light-years while the outside world ages only a few days.

But if time is speeded up so very much on board a starship, the trips will seem to the crew a lot longer than to outside observers. In fact, they will seem to take as long as a trip using the field drive and no time warp would take.

If the field drive can only produce a speed of 0.0091428 C, then any trip will take a period of time equal to the distance in light-years divided by 0.0091428. A trip of 1 light-year will take 109.37568 years.

If the speed produced by the field drive varies and the time warp remains at 56,000 times, then the time a 1-light-year trip will take will vary with the warp factor. At warp 1, and a speed of 0.0000178 C, a trip of 1 light-year will take 56,179.775 years, ship's time; though to outside observers, it will seem to take just one year. At warp 4, it will seem to take 875.04375 years to those on board, and only 5.7 days to outside observers. At warp 8, it will take 109.37568 years to those on board, and 17.21 hours to outside observers.

However, there is a simple solution. An inner time warp field is created which encloses the passenger quarters of the ship, and slows down time to a rate equal to that at which the outer warp speeds it up. Thus the crew ages no faster than those in the outside world, and can have conversations with outsiders via subspace radio without differences in the time rate messing things up.

If that is the case, the inner time warp does not neutralize the effects of the main one—otherwise the passenger quarters would be traveling at a fraction of the speed of light while the main body of the ship was traveling at hundreds of times the speed of light, and the ship would be destroyed. Instead the inner warp superimposes its effect on that of the main time warp.

I suppose that it is normal to have the inner time warp adjusted so that time will seem to pass at the same rate as in the outside universe. That allows for conversations via subspace radio with persons on various planets. However, it is possible that the time rate is the same as that in the outside universe only while such conversations are taking place, and is different the rest of the time.

In "Menagerie," Kirk said that Talos IV was only six days from Starbase 11 at maximum warp, a figure which must have been accurate unless for some reason the Talosians were making him say things which weren't true. The episode began at Starbase 11 at stardate 3012.4; the court-martial on board the *Enterprise* began at 3012.6; at 3013.1, Kirk spoke of the startling events of the past twenty-four hours (since 3012.1); and yet it was only 3013.2 when the *Enterprise* was only one hour from Talos IV. Thus the trip seemed to start between 3012.4 and 3012.6 and to end about 3013.2416, taking between 0.84 and 0.64 days instead of six days.

Either Spock knew of a shorter and faster route through the space warps to Talos IV, or the Talosians were making Kirk think that time was not passing as fast as it was (so he wouldn't be as likely to find a way to turn the ship); or else it is normal procedure for the internal time warp to slow down time more than the main warp speeds it up, so that time seems to pass at a slower rate for the crewmembers than for outside persons.

If that is the case, in the voyage to Talos IV time seemed

to pass 7.129 to 9.351 times as slow on the *Enterprise* as in the outside universe.

Thus it is possible that Starfleet members age slower on the average than most members of their societies, since time passes slower for them.

During emergencies, however, the inner time warp must be shut off so that the effect of the main time warp is not diminished. The sensors of the *Enterprise* (which must use a form of radiation which travels much faster than warp 15) must have turned off the inner warp automatically as soon as Nomad's energy bolts were detected in "The Changeling." This must be standard procedure during emergencies.

Thus during emergencies, time aboard the crew's quarters must pass about 56,000 times as fast as the outside flow of time. That enables the captain and officers to react 56,000 times as fast as they would when time was flowing normally.

Whatever the time rate in the crew's quarters, during space battles the phaser stations must always be under maximum time-warp acceleration, with no compensating time slow down. That way the power of the phaser beams will be intensified tremendously.

When the phasers are fired at maximum strength during a period of time acceleration, there will be a certain intensity of energy per unit cross section of the beam per second. But as the particles of energy pass into the space outside the time warp (the space where time is passing much slower), the energy particles which were fired over a period of one second of the ship's time will strike any object in their way over a period of 1/56,000 of a second, and thus the energy density of the beam will appear to be increased 56,000 times.

Similarly an external beam fired into the starship's time warp will have its energy spread out over a period of time 56,000 times as long as the period over which the beam was being fired in the external universe, and will have its energy density per second reduced 56,000 times.

The time differential makes even a flashlight beamed from a starship in full time warp seem like a deadly energy beam to any ship in normal time which is hit by it, and will make a deadly phaser beam from a spaceship at a normal time rate seem like an innocent searchlight to a starship under full time acceleration. Only a battle between two starships at the same time warp would be a fair fight.

I seem to remember that in the various battles of the *Enterprise* enemy vessels traveling at warp speed seem to take minutes instead of split-seconds to travel distances of a few dozen or hundred thousand kilometers.

This indicates that the bridge crew of the *Enterprise* was experiencing time warps which made seconds seem like hours. No doubt the precise figures from time warp deduced from information given will vary from episode to episode, as the precise amount of time acceleration to be used in battle may vary with circumstances.

Phaser beams seem to use energy which travels faster than light, or else ships could outrun them. They may work by simply concentrating so much of that energy that any object it hits is heated up and vaporized, as modern lasers use intense amounts of ordinary light to vaporize metal.

But it is possible that phaser beams are compound, containing several different forms of energy with different effects on the objects they hit, like some of the deadlier beams in Doc E. E. Smith's space epics.

One of those components of phaser beams might be a series of alternating tractor and deflector beams. The tractor beams would attract the part of the enemy ship that was struck, then the deflector beams would push on it. . . . Such a series, if the beams were of great strength and alternated rapidly, would soon shake a target to pieces, as the "rattlers" in James White's hospital-station series do.

Only when the targets have internal acceleration compensators like that of the *Enterprise* would such an attack be ineffective, as they would manage to neutralize the shaking of the alternate attraction and repulsion. And the time warp of the *Enterprise* speeds up time within the ship 56,000 times, so that a fast cycle of ten tractor beams and ten deflector beams per second becomes a slow cycle of one tractor beam and one deflector beam every 1.5 hours, for example.

Even with the internal acceleration field, and even with the time warp speeding up time 56,000 times, the effect of the "rattler" component of phaser beams of an enemy is enough to throw the bridge crew members off their feet. If it was just a tiny fraction more powerful, the first phaser burst would destroy the entire *Enterprise!*

If the internal gravity field was just a little less powerful, or if the time warp could accelerate time just a little less than it can, the *Enterprise* would be destroyed. A ship without one or the other of those defenses—or without either—would be destroyed by the first shot from the *Enterprise*.

The present situation in which the offensive power of the phasers and the defensive power of the deflector screens, internal gravity control, and time warp are almost exactly equal must be just a temporary stand-off in the never-ending struggle between offense and defense.

There must have been times—and there will be times again—when the alternating tractor and deflector beams were powerful enough to shake a starship to pieces instantly. There must have been times—and there will be times again—when the defenses of a starship were totally immune to the effects of that component of phaser beams.

Current scientific theories know of several methods, such as intense gravitational forces and acceleration to high velocities, to slow down the passage of time within an area or objects—such effects have been measured. As far as I know no theory suggests how the passage of time may be speeded up, though the usual symmetry of the universe suggests that there may be methods which no one has imagined yet.

At present, we cannot guess how the main time warp of the *Enterprise* speeds up time, nor how the inner time warp slows it down—for none of the known methods of slowing down time seem to apply.

In "The Naked Time," Spock spoke of a theoretical relationship between antimatter and time. I believe that was a hurried way of saying that there is a theoretical relationship between the mutual annihilation of matter and antimatter and the flow of time. The warp-drive engines normally use a different relationship between matter-antimatter reactions and time. But the untested formula was tried during the emergency—and resulted in travel back in time.

Thus it would appear that the warp engines do not annihilate matter in order to provide the power needed to warp time. Instead they annihilate matter because the matter-antimatter reactions cause a side effect which warps time. This effect has yet to be noticed by our scientists because of the small scale of all present-day matter-antimatter reactions. In addition, the annihilation of matter no doubt provides the power to fuel various highly esoteric devices which control and manipulate the time warp.

If the supposition that one second of time at the normal rate of flow is equal to 183,000 miles (the distance light travels in a second), rough calculations of the power requirements might be made. To enable time to be increased 56,000 times, you would need enough energy to accelerate the ship 56,000 times the speed of light, if my figuring is correct.

But if relativity has any meaning, it would take an infinite amount of energy to accelerate to the speed of light, to say nothing of 56,000 times the speed of light, or warping time to become 56,000 times as fast!

Perhaps the energy needed to speed up time 56,000 times is not equivalent to that required to reach 56,000 times the speed of light according to Einsteinian physics but rather according to Newtonian physics. In that case the energy required to speed up the time rate of one gram of matter 56,000 times is about 1,668,408,000,000,000 ergs; or that released by the total conversion of 0.000016 grams of matter into energy.

There are other ways the energy consumption may be calculated. Theories about hypothetical tachyons (faster-than-light particles) say they should require less energy to go faster. Perhaps the amount of energy required to speed up time 56,000 times is equal to that of a tachyon traveling 56,000 times the speed of light.

It would appear that the stored antimatter and matter are separated from the walls of their containers by gravitational force fields—which is necessary in the case of the antimatter, at least. The storage would also be at a comparatively cold temperature.

To move them into the reaction chambers, they are heated up until they become ionized plasmas which can be manipulated by electromagnetic fields, which are apparently far more flexible than the gravitational fields. Because the matter and the deadly antimatter must be in the superheated plasma state to be manipulated, Scotty says in "Naked Time" that it is impossible to mix matter and antimatter cold without an (uncontrollably violent, instead of controlled) explosion.

Most of the fuel is stored in the form of ordinary matter, the needed amounts of antimatter being provided by transforming some of the ordinary matter into antimatter somehow, whenever it is needed for the reaction. This makes fuel storage much safer.

However, some antimatter must be kept on hand at all

times, for a certain amount is needed for the engines to "regenerate" antimatter (convert ordinary matter into antimatter), according to "One of Our Planets Is Missing."

There is no information about the size of the fields in which the time warps of the starship are effective, except that the inner time warp must include the main saucer and other parts of the ship, but must not include the engines.

It would be simplest to assume that the time warps are spherical and their effects diminish with distance, being proportional to the square of the distance. But in that case, a part of the ship 100 feet from the warp drive would have its time rate speeded up twice as fast as the time rate of a part of the ship 200 feet from the time warp, which would have its time rate speeded up twice as fast again as that of an area 400 feet from the engines.

And that would mean that the parts of the ship 100 feet from the engines would be traveling twice as fast as the parts 200 feet away, which would be traveling twice as fast as the parts 400 feet away. That would not work very well.

Thus it may be concluded that the effect of the time warp is uniform over the entire volume of space it affects, and that it has a sharply defined edge at its boundary with the volume of space in which time passes at its normal rate.

The location of the engine room is not known, though it is logical to assume that it is the engineering section in the secondary hull, as close as possible to the engine nacelles.

The *Enterprise* blueprints put the familiar engine room we all know at the back of the saucer-shaped primary hull where the impulse engines are supposed to be, and says that it is, indeed, the impulse engine room. But we have all seen shows in which the warp drive was controlled from that engine room, and in which the great engines were obviously in action while the warp drive was running. And the corridor outside that engine room is curved, like one in the primary hull, instead of the straight corridor we would expect to find in the secondary hull.

The dilithium crystals are said to have some use in the control of the ship's power, which is apparently channeled through them.

The element lithium is a white metal with a silvery luster, not a jewel-like crystal. It can probably be assumed that dilithium crystals are not some form of pure lithium but more likely a complex compound of many elements.

This compound no doubt closely resembles some other compound, except for having two lithium atoms where the other has but one; and so is called dilithium ——, commonly shortened to the word "dilithium," and more rarely, just "lithium."

There is a lithium-cracking station on Delta Vega, an automated factory-mining-refinery complex which produces enough ore in twenty years for a freighter to come for. It does not seem likely that the output of that factory had anything to do with dilithium crystals, which seem to be mined ("Mudd's Women," "Elaan of Troyius," "Journey to Babel") rather than manufactured or processed. More likely the complex produces some other form of lithium or some compound containing it.

Still, it seems strange that a lithium-refining complex would be built on a distant planet. No doubt—whatever product is refined there—the site makes sense in the time of Star Trek.

It is possible that the dilithium crystals which are dug up on various worlds in the time of Star Trek are in fact artificial, having been made by some supercivilization which left them where other beings would find them and use them. I find it easier to believe that such as yet unknown, unusual, and highly useful substances were artificially created than that they just naturally occurred.

It can easily be seen that the warp drive and other aspects of the *Enterprise*'s technology produce some highly complicated and unusual physical conditions on board. While it would be fun to travel in such a perfected and developed vehicle as the *Enterprise,* it would not be too wise to volunteer as a test pilot in any of the ships in which the various devices were first tested.

31. TREK FAN POLL RESUTS
by Walter Irwin and G. B. Love

In the back of the seventh issue, we ran a filler page which was a simple series of questions about our readers' major likes, dislikes, and attitudes about Star Trek. We expected enough of a response to this poll to fill up another page or two in the following issue, providing our readers with an interesting, but still relatively minor, look at how their peers felt. Well, were we surprised when literally hundreds of responses to our poll began pouring in! What was to have been a short feature had suddenly become the greatest mail-puller in our history, so we immediately decided to devote a full-length article to the results of the poll. Again and again, we have touched on the theme of diversity among fans as being the most outstanding characteristic of Star Trek fandom, and the results of our poll only confirmed our beliefs.

As most of you know, last issue we ran the first of a series of Fan Polls which are designed to gauge the opinions of ST fans about certain aspects of the show in general. Since a new TV series is now in preparation, the results are being forwarded to Gene Roddenberry and his staff to help them implement any changes and refinements in the forthcoming shows.

The results were just as we expected—plenty of surprises. Star Trek fandom is such a diverse lot, we knew that any preconceptions of how the poll would turn out weren't worth the time it took to consider them. But even being ready for the unexpected, some of the answers still surprised and delighted us.

All of the results are given in percentages, with the exception of the most-liked and most-disliked shows, which were given weighted point values, according to their place on an individual's list.

One other point before we go on to the results: With only one exception, no question has a decisive resolution. When a majority of votes was reached, there were still enough opposing votes to represent a very large segment of fans. Which goes to prove that you can't please everyone, or more optimistically, in difference there is beauty.

1. Name the top ten episodes in the order of your preference.
    1. "City on the Edge of Forever"   232
    2. "Amok Time"   192
    3. "Journey to Babel"   141
    4. "The Menagerie"   127
    5. "The Trouble with Tribbles"   125
    6. "Shore Leave"   118
    7. "Balance of Terror"   100
    8. "The Enemy Within"   92
    9. "The Naked Time"   84
   10. "Mirror, Mirror"   81

There was no surprise with the result, as far as number one goes. "City" was on almost every list we received. Perhaps our biggest surprise was the high finish of "Amok Time," which is not usually discussed when the subject of most popular episodes comes up. And almost as great a surprise was the tenth-place finish of "Mirror, Mirror." It was first on many lists.

A careful examination of the list will show that it somewhat leans toward "Spock" shows. Whether this is due to the fact that our readership is mostly Spock fans, or the best episodes are those which feature him prominently, we leave for our readers to discuss.

2. Who is your favorite Star Trek character?

Another surprise. One would figure that either Kirk or Spock would beat the others out by a narrow margin, but it turned out to be even closer than that! Yep, that's right, a draw! Each took 43% of the vote, while the remaining 14% was divided between McCoy (8%), and Scotty, Janice Rand, and Chekov (2% each). Oddly enough, Uhura and Sulu got no votes at all. Where were all the "Uhura for Captain" button wearers?

3. Which actor do you feel contributed the most to Star Trek?

Again, the vote was split between Shatner and Nimoy, with Shatner finishing with a lead of 56% to Nimoy's 44%. Although no one else got any votes, many respondents answered the question with all of the cast, stating that they felt the success of Star Trek was a joint effort, and that no one actor could be singled out as having contributed more than any other. It is also interesting to note that Shatner gathered up almost all of the "other character" votes from question number two, which gave him the edge over Nimoy.

4. Who is your favorite villain?

This must have been a tough one for many fans, since there are just so many rotten, lovable baddies to choose from. The leading vote-getter was the inimitable Leo Walsh; yes, Harcourt Fenton Mudd got a solid 25% of the votes cast. A surprising second place was Mark Lenard's superb portrayal of the Romulan commander in "Balance of Terror," with 14%. Squire Trelane of Gothos came in third with 11%, followed by two Klingon baddies—Kor ("Errand of Mercy") with 9%, and Kang ("Day of the Dove") with 7%. The remaining 34% of the vote was just about equally divided between the Horta, the Keeper, Koloth, Khan, the Theleb, Dr. Simon Adams from "Dagger of the Mind," and the Romulans and Klingons in general.

5. Who is your favorite male guest star?

Mark Lenard tops the list with 35% of the vote, almost all of which gave him top spot for both roles as the Romulan and Sarek. William Campbell was in a similar situation, gaining votes both for Trelane and Koloth. He finished second with 13%. Third place was a tie, with Roger C. Carmel and William Windom each gleaning 11%. Fourth was Ricardo Montalban with 10%. Gary Lockwood and Robert Lansing tied for fifth with 5% each, and the remaining percentages were tied between David Soul, Mike Forrest, Robert Walker, Jr., Percy Rodriguies, Jeff Hunter, Bruce Mars, Logan Ramsay, and John Colicos.

6. Who is your favorite female guest star?

Garnering the largest percentage was Joan Collins, with

21% of the vote. Jane Wyatt impressed many fans as Spock's mother, Amanda, enough so that she came in second with 10%. A four-way tie marked third place, with Diana Muldaur, Sabrina Scharf, Joanne Linville, and Mariette Hartley each getting 8%. Fourth was Kim Darby with 6%. Fifth place was also a tie; Susan Oliver, Arlene Martell, Jill Ireland, France Nuyuen, Terri Garr, Karen Steele, Emily Banks, and the impeccable T'Pau, Celia Lovsky, all sharing 30% right down to the fractions. And receiving 1% of the vote each were Barbara Luna and Kathryn Hays.

7. What do you think is the most believable piece of equipment aboard the *Enterprise?*

Another difficult one to answer, as you had to consider not only the scientific possibilities of any given device, but also the fact that many of these devices were necessary to the basic concept of the show. The dilemma here was obviously which to choose, since something which was believable in the series might not be practical in real life. However, the fans considered the question, and their answer came through loud and clear.

The handy communicator and the versatile phaser tied for first place with 18% of the vote each. The transporter was second with 16%, and third was a tie between the diagnostic bed and the main computer at 14% each. They were followed by the communications panel, the shuttlecraft, and the bridge with 5% each. The remaining 5% went to the warp drive, the spray hypo, the sickbay, the viewscreen, and the helm controls.

8. Who do you think is the best overall Star Trek writer?

Another difficult question for many fans. Some considered the question on the basis of one episode, while others used the term "overall" to mean those who have been the most prolific, and narrowed their choices to them. However, the fans proved themselves knowledgeable with their selection of Dorothy C. Fontana for first place with a whopping 40% of the vote. D. C. obviously garnered most of the votes not only for her own scripts, but for the rewrites and polishing she did with many others. Coming in second was the Great Bird himself with 20%, and third place went to Theodore Sturgeon's 13%. The late Gene L. Coon placed fourth with

11%; and a three-way tie was fifth with Paul Schnieder, Jerome Bixby, and Richard Matheson getting 4% each. The remaining 4% was divided between James Blish, Robert Bloch, Art Wallace, and David Gerrold. It was rather strange that James Blish received as many votes as he did, since his ST writing was confined to the paperback adaptations and the one original novel he did for Bantam books. Another interesting sidelight: Although "City on the Edge of Forever" finished first in the favorite-episode poll, Harlan Ellison did not receive even one vote for best writer.

9. Do you think that Arex and M'Ress should be included in the Star Trek movie?

This is the only question on the poll to which there was a clear and resounding mandate, and it was a definite *no*, with the nays occupying over 80% of the votes. Perhaps the response to this question was the fear of many that Uhura, Sulu, and especially Chekov would be slighted if the two aliens were included.

10. When Star Trek returns, should the series take up where it left off, or should the intervening years be accounted for?

This was a close one, with those fans who wanted the intervening years accounted for holding only a 54% margin. Most fans simply stated that they just wanted the show back on the air and couldn't care less when it began.

11. Do you prefer action-oriented shows or "think" shows?

Think shows won this one by a resounding margin (71%), but almost every letter yelled "Foul" for making them choose, since their contention was that a good episode has elements of both. Many fans even refused to answer in one way or another.

12. Do you think that the regular characters should die, marry, or otherwise undergo major changes?

A small majority (57%) were against any changes taking place. But almost every vote—regardless of whether the

voter was in favor of change or not—said that they definitely did not want to see any of the major characters die.

13. Name the five worst Star Trek episodes in the order of
your distaste.

This was yet another toughie, since there are (yes, even in
Star Trek!) many episodes which are despised by thousands
of fans. The amazing thing about this section of the poll
was the large number of episodes which are generally not
considered bad (many, many of which showed up in the best
poll) that fans chose as their least favorites. But the final
results looked like this:
1. And the Children Shall Lead
2. The Way to Eden
3. Spock's Brain
4. Spectre of the Gun
5. The Omega Glory

As you can see, the list (with one exception) is drawn
exclusively from the third season. The absence of the creative leadership of Gene Roddenberry is thus more graphical-
ly pointed out in that a majority of the worst shows in our
poll also came from the third season's episodes.

Well, what does it all mean? We see it like this:

Favorite episodes all are those which have a strong dramatic conflict, some humor, and involve the major characters in a very tense situation. This is what every television
show strives for, as these elements are vital to a successful
script. Each and every one of them has a point or moral,
yet each is notable for its subtlety in making its message
known to the viewer. So in future ST shows the producers
would be wise to avoid "Preachy" stories, those with mindless violence or action, and those which do not feature one
or more of the regular players prominently. Fans' comments
on this question went like this: "Only *ten?,*" "Hardest
question I ever answered. Finally, after 100 changes, here it
is." And many fans couldn't bear not to mention several
more favorites as "honorable mentions."

A warning of sorts to Gene Roddenberry: You had better
not make the Star Trek movie without William Shatner as
Kirk and Leonard Nimoy as Spock. If you do, then you will
lose about half your audience!

Seriously, our poll showed that these two men and the

characters they played are indispensable to what made Star Trek great. And it is a good thing for ST fandom, we feel, that the votes were divided so sharply between the two. We are looking for heroes today, and where else can you find two of them together but in Star Trek? And even though these two got the majority of the votes, the fans who voted for other members of the crew were just as adamant in their reasons. A consensus drawn from this would most probably be that Star Trek truly was a team effort; and while one particular actor or character may appeal to a person, things would simply not be the same if any of the regulars were missing.

Fan comments: (Shatner, Kirk:) "He breathed life into the character and made it better with each episode"; "He spoke with his eyes"; "Through Kirk we came to know the many sides of Spock."

Nimoy, Spock: "It's not every TV show on which you can see a very intelligent alien being accepted and loved by humans"; "Logic, precise, and, underneath his surface, he's feeling emotions!"

Kelley, McCoy: "He may not have been logical or rational, but he sure made things interesting."

For the group effort: "Each was a perfect foil for the other"; "It was the counteraction of the main characters"; "Not fair! Star Trek was all eight of the continuing characters. Leave one out, and you have a good show, but not Star Trek!"

Mark Lenard is a favorite with the fans by a wide margin. It is unthinkable that he not make at least an appearance in the Star Trek film. As far as the rest of guest stars and villains go, it seems to be a mix, with the humorous Harry Mudd a strong favorite, and the Klingons and Romulans giving a strong showing also. This is no surprise, since the "adversary" relationship must be retained to keep the *Enterprise* in conflict not only with the universe itself, but also with its more irresponsible citizenry. Some comments: "I do not consider Mark Lenard a guest!"; "Kor—he even looked mean"; "The Horta, because it turned out not to be a villain at all, just a mother protecting its young"; "William Campbell, but he's dead—so Robert Walker, Jr."

Joan Collins fared better with her performance in "City" than Harlan Ellison did for writing it. She proved the most popular female guest star. Only Jane Wyatt got enough of the vote to be considered a clear choice also. So the assumption here can only be that female Star Trek guest stars must depend on the popularity of the episode they are in to gain any sort of recognition. And it would also follow that whoever was cast in a woman's part (except for a returning character from an earlier show) would be all right with the fans.

Although the poll for favorite female guest star produced only one overwhelming favorite, it did account for a larger part of the "tie" votes we received. Apparently, many fans could not decide which lady they liked best.

(A note: Whenever in our poll our readers told us that they simply could not choose between two or even more persons, we gave each of the people they voted for a full point. This may not be strictly fair, but we believe that the readers who couldn't make up their minds were sincere about their dilemma, and that if their favorites were close enough to tie, then they were important enough to be counted in full.)

In general, our fans feel that the entire ship is a believable piece of equipment. Again, we see the effect that careful planning and working from logical progression of known scientific facts can produce. This ability of Star Trek fans to be able to completely "get into" the universe of the *Enterprise* is another salute to the skills of Roddenberry and company. Comments usually stated that everything aboard the ship was indeed believable, regardless of what was singled out for the poll.

It is obvious that fans prefer writers who are familiar with Star Trek, since the highest ranking were usually those who did more than one episode. It would be wise for the producers to make certain in the future that any writer assigned a Star Trek script has a full and sympathetic understanding of the series, its aims, and its framework. There were also many "ties" in this question. One fan spoke for all: "This was a very hard question!"

When one considers that the basis of Star Trek's popularity lies in its acceptance of things alien and different, it is very strange that fans should so strongly reject having Arex and M'Ress featured in the ST movie. We feel that two factors contributed to this general feeling (besides the stated fear that other regulars would be slighted).

First, the cartoon ST was not considered to be "real Star Trek" by many fans, and they fear that any carryover from the animated version would hurt a live movie or program's credibility.

Second, some fans said that they didn't think that the two aliens could look believable in the makeup required in a live episode. We agree as far as Arex is concerned, since it would be very easy for his multilimbed body to look very much like a fake. But in the case of M'Ress, there would be absolutely no problem at all, her makeup being hardly more involved than that of, say, an Andorian. And the effect would be striking and quite beautiful.

Fan comments: "Would it add to the relationships that already exist?"; "If there's one alien (Spock) on board, shouldn't there logically be others roaming about here and there? Sure! More fun that way!"; No, because it would limit Uhura's and Chekov's parts and I would rather see them."

When discussing at what point in "Star Trek time" the series should be picked up, things are always likely to become hot and heavy. Fans are about evenly split on this question, and good arguments are available to each faction. And this question logically ties in with whether or not there should be major changes in characters.

If the time passage (and the age differences in the actors) is accounted for, then there would and should be changes. Ten years is a very long time, and it would be absurd to assume that the entire crew remained exactly as they were.

No less an authority than Gene Roddenberry himself has advocated accounting for the passage of time in his original script for the movie. And there were major changes in each and every character in that screenplay.

However, if the time difference is written into a new series format, it very well could destroy the delicate balance and chemistry of personalities which made Star Trek so successful. This is also an excellent argument for not having the characters change in any major way.

Fans see it thus: "Everyone knows the show has not been in production during this time, and the people who have portrayed the continuing characters have changed in their own lives during this time, and so would their namesakes"; "I think that pretending that no irreversible personal events ever occurred aboard the *Enterprise* would detract from the integrity of the drama"; "Nobody went to any great trouble to account for intervening time between episodes before. And we didn't find it particularly distracting then, did we?"; "We selfishly like to keep them to ourselves the way they are"; "Only to the point that the change keeps the characters interesting"; *"No major changes!"*

As to action-oriented shows versus think shows, the think shows won the poll, but most fans indicated that their favorite shows were those which combined elements of both. Again, it goes back to what constitutes a well-written show, and fans have shown their preference for these many times over.

And as for the worst episodes: Well, you know what they are, and what they are like. But they are in general ones in which fans cannot really believe, ones which fail to make the jump from a fictional show to a familiar universe. Only careful (and caring) production can reduce the number of clinkers. They cannot be eliminated entirely, unfortunately, since it is in the nature of TV for every series to have a certain number of lesser shows. It is the responsibility of fans to keep their letters and comments on the show coming to help those in charge know what we want to see.

So those are our poll results. We promised to send these results to Gene Roddenberry and we did. But to keep strictly to the results of the poll, the recommendations would be:

1. Use stories which are superbly well written, containing elements of drama, action, humor, and a subtle message.
2. Feature Kirk and Spock prominently, but use the extraordinary chemistry between the regulars to full advantage.
3. Mark Lenard, Roger C. Carmel, Joan Collins, and Jane Wyatt should be featured prominently.
4. Change the ship's equipment only to make it more believable and efficient.
5. Use yourself and D. C. Fontana to fullest advantage on the scripts.
6. Do not have Arex and M'Ress in the movie.
7. Have the intervening years accounted for, but have no major changes in the regulars.

8. Avoid any resemblance at all to "The Children Shall Lead."

We would like to give special thanks to all of our readers who responded to this poll. We know it took time and effort to do so, but we feel that it was worth it.

About the Editors

Walter Irwin is a graduate of the University of Houston with a degree in Journalism, and has been involved in newspaper work, films, and free-lance writing. He is the Executive Editor of *Trek*, has been active in Star Trek and comics fandom for several years, and was one of the planners of Houstoncon '76. Besides working on *Trek*, Walter is currently putting the finishing touches on his soon-to-be-published first novel, doing a series on famous detectives and adventure heroes, and laying plans for a Star Trek parody. He is twenty-seven, single, and lives in Houston, Texas

G. B. Love started the first comic-book ad-and-fanzine, *The Rocket's Blast—Comiccollector*, in 1960, and is credited with being a major force in the development of comics fandom. Until 1974, G. B. was responsible for the publication of literally hundreds of comics, nostalgia, and Star Trek fanzines, books, posters, and other collectibles. Having tired of the daily grind of putting out a magazine, G. B. "retired" in '74. But when *Trek* was on the drawing boards, he couldn't resist the excitement and challenge of the first professional Star Trek magazine, and he once more returned to publishing. G. B. currently adds his years of experience to *Trek* as the Managing Editor. He is thirty-eight, single, and lives in Houston, Texas.

SIGNET and MENTOR Science Fiction Readers

Buy them at your local

bookstore or use coupon

on next page for ordering.

More Science Fiction from SIGNET